Lifestyles of the Elderly

Diversity in Relationships,
Health, and Caregiving

Lifestyles of the Elderly

Diversity in Relationships, Health, and Caregiving

Edited by
**Linda Ade-Ridder, Ph.D.
and Charles B. Hennon, Ph.D.**

*Miami University
Oxford, Ohio*

 HUMAN SCIENCES PRESS, INC.

Library of Congress Cataloging in Publication Data

Lifestyles of the elderly.

Bibliography: p.
Includes indexes.
1. Aged – United States – Attitudes. 2. Life style. 3. Aged – United States – Family
relationships. 4. Aged – Health and hygiene – United States. 5. Aged volunteers –
United States. I. Ade-Ridder, Linda. II. Hennon, Charles B.
HQ1064.U5L55   1989   305.2'6'0973   88-8997
ISBN 0-89885-447-4

Chapters 2–20 in this volume are reprinted with minor
modifications from *Lifestyles: A Journal of Changing
Patterns,* Volume 7, Numbers 2 and 4, and Volume 8,
Numbers 3 and 4.

© 1989 Human Sciences Press, Inc.
A Subsidiary of Plenum Publishing Corporation
233 Spring Street, New York, N.Y. 10013

Printed in the United States of America

This book is dedicated to
Mary Keller Ade, M.D., and C. Hamilton Ade, M.D.
and to
Bernice Hennon
who have shown us how to grow older gracefully,
and to
Glenn Hennon
who never had the opportunity to experience the rewards of a
long life.

"The older we get, the more like ourselves we become."
—Mary Keller Ade, M.D.

Contributors

Linda Ade-Ridder
*Department of Home Economics
and Consumer Sciences
and
Family and Child Studies Center
Miami University
Oxford, Ohio 45056*

Leland V. Axelson
*Department of Family and
Child Development
Virginia Tech
Blacksburg, Virginia 24061*

Charles M. Barresi
*Department of Sociology
and
Institute for Life Span
Development and Gerontology
The University of Akron
Akron, Ohio 44325*

Dolores Cabic Borland
*Department of Family and
Child Ecology
Michigan State University
East Lansing, Michigan
48824-1030*

Ellie Brubaker
*Department of Sociology
and Anthropology
Miami University
Oxford, Ohio 45056*

Timothy H. Brubaker
*Family and Child Studies Center
Miami University
Oxford, Ohio 45056*

Margaret A. Bugaighis
*Department of Family and
Child Development
College of Home Economics
Kansas State University
Manhattan, Kansas 66506*

Jane M. Cardea
*School of Nursing
Azusa Pacific University
Azusa, California 91702*

Charles Lee Cole
*Department of Family
Environment
Iowa State University
Ames, Iowa 50011*

Janette M. Copeland
*Department of Family and
Child Development
College of Home Economics
Kansas State University
Manhattan, Kansas 66506*

Mary Dellman-Jenkins
*Department of Individual and
   Family Studies and
   Gerontology
Kent State University
Kent, Ohio 44241*

Jean L. Engelhardt
*Southwest Ohio Development
   Center
Batavia, Ohio 45103*

Ron W. Eskew
*Department of Psychology
Buffalo Psychiatric Center
Buffalo, New York 14213-1298*

Mary L. Franken
*Department of Home Economics
University of Northern Iowa
Cedar Falls, Iowa 50613*

Charles B. Hennon
*Department of Home Economics
   and Consumer Sciences
and
Family and Child Studies Center
Miami University
Oxford, Ohio 45056*

Pat M. Keith
*Department of Sociology
Iowa State University
Ames, Iowa 50011*

Beth I. Kinsel
*Family and Child Studies Center
Miami University
Oxford, Ohio 45056*

Karen A. Kohlhepp
*Kennebec Valley Mental
   Health Center
Augusta, Maine 04330*

Mary S. Link
*Department of Home Economics
   and Consumer Sciences
Miami University
Oxford, Ohio 45056*

Martha Lopez
*Struthers High School
Struthers, Ohio 44471*

Victoria D. Lutzer
*188 Lewis Roberts Way
Williamsburg, Virginia 23186*

Carol E. MacKinnon
*Department of Child
   Development and Family
   Relations
University of North Carolina
   at Greensboro
Greensboro, North Carolina
   27412*

Robert F. MacKinnon
*Department of Child
   Development and Family
   Relations
University of North Carolina
   at Greensboro
Greensboro, North Carolina
   27412*

Donna Jo McConnell
*Mahoning County Transitional
   Homes
Youngstown, Ohio 44504*

Diane Papalia
*Department of Psychology and
   Pediatrics
University of Pennsylvania
Philadelphia, Pennsylvania
   19104*

Karen A. Roberto
Gerontology Program
University of Northern Colorado
Greeley, Colorado 80639

William Rudman
Department of Sport
Management
Ohio State University
Columbus, Ohio 43210

Gregory F. Sanders
Department of Child
Development and Family
Relations
North Dakota State University
Fargo, North Dakota 58105

Walter R. Schumm
Department of Family and
Child Development
College of Home Economics
Kansas State University
Manhattan, Kansas 66505

Jean Pearson Scott
Department of Human
Development and Family
Studies
Texas Tech University
Lubbock, Texas 79409

Michael J. Sporakowski
Department of Family and
Child Development
Virginia Tech
Blacksburg, Virginia 24061

Clifford H. Swensen
Department of Psychological
Sciences
Purdue University
Lafayette, Indiana 47907

Georgeanna M. Tryban
Department of Sociology
Case Western Reserve University
Cleveland, Ohio 44106

Concetta M. Tynan
Handmaker Jewish Geriatric
Center
Tucson, Arizona 85712

James Walters
Child and Family Development
Department
University of Georgia
Athens, Georgia 30605

Acknowledgments

Many individuals have assisted in the production of this book. Timothy H. Brubaker contributed immeasurably through his editing efforts of the original journal publications and through his ideas and efforts in bringing this volume to the final compilation stage. Editing and typing responsibilities have been expertly performed by Mary Tharp of the Family and Child Studies Center with the assistance of Debbie Bodey, Jennifer Bollinger, Robin Heltzel, Samantha Inskeep, Justine Kennedy, Amy Pilarcik, and Susan Takigiku in the Department of Home Economics and Consumer Sciences, Miami University.

Special thanks also go to the many people involved in the publication of the original special issues of *Lifestyles* (Volume 7, Numbers 2 and 4, and Volume 8, Numbers 3 and 4), from which the chapters in this book have been drawn. First, thanks to the contributors, whose work and dedication provide clearer understanding of the richness and diversity of lifestyles of today's elderly. Thank you to the reviewers who contributed their comments and suggestions to the manuscripts: Karen Arms, Rosemary Blieszner, Charles L. Cole, Sherry Corbett, James DeBurger, Paula Dressell, Rhonda Montgomery, and Edward A. Powers. Cheryl Chauncey, graduate assistant in the Department of Home Economics and Consumer Sciences, also assisted in the preparation of *Lifestyles* Volume 8, Numbers 3 and 4.

Miami University's Family and Child Studies Center and Department of Home Economics and Consumer Sciences provided support for the publication of the *Lifestyles* special issues and to this book. We appreciate the efforts of all who assisted with the many phases of this publication.

Linda Ade-Ridder
Charles B. Hennon
Family and Child Studies Center
Miami University
Oxford, Ohio

Contents

xiii

PART IV: CAREGIVING ISSUES

Chapter 1

Introduction
Diversity of Lifestyles among the Elderly

Linda Ade-Ridder and Charles B. Hennon
Department of Home Economics and Consumer Sciences
and
Family and Child Studies Center
Miami University
Oxford, Ohio 45056

As the incidence of older people increases in society, so does the necessity to better understand their needs, feelings, thoughts, and behaviors. Only through increased knowledge of the many and diverse facets of the aging process can changes be implemented that will enable the older citizens of today and tomorrow to lead more fulfilling lives. There is no one correct way to grow older; diversity of lifestyle is as evident among the elderly as it is among younger generations. Societal change touches all age groups, including our elders. Many older people live alone with their spouses, others live by themselves, and a few live in multigenerational households. Medical science and better health habits have increased the quantity of life; this book offers an understanding of the ways in which today's elderly enhance and maintain the quality of their lives. *The primary objective is to present research about the diverse lifestyles of older people.*

Studying the lives of older persons provides a road map for all who are fortunate enough to be able to make that journey. This book draws together knowledge about the heterogeneous lifestyles of the elderly in order for the professionals who work with them (e.g., gerontologists, family life specialists, physicians, nurses, therapists, social workers, clergy) to expand their knowledge base and find ways to improve their service delivery to this population. These readings provide students a better understanding of the diversity of lifestyles among the elderly. Challenges for new research are offered.

The readings are divided into four parts, each one exploring a different type of lifestyle diversity. Part I examines long-term marriage, the goal of nearly every couple embarking upon a marital career. The importance of relationships with family and friends is the focus of Part II of the readings. Part III considers the importance of health for the quality of later life. Finally, in Part IV, caregiving issues are discussed. Particular attention is directed toward living situations that influence the behavior of older persons.

Long-term marriage is an issue of special concern. One of every five first marriages will survive to celebrate a 50th wedding anniversary (Glick & Norton, 1977). These couples are survivors—of the rigors of marriage, and of life itself (Brubaker, 1986). Research on long-term marriages is the focus of the first part of this book. Examination of marital relationships of 30 years' duration or longer provides insight into the factors that contribute to successful long-term relationships, and about ways that quality of later life can be maintained and enhanced.

Michael J. Sporakowski and Leland V. Axelson (Chapter 2) review the research and call for a standardization of measures used in studying long-term marriages. The past heterogeneity makes comparisons difficult. In order to identify the unique characteristics of long-term marriages, more comparisons are needed between shorter and longer relationships.

Marriages of 30 years' duration and longer are contrasted with one of shorter length by Janette M. Copeland, Margaret A. Bugaighis, and Walter R. Schumm (Chapter 3). Four samples of rural and urban families, married couples, and wives are drawn upon in this study of marital quality and length of marriage. The importance of communication is discussed.

Marital quality, morale, and sexual behavior are examined in a sample of older couples married an average of 41 years and living in a comprehensive retirement community. Linda Ade-Ridder (Chapter 4) compares the couples who have celebrated their 50th wedding anniversary with those in marriages of shorter duration. Interactions with friends are contrasted by length of marriage in this sample of healthy older people.

Robert F. MacKinnon, Carol E. MacKinnon, and Mary L. Franken (Chapter 5) report their findings about family strengths from a sample of couples married an average of 46 years. These couples are examined in terms of family satisfaction, quality of life, family coping strategies, and family enrichment. Couples with "high family strengths" are compared with couples with "low family strengths."

Charles Lee Cole (Chapter 6) presents findings about the relationship dynamics in long-term marriage. Marital quality is measured in samples of couples enrolled in marital enrichment classes with those seeking marital and family therapy. Case studies are presented to illustrate different coping styles. A typology of relationship dynamics differentiating low-quality marriages from high-quality marriages is proposed.

The importance of the love relationship is underscored by Clifford H. Swensen, Ron W. Eskew, and Karen A. Kohlhepp (Chapter 7) in their study of retired couples married an average of 40 years contrasted with nonretired couples married an average of 31 years. Sex, retirement status, relationship to children, commitment to each other, and stage of ego development are compared between these two samples.

Georgeanna M. Tryban (Chapter 8) inspects the marriages of 21 retired working-class couples to determine the effects of retirement on the marriage's social integration, happiness, involvement, and satisfaction. She reports apparent relationship benefits for dual-earner couples compared with traditional couples.

Finally, Timothy H. Brubaker and Beth I. Kinsel (Chapter 9) explore the division of responsibility for household tasks within a sample of golden wedding couples. At least one partner is under age 75. Even though some tasks are shared, these couples have developed interdependent, gender-differentiated divisions of household tasks. Expectations are compared with actual incidence of task performance.

Part II explores the diversity of relationships with family and friends. Most elderly are not abandoned; only 3% are kinless (Shanas, 1980). Few older people live with other family members, although friendships and family relationships are important in maintaining a high quality life among the elderly. Friendships contribute to morale (Wood & Robertson, 1978), and close ties are maintained between the elderly and their children, including frequent visit and the exchange of mutual aid (Lee & Ellithorpe, 1982).

Gregory F. Sanders and James Walters (Chapter 10) study the family interaction quality of married elderly with their children. They also examine the life satisfaction of these older persons. Life satisfaction is explained by factors that differ for men and for women. Important variables include health, job prestige, and financial help given.

Ellie Brubaker and Linda Ade-Ridder (Chapter 11) investigate factors related to marital quality for 335 elderly couples living in two residential environments. Interactions with friends and frequency of visits with children are contrasted between couples living in a retirement community setting and in the community at large. Implications for applied gerontologists are suggested.

Friendship patterns are compared for older rural and urban residents. Karen A. Roberto and Jean Pearson Scott (Chapter 12) conclude that for these 258 elderly persons, differences in residential location are related to participation in different kinds of activities and to helping behaviors given by friends.

The grandparenting role is explored by Mary S. Link (Chapter 13). She reviews the literature on grandparenting with particular attention to the roles of grandparent and grandchild. Intervention programs are suggested, such as foster-grandparenting.

Mary Dellmann-Jenkins, Diane Papalia, and Martha Lopez (Chapter 14) report data from 225 high school students about their interaction with their grandparents. Evidence suggests that teen-grandparent relationships are not only viable, but strong. Primary avenues for grand-parent-teen grandchild interaction include companionship and advice.

Health influences lifestyle diversity among the elderly. The three chapters of Part III explore different facets relating health to quality of life. Health is a major predictor of life satisfaction and morale (Lee, 1978), and four-fifths of the over-65 population has at least one chronic health condition that could negatively influence life satisfaction (Riley & Fonner, 1968). Marriage itself positively effects health maintenance (McKain, 1969). This part discusses additional ways to maintain a high quality of life through health maintenance.

Jane M. Cardea and Concetta M. Tynan (Chapter 15) focus upon home safety and health issues in later life. An assessment was done initially with 125 older individuals in their homes; recommendations were made to improve health and safety. Three months later, the interviewers returned to conduct a follow-up assessment. Most recommendations emphasized changes in activities or in the environment to avert falls or reduce medication use. The applicability of this model to other communities is discussed.

Longitudinal analysis of data of 375 unmarried men by Pat M. Keith (Chapter 16) explores the reasons for the postponement of health care by 30% of the males in her sample. Marital status (widowed, divorced, or never-married), reasons for postponing treatment, factors associated with delaying care, and changes in health care behavior over a 10-year period are examined.

William Rudman (Chapter 17) looks at a new model for health maintenance after retirement—corporate fitness programs. He interviewed 13 retired employees of the Campbell Soup Company who have participated in Campbell's Corporate Fitness Program. Not only are physical fitness needs met by this type of program, but social and emotional needs seem to benefit as well.

Part IV explores three diverse caregiving issues. One caregiving issue that is often overlooked is when the aging adult is a caregiver to a disabled adult child. Typically, the topic of caregiving focuses upon meeting the needs of the older person. Most elderly live independently. As age advances, the likelihood that the older person will require some assistance in daily living increases. Estimates are that by 1990, 6.6 million people living in their own homes in 1981 will require assisted living (U.S. Senate Special Committee on Aging, 1981). Institutions cannot keep pace with the increased demand. Needed are other ways to maintain the elderly within the community environment.

Jean L. Englehardt, Victoria D. Lutzer, and Timothy H. Brubaker (Chapter 18) surveyed 155 families with a developmentally disabled adult being cared for by older parents. They discuss the underutilization of nonfamilial caregivers by these families. The lack of qualified caregivers and financial hardship are cited as reasons for going it alone.

Dolores Cabic Borland (Chapter 19) explores the sibling relationship as a housing alternative to institutionalization in later life. Siblings prefer to assist one another, according to the 41 older individuals in her sample. Sisters are the most frequent recipient of a sibling requiring assistance, and most rank living with a sibling equal to living with a child.

The final chapter by Charles M. Barresi and Donna J. McConnell (Chapter 20) looks at adult day care as an alternative for impaired older people. A sample of 35 impaired elderly day care participants are compared with 116 impaired older citizens in typical community settings. Those who utilize day care are more likely to be labeled as dependent by their families and to differ in social and economic resources, as well as in mental health.

Together these readings represent a diversity of lifestyles and relationships. Older people cope with advancing age and the situations in which they find themselves in a variety of ways. There is no right way to age. Quality of life can be maintained by most older individuals within the community environment. Support from one's spouse, family, and friends are key to maintaining health and happiness in later life.

> Grow old along with me!
> The best is yet to be,
> The last of life, for which the first was made:
> Our times are in His hand . . .
>
> Robert Browning
> *Rabbi Ben Ezra*

Part I

Long-Term Marriages

Chapter 2

Long-Term Marriages

A Critical Review

Michael J. Sporakowski
  Department of Family and Child Development
  Virginia Tech
  Blacksburg, Virginia 24061
Leland V. Axelson
  Department of Family and Child Development
  Virginia Tech
  Blacksburg, Virginia 24061

Long-term marriages, defined here as those of 20 or more years in length, are a relatively new phenomenon in the history of the United States. Although Glick and Norton (1977) indicated that one marriage in five will see its 50th anniversary, Peterson (1975) noted that at the turn of the century most marriages were terminated during middle age by the death of one of the spouses.

Swenson and Moore (1979, p. 250) stated: "The average couple marrying today and living out their expected span of years, well into their seventies, can expect a marriage lasting about 48 years." Census data (U.S. Bureau of the Census, 1977, 1982) convey a picture of an increasing number of married-couple households[1] where members are 65 years of age and over. In 1977, persons 75 years of age or older made up 3.61% of married couple households; in 1982, the percentage had increased to 4.36%. Similarly, for married couple households with persons 65 to 74 years of age, the percentages were: 1977, 8.05%; 1982, 9.00%. As individual longevity increases, it would seem logical that the potential for marriages of long duration would also increase, assuming of course that rates of marital dissolution do not dramatically increase in the foreseeable future. Even if rates of divorce remain at their current historical highs, with longevity remaining constant or increasing, the opportunities exist for remarriages as well as first marriages to meet the time criterion of long-term relationships.

Although many studies have defined long-term marriages as those lasting in excess of 40 years (Ade-Ridder & Brubaker, 1983b; Bain, 1974; Friedman & Todd, 1983; Roberts, 1980; Sporakowski & Hughston, 1978; Swenson, Eskew, & Kohlhopp, 1981; Todd, Friedman, & Lomranz, 1983), a number of studies reviewed here have used 18, 20, or 25 years as the lower boundary of long-term marriage (Fields, 1983; Medling & McCarrey, 1981; Rowe & Meredith, 1982). This variability undoubtedly accounts for the many problems of generalization in studies examining long-term relationships.

With the above in mind, it is the authors' purpose to critically review studies with the intent of developing guidelines necessary for research needed in this area. As will be seen, the heterogeneous nature of studies—their samples, variables, and modes of assessment—has provided a diverse mix of findings and conclusions about marriages of long duration.

Growing Old Together

The following is an overview of many life experiences that are likely to be part of the long-term marriage process. Some of the features of the aging process presented are external to the marriage itself.

As couples grow old, forces not of their own making begin to have an impact upon their relationships and life satisfactions. These forces may include the real consequences of the aging process, such as debilitating disease, deafness, poor eyesight, and/or loss of stamina. Events in the lives of their children and other kin, which might include divorce, desertion, economic deprivation, and the death of a loved one, as well as significant passages in their own lives, such as retirement and the possible loss of financial independence, are important events in the lives of the elderly. These elements have a potentially strong impact upon the marital happiness and life satisfaction of the older married couple.

Resources

Data from Current Population Reports, Series P-20 (U.S. Bureau of the Census, 1977, 1983) indicate that in March of 1982, of married-couple households in which the householder was 65 years old or older, 87.6% lived in their own house (p. 31). This was up from 82.8% in 1976 (p. 49).

For whites in 1982, 88.8% owned their homes as did 76.5% of black families. In 1976, 83.2% of whites owned their own home compared with 75.5% of blacks. For married-couple households in which both of the spouses were 65 years old or older in 1972, slightly over 18% had at least one member of the household employed: in 3.75% of the households wives were employed, and 11.5% of the husbands were employed; and in 3% both were employed. These figures are of importance, because the financial welfare of the couple is likely to have a significant impact upon their marital and life satisfaction.

Hill and Dorfman (1982), in a study of housewives whose husbands had recently retired, found a statistically significant association between income and the wife's life satisfaction, but no apparent association with marital satisfaction. Heyman and Jeffers (1968) found that wives from the upper socioeconomic statuses were more likely to be "glad" their husbands had retired.

The financial status of a couple can also have a potential impact upon the couple's interaction with its children. Simos (1973), in a study of 50 adult children reporting on 60 of their aging parents, found that a small group of children (20%) were bitter that medical expenses had exhausted their parents' savings and deprived them of what they considered to be "their rightful" inheritance. Most of these children did not blame their parents for their financial difficulties but blamed the "system." For the most part, these offspring felt little financial obligation to their parents, but saw their primary obligation to be to their own nuclear family.

Feelings of happiness may also be affected by one's financial situation. Hutchinson (1975) in a study of the low-income elderly, found that among married females, those who were defined as belonging to the "poverty group" were less happy than their counterparts with "low incomes." For husbands, there were no differences in reported happiness between these two economic groups.

Physical and Mental Health

Health seems very important in predicting life satisfaction and it is probably an intervening variable in determining the status of a marriage. Heyman and Jeffers (1968) found strong evidence supporting the hypothesis that wives with healthy husbands were more likely to be glad that their husbands had retired. They also found these wives to be happier in their marriages. Because of increasing poor health, an individual will, on occasion, reject a spouse. Decreasing unhappiness of parents, frequently exaggerated by chronic depression and general anxiety, increases their difficulties in relating to their children (Simos, 1973).

The level of morale of retired and older couples in large measures depends upon the adjustment of the retired male to his new social environment. As has been already noted, wives in families in which the husband retires because he believes it is time and he is in good health, make better adjustments to their husband's retirement (Heyman & Jeffers, 1968). The male's morale and his marital adjustment also remain high if he accepts the responsibility of sharing household activities (Lipman, 1961). Ballweg (1967) found little differences in shared household tasks between spouses when interviewing housewives whose retired husbands were 65 years old or older. On the extreme of his continuum, he found wives decreasing their household responsibilities and husbands increasing theirs. Mancini (1979) also found that among 14 individuals who had been married more than 50 years, there existed a high level of morale in conjunction with a high level of marital satisfaction.[2]

Gubrium (1974) and Hutchinson (1975) each found that married individuals were less likely to experience loneliness. They also reported evidence suggesting that wives, more than husbands, will most likely experience some form of loneliness.

Regarding the general outlook toward life of the elderly, Harris and associates (1981) discovered that when comparing the attitudes of people 65 and over in 1974 with those in 1981, a decreasing percentage of the elderly thought that, "Things seem better as I grow older." Fewer thought they were as happy as they were when younger; more thought that life could be happier; and still more thought that the lot of the average person is growing worse. So much for health in the "golden years."

Marital Happiness/Satisfaction

The common finding that older couples report their marriages to be very satisfying must be interpreted with caution. In a very early study, Pineo (1961), using 400 respondents from the Burgess and Wallin (1953) study, found a general drop in marital satisfaction as one approached the 20th year of marriage. There was a loss of intimacy and a reduction in the frequency of sexual intercourse. He also found that these shifts in behavior did not seem to affect the personal adjustment of the individuals involved. More recently, papers reviewing marital quality across the life cycle (e.g., Rollins & Cannon, 1974; Spanier, Lewis, & Cole, 1975)

indicated the curvilinearity of the relationship of duration with happiness and satisfaction, which varies from a high during the early years of
marriage, lowers during the childrearing years, and increases as the
children leave home. This research suggests that couples refocus on their
marriage in later life.

Mancini (1979) found that 13 of the 14 individuals married 50 or more
years thought that things went well between them and their spouses
"most" or "all of the time." Rowe and Meredith (1982) found that among
those married 50 or more years, 80% recalled their marriages as being
happy from their wedding day to the present. Yet these same individuals,
when asked, selected their spouses as one of their three closest intimates
only one time in four (28%). They also found that only 11% of the partners
selected each other in common as their closest intimate. Nearly two-
thirds of the group married 50 years or more did not select their spouse
at all. It is difficult to comprehend the social mechanisms functioning
that permit individuals to record their marriages as happy to very
happy, yet not select their spouse as the first, second, or even third
closest intimate.

Harris and associates (1975) asked men and women over 65 to identify
someone they felt "close enough to" to talk about things that really
bothered them. Of the men responding, 60% selected their spouse.
Women selected their children first (39%) and their friends second
(29%), before they selected their husbands (25%). Unfortunately, the
percentage of marrieds among these men and women was not indicated.
Suspicion that long-term marriages are not as happy as reported is
aroused when 94.9% of the elderly respondents (Stinnett, Carter, &
Montgomery, 1972) reported their marriages to be very happy or happy,
yet when these same individuals were asked to indicate the "most troublesome aspects" of their present marriage relationship, 12.5% indicated
a lack of mutual interests with their spouse, and 13.8% reported differing
values and life philosophies from those of their spouse.

Intimacy may also be evidenced in the sexual relationship of couples
married over 50 years. Ade-Ridder and Brubaker (1983b) found that
there was a positive correlation between interest in sex and marital
happiness.

Chiriboga (1982) offers possible insight into the intimacy dilemma. In
his study of marital separation in later life, he found that women begin to
shift their balance of satisfaction and dissatisfaction with their marriages well before their spouses. Utilizing techniques developed by Lowenthal, Thurnher, Chiriboga, and associates (1975), he was able to
develop a "life evaluation chart" sensitive to early signals of discontent

prior to a couple's decision to divorce. It may well be that a modification of this method would allow researchers to bypass the socially acceptable responses of many elderly couples.

Internal and External Family Relations

Simos (1973) explored a broad range of social, financial, and physical problems and their influences upon intragenerational and intergenerational interaction. Zube (1982), in a review of the research literature on rates of personality change, social involvement, and shifting roles of adults in the later years, noted the difficulties that the shifting and uneven development of personalities have upon spousal relationships. The fact that older parents can have a positive effect on the "psychological well-being" of a widowed daughter emphasizes the reciprocity of generational contacts (Bankoff, 1983). A shift in power held by husband and wife can well be expected upon the retirement of the husband. One interpretation of the Hill and Dorfman (1982) study cited above could be that, as the roles within the household begin to shift, there is a greater balance of responsibility leading to greater equity in the decision-making process.

The Long-Term Marriage

Table 2.1 presents a summary of the studies published since 1970 and reviewed for this chapter. As can been seen at a very cursory level, the sampling procedures, actual samples secured, ages of individuals and length of marriages, variables investigated, and findings are diverse. Some can best be categorized as studies of older persons, some of whom were in long-term marriage relationships (Atchley & Miller, 1983; Maas & Kuypers, 1974; Mancini, 1979; Stinnett et al., 1972; Stinnett, Carter, & Montgomery, 1970; Swenson et al., 1981). Others (Ade-Ridder & Brubaker, 1983; Atchley & Miller, 1983; Bain, 1974; Fields, 1983, Friedman & Todd, 1983; Medling & McCarrey, 1981; Roberts, 1980; Rowe & Meredith, 1982; Sporakowski & Hughston, 1978; Swenson & Moore, 1981; Todd, Friedman & Lomranz, 1983) appear to be focused primarily, if not exclusively, on long-term couple relationships.

Of the studies cited, 63% (ten) involved data derived from couples as the primary focus of analysis, whereas 37% (six) were based on individuals who were involved in long-term marriages. Data were typically gathered using questionnaires and/or interviews. One notable exception

Table 2.1

Chronological Summary of Studies Involving Long-Term Marrieds

Authors	Sampling techniques	N	Ages	Couple status	Length of marriage	Variables studied	Findings/conclusions
Stinnett, Carter, & Montgomery (1970)	Responses to mailed questionnaires from senior citizen lists (26% return rate)	227	60–89	Married persons but not analyzed as couples	1–50 years (52% married 40–49 years)	Marital need satisfaction Morale (Life Satisfaction Index-Z) Self-Image (Self-Image Scale) Personal aspiration (Ori Scale)	Men had higher marital need satisfaction than women. Wives' lowest subscore on communication; husbands' on respect; 52% said the present time was the happiest. Persons who rated marriages very happy had highest marital-need satisfaction scores; 53% said marriage improved over time. Marital need satisfaction significantly correlated with morale and not self-image or personal orientation scores. Moderate interaction with children was positively related to marital need satisfaction. Love is the greatest area of marital need satisfaction for both men and women.

(continued)

Table 2.1 (*Continued*)

Authors	Sampling techniques	N	Ages	Couple status	Length of marriage	Variables studied	Findings/conclusions
Stinnett, Carter, & Montgomery (1972)	Responses to questionnaires mailed to persons on senior citizen center lists in Oklahoma	408 (51% males)	60–89	Married persons but not analyzed as couples	Not reported	Morale (Life Satisfaction Index-Z) Marital happiness (self-rating) Perceptions of marriage, health, problems, happiness	Marital happiness positively related to morale. Morale correlated with marriage improving or worsening over time. The present was the happiest period of time in life. Choosing it as such correlated with high morale. Poor health, housing, and money were the most significant problems. 94.9% rated their marriages happy or very happy.
Bain (1974)	Convenience-newspaper announcements, "word of mouth" Roanoke, VA; Toledo, OH; Worcester, MA	69	65–100	31 couples	50–60 yr. ($\bar{x} = 51.13$)	Family life cycle adjustment Marital adjustment (Locke-Wallace)	Husbands and wives agreed on problems over the life cycle (97.5%). Males had slightly more problems overall than females.

Study	Method	N	Age	N couples	Length	Variables	Findings
Maas & Kuypers (1974)	Longitudinal over 40 years. Parents of children born 1928-1929. Sampling of children initially representative of area, 1 in 3 births	142	60-89 ($\bar{x}$ males = 71; $\bar{x}$ females = 69)	Included 47 couples	40 or more years	Lifestyles personalities	Aging lifestyles of fathers and mothers married to each other develop quite independently of each other. No personality matching evidenced across the couples.
Sporakowski & Hughston (1978)	Convenience-newspaper announcements "word of mouth" Roanoke and Reston, VA (35% participation rate)	80	66-93	40 couples	50-68 years ($\bar{x}$ = 52.7)	Marital adjustment (Locke-Wallace) Family life cycle assessment Personality congruence (Interpersonal checklist)	Maritally well-adjusted tended to have greater congruence of personality perception. Couples whose perceptions of problems over the life cycle agreed had better marital adjustment. Childbearing stage was seen as both most and least satisfying. Religion, love, permanence, and cooperation were seen as most important factors in making a marriage work.

(continued)

Table 2.1 (*Continued*)

Authors	Sampling techniques	N	Ages	Couple status	Length of marriage	Variables studied	Findings/conclusions
Mancini (1979)	Random selection using census data, urbanized area proportioned into year-round dwellings (67% participation rate)	104 (54% female)	65 or older (30% over $\bar{x}$ = 72.5)	57 currently married and living with spouse	$\bar{x}$ = 39.6 years (14 respondents married 50 or more years)	Perception of marital competence Marital satisfaction Marital longevity Perceptions of parental competence Morale (The Philadelphia Geriatric Morale Scale)	Marital competence, marital satisfaction and parental competence associated with high morale. The greater the number of children, the lower the moral score. 50 year marrieds indicate high marital satisfaction and high morale.

Study	Sampling	N	Mean age	Variables	Findings
Swenson & Moore (1979)	Nonrandom from churches, senior citizens centers, retirement groups, and friends Interviews Indiana, Florida, Pennsylvania, Oklahoma (40% of those contacted cooperated)	224 couples in 2 groups, pre- and post-retirees	$\bar{x} = 54.9$ $\bar{x} = 67.5$ Couples	Retirement status Relationship with children Love (Love Scale) Marriage problems (the Scale of Marriage Problems)	$\bar{x} = 31.54$ years $\bar{x} = 40.13$ years — High-commitment marriages have fewer problems and agree on what they are. Couples in postretirement group had less love expression but also fewer marital problems than the preretirement group. Interaction with children has little effect on the marriages of older couples.
Roberts (1980)	Nonrandom	50 couples	$\bar{x}$ males = 80.4; $\bar{x}$ females = 77.9 Couples	Marital adjustment (Locke-Wallace) Perception of health Life satisfaction (Life Satisfaction Index-Z)	50–65 years ($\bar{x} = 55.5$) — Commitment to marriage increases contentment and fulfillment in later years. Independence, commitment, companionship, and caring were significant elements in long-term marriage. 50% had been sexually active during the past 5 years. Scores on three general variables—marital adjustment, life satisfaction, and perception of health were all high. Most had never seriously considered divorce.

(continued)

Table 2.1 *(Continued)*

Authors	Sampling techniques	N	Ages	Couple status	Length of marriage	Variables studied	Findings/conclusions
Medling & McCarrey (1981)	Cross-sectional Census tract, Nepean, Ontario, Canada Hand-delivered questionnaires (26.4% return rate)	172 couples	$\bar{x}$ = 44.4	Couples ($\bar{x}$ = 20 years): One third married 1–12 years One third married 13–24 years One third married 25–50 years	$\bar{x}$ = 20 years	Marital adjustment (Dyadic Adjustment Scale) Values (Rokeach) Years married (see categories under couple status)	High value similarity significantly correlated with high marital adjustment for longest-term marriages but not shorter ones. Value similarity across the life cycle accounts for very little of marital adjustment scores.

Study	Sample	Age	Variables	Findings
Swenson, Eskew, & Kohlhepp (1981)	Nonrandom from church, social, and civic organizations in a midwestern metropolitan area of over 100,000 population 5 subsamples representing various stages of the family life cycle (FLC)	436 individuals in stages 7 and 8 of the FLC	$\bar{x} = 54.96$ (stage 7) $\bar{x} = 67.50$ (stage 8)	Love (Love Scale) Marriage problems (the Scale of Marriage Problems) Sentence completion test Ego development level	Love scores decreased with subsequent FLC stages. Marriage problems decreased after empty nest stage. Over the course of marriage, devitalization occurs. Less husband-wife interaction and satisfaction. Postconformists (ego development is higher) tend to have more positive marital adjustment. Conformists are habituated and lack skill and sensitivity to overcome estrangement in marriage over time.
Rowe & Meredith (1982)	Convenience-newspaper sample in Midwest (71% return rate) of persons married 25 or more years.	71 couples	Age by group: (1) $\bar{x} = 51$; (2) $\bar{x} = 65$; (3) $\bar{x} = 77$	Couples (3 groups): 25-62 years Length within groups: 25-34 (one third) 35-49 (one third) 50 or more (one third)	Level of marital quality Level of perceived marital happiness Reasons for remaining married	With age, the spouse is less often chosen as someone in the "top 10 intimates." Married 50 or more years, marital happiness was high over time and remained so. Less than 50 years, high at beginning, low, then higher. Love was the major reason for staying married.
Ade-Ridder & Brubaker (1983b)	164 couples in general community 79 couples in retirement facility	Individuals	$\bar{x} = 42.9$ years	Marital happiness Sexual activity Residence	The maritally happier are more interested and active in sex. Adjustment not related to residence in the general community or retirement facility.

(continued)

Table 2.1 (*Continued*)

Authors	Sampling techniques	N	Ages	Couple status	Length of marriage	Variables studied	Findings/conclusions
Atchley & Miller (1983)	Subsample from a larger sample of persons 50 years of age or older involved in a longitudinal study of adaptation. Small (25,000) Ohio township. Larger sample base on postcard census of voter registrations (which had a 71% return rate).	208 couples	Males (Md[a] = 63) Females (Md[a] = 61)	Couples		Life satisfaction Health Family interaction Values	Retirement had no effect on life satisfaction of either couple member. Life satisfaction was generally high and correlated positively with good health. Most couples placed high value on intimacy, family ties, and frequent interaction with children and grandchildren. Spouses were quite similar on values and activities. Most couples were family-centered as opposed to couple-centered or individually self-centered.

Study	Recruitment	Sample	Age	Unit	(Age)	Variables	Results
Friedman & Todd (1983)	Response to flyers and announcements in senior citizen centers and apartments and apartment homes in Los Angeles and Tel Aviv.	30 couples	59-92 $\bar{x}$ = 71.24	Couples	45-66 years ($\bar{x}$ = 50.38 years)	Power Marital happiness Intimacy	Husbands had higher marital happiness ratings than wives. Husbands more powerful than wives in happier marriages. Intimacy was less important than power, though important to marital happiness.
Todd, Friedman, & Lomranz (1983)	Clinical interviews of persons responding to advertisements (paid $15).	20 U.S. couples, 8 Israel couples.	61-92 $\bar{x}$ = 71.9	Couples	47-66 years ($\bar{x}$ = 51.2 years)	Intimacy, power, marital happiness, retirement status	Retirement reduced power held by husbands (in the relationship) and power increased for wife. 28% of husbands and 75% of wives said marital happiness was greater after husband's retirement. If they were able to live life over again 18% of husbands would choose retirement, 68% of wives would. Intimacy increased only slightly after retirement; for those who had had intimacy before retirement, it tended to increase; for those who had little before, it decreased.

(continued)

Table 2.1 *(Continued)*

Authors	Sampling techniques	N	Ages	Couple status	Length of marriage	Variables studied	Findings/conclusions
Fields (1983)	Questionnaires to 1,200 members of 3 synagogues in Los Angeles (24% usable return rate)	145 couples	Females $\bar{x}$ = 45.48 Males $\bar{x}$ = 48.56	Couples	18–34 years	Marital satisfaction Congruence of mates' perceptions Sexual satisfaction Trust Parents' marital satisfaction Feelings toward parents	High correlations within pairs on marital satisfaction, trust, sexual satisfaction, and congruence of mates perceptions. Women held a more positive view of their husbands than did men of their wives. Women, more than men, were likely to enjoy sharing feelings with their spouses. Congruence of spousal perceptions was more highly correlated with other variables for women than men. Feelings toward parents and parents' marital satisfaction were more highly correlated with females' scores on other variables than males.

[a] Md, Median.

to the cross-sectional approach was the Maas and Kuypers (1974) study, which was based on longitudinally gathered materials, as well as current interviews.

The length of marriages studied ranged from 20 to 55.5 years with most over 40 years. Individuals in the marriages were, typically, 60 years of age or more, with males generally about two years older than females—in both individual and couple samples.

Variables studied frequently included: Marital happiness/satisfaction/ adjustment (n = 12); Intimacy/Love (n = 5); Personality (n = 5); The Family Life Cycle—problems or tasks across stages (n = 3); Morale (n = 3); and Power (n = 2). Measures were most often ones unique to the particular study/researcher rather than the preferred standardized instruments of wide usage.

Significant findings are summarized in Table 2.1. Positive ratings on health, morale, and need satisfaction were correlated with positive marital quality. Agreement between spouses on problems, needs, and personality perceptions were positively related to marital quality. Commitment, value similarity, and love tended to be positively related to marital quality, although one study (Swenson et al., 1981) indicated that love expression decreased over the family life cycle. Interestingly, intimacy with spouse (or rating the spouse highly on one's list of intimates) was not typical of the long-term marriages studied by Rowe and Meredith (1982).

Retirement was generally viewed as more favorable by wives than by husbands, possibly because of a perceived gain/loss of power (Todd et al., 1983). Marriages where the husband held or maintained more power than the wife were generally viewed as happier, perhaps indicating a stereotypically traditional relationship. Overall, across studies, the common factor binding the marriages together was time: endurance, tolerance, enjoyment, perseverance, fulfillment over the years.

Critique

In reviewing the state of research on enduring marriages, it became apparent to the authors that a number of problems exist in the collection and analysis of the data. First, there is little agreement about the minimum number of years married that is considered to denote a long-term relationship. In the materials reviewed here, the range in years married varied from a minimum of 1 (Medling & McCarrey, 1981; Stinnett et al., 1970) to 68 (Sporakowski & Hughston, 1978), with most studies investigating marriages of 40 or more years in length. This was probably the result of a variety of factors, including but not limited to subject availability. The data were also often extracted from larger bodies of information not expressly gathered for the purpose of studying long-term relationships (e.g., Maas & Kuypers, 1974; Mancini, 1979).

A second problem is that many studies (Maas & Kuypers, 1974; Mancini, 1979; Stinnett et al., 1972; Swenson et al., 1981) report data about enduring relationships gathered from individuals—but analyses did not match respondents with their spouses. The reports by Stinnett et al. (1970, 1972) seem to illustrate this point best. It is difficult to know whether the failure to match the spouses is the result of deliberate planning or oversight. Nevertheless, it would seem that significant information and comparisons were lost, or were made unavailable because couple members in the data set were not or could not be paired.

Third, we found most information to be based on cross-sectional studies. Few attempts have been made to follow couples or families as groups even over a time frame as short as five years. The longitudinal work published is often not a primary focus of the original study or cannot be criticized on the grounds discussed above. The comparisons or findings are often only marginally related to the topic at hand, or analyses are based on afterthought rather than preplanning.

A fourth criticism is that the conceptual frameworks of studies often did not allow for couple analysis because they were primarily focused on individual issues. The Maas and Kuypers (1974) study is an example. The study was based on children born in 1928–29. Data were gathered on the families of these children, and individual personal typologies were generated which categorized mothers, fathers/husbands, and wives. Analyses did include material on marriage, work and leisure, and parenting among other issues, but did not look at the marriages per se. This is most unfortunate because these are some of the few longitudinal data. Of the 142 individuals in the report, 47 intact couples married at least 40 years were included. The study is an excellent example of how data originally gathered for other purposes might have potential secondary or tertiary analyses. Nevertheless, it has little apparent utility because of the constraints placed upon it by the analytic model developed at the beginning of the project.

A fifth concern is the lack of consistency in the variables studied, the instruments used, and methods employed in gathering data. Only the Life Satisfaction Index-Z (Neugarten, Havinghurst, & Tobin, 1961), used to measure morale/life satisfaction, the Locke-Wallace Short Marital-

Adjustment Test (Locke & Wallace, 1959), used to measure marital adjustment, and the Family Life Cycle (Duvall, 1975), used as a framework for viewing tasks, problems, and concerns over time, were used in two or more of the studies cited. Obviously, the divergent kinds of data gathered and the variety of conclusions resulting from varied analyses are often not comparable.

Sixth, the response rates are uniformly low. Many studies find marital satisfaction/happiness relatively high among long-term marrieds, yet few report response rates as high as 50%. Could it be that those who have unhappily stayed together for 40 or more years do not choose to participate in such research out of fear of jeopardizing their secret or having to answer for their unhappiness? Perhaps as Spanier, Lewis, and Cole (1975, p. 2) stated, "Older married persons may see themselves as being more satisfied with their marriages than do younger or middle-aged persons because of their long investment of time, energy, and other resources into the relationship." Perhaps the designation "enduring marriages" would be more appropriate than long-term marriages, so as to better suggest toleration or long-suffering involvement.

A Proposal for Future Research

Although many authors (e.g., Pineo, 1961; Rollins & Cannon, 1974; Spanier et al., 1975) have discussed marital adjustment, happiness, or satisfaction over the life cycle, relatively little data has been gathered about couples in the retirement/aging stage. Much of what has been gathered has been based on *individuals* who have been married 40 or more years. Few studies have used couple comparisons as a primary focus. Where longitudinal data are being gathered, an attempt should be made to include information about couple behaviors, perceptions, satisfactions, and adjustments, not just those of individuals.

A standard set of measurement techniques and devices should be included in the data-gathering process, in addition to any specific or unique measures the research might require. Currently available materials might include *The Dyadic Adjustment Scale* (Spanier, 1976), the *Life Satisfaction Index-Z* (Neugarten et al., 1961), or other instruments that have been used in a number of studies and thus have an established reliability and validity. Where appropriate, criss-cross or spouse-ratings-of-spouse assessments might also prove valuable. These assessments offer the potential for cross-checking spousal perceptions and establishing couple-based normative scores.

Although not the most perfect means of sample selection, utilization of published reports of long-term marriages might prove to be the most efficient method of obtaining subjects for research. Newspapers frequently include names of couples celebrating a "Golden Wedding" or subsequent anniversaries. Although this source may not provide a complete listing of all such marriages, newspapers currently available indicate sufficiently large numbers of couples to warrant study. Over the period 1977-1983, the first author compiled a list of over 400 couples married 50 or more years from a newspaper that served an area with a population of 250,000.

The stage has been set for potentially important work in the development of a better understanding of long-term marriages. It is time to go beyond speculation, conjecture, and editorializing about enduring relationships, and instead begin to fit some of the pieces of the puzzle together to build a comprehensive and comparable data base on long-lasting marital relationships.

Notes

1. Through 1979, these data included husband-wife families; currently, the listing is for married-couple households.
2. Dr. Jay A. Mancini was kind enough to reexamine his data, looking only at those respondents married 50 years or more.

Chapter 3

Relationship Characteristics of Couples Married for 30 Years or More
A Four-Sample Replication

Janette M. Copeland, Margaret A. Bugaighis, and Walter R. Schumm
Department of Family and Child Development
College of Home Economics
Kansas State University
Manhattan, Kansas 66506

Introduction

Rice (1983) has echoed the Maces' observations (Mace, 1972; Mace & Mace, 1974) that marriages have become more *intrinsic* than in the past, with greater emphasis on love, open communication, and companionship. In Wampler and Powell, (1982), the latter concepts have been approximated more formally by the concepts of positive regard, congruence, and empathy (Barrett-Lennard, 1962). If Rice and the Maces are correct in their assumption that older marriages are less intrinsic, then we would expect that relatively intrinsic variables such as regard, congruence, and empathy would be weaker predictors of overall marital satisfaction among older marriages as compared with marriages contracted more recently.

At the same time, research (Anderson, Russell, & Schumm, 1983) often has found a curvilinear relationship between marital quality and stage in the family life cycle with the very youngest and the very oldest couples reporting higher marital quality. In most cases, such research has used only marital adjustment as the dependent variable without evaluating the effect of duration of marriage upon more specific aspects of marital communication such as regard, congruence, and empathy. Therefore, we

The preparation of this paper was supported in part by the Kansas Agricultural Experiment Station, Contribution No. 84-516-J.

elected to test the following hypotheses regarding couples in long-term marriage relationships:

Hypothesis 1

Marital quality will be curvilinearly related to duration of marriage with couples who have been married 30 years or more and those couples married less than 10 years reporting the highest levels of marital quality.

Hypothesis 2

Regard, congruence, and empathy will be weaker predictors of overall marital satisfaction among couples married 30 years or longer as compared with more recent marriages.

Method

Measurement

In each of the four samples described below, we had measures of marital satisfaction, positive regard, and congruence. Three samples also included a measure of empathy. Marital satisfaction was measured by the Kansas Marital Satisfaction (KMS) Scale, a three-item measure that has shown high internal reliability (Grover, Paff-Bergen, Russell, & Shumm, 1984; Nichols, Shectman, & Grigsby, 1983; Shumm, Scanlon, Crow, Green, & Buckler, 1983) and test-retest reliability (Mitchell, Newell, & Shumm, 1983) as well as concurrent validity with the Dyadic Adjustment Scale (Spanier & Filsinger, 1983; Grover et al., 1984). Positive regard, empathy, and congruence were measured by abbreviated subscales from the Barrett-Lennard (1962) Relationship Inventory (Schumm et al., 1981; Schumm et al., 1983).

Samples

The aforementioned measures were administered in a variety of surveys of the general population of married persons residing in various communities within Kansas. Data were available from a sample of 83 rural families surveyed in the fall of 1977, a sample of 98 urban families surveyed in the spring of 1978, a sample of 212 wives surveyed in 1979, and a sample of 79 married couples surveyed in 1981, as described respectively in previous reports (Schumm et al., 1981; Schumm, Anderson, et al., 1983; Schumm, Scanlon, et al., 1983). The samples are best described here as middle class, white, predominantly Protestant, and rather typical of midwestern families. The characteristics of the spouses married for 30 years or more within each of these samples are presented in Table 3.1. Thirty years of marriage was chosen as our cutoff point because our random samples had yielded very few couples who had been married longer. In additon, we felt our hypotheses could be best evaluated with couples married at least this length of time.

Table 3.1
Demographic Characteristics of Four Samples of Husbands and Wives

	1977		1978		1979	1981	
Characteristics	Husbands (n = 83)	Wives (n = 83)	Husbands (n = 98)	Wives (n = 98)	Wives (n = 212)	Husbands (n = 79)	Wives (n = 79)
Age in years[a]	54.3(2.90)	52.3(2.80)	58.8(4.27)	53.7(4.29)	63.5(7.92)	64.4(11.33)	61.8(11.4)
Duration of marriage in years[a]	32.8(2.01)		33.9(4.17)		40.8(7.28)	39.9(7.23)[b]	40.1(7.34)
Number of children	4.09[c]		2.77[c]		2.74(1.56)	0.31(0.63)[d]	
Education (%)							
High school or less	83.3	66.7	69.2	69.2	38.2	38.5	61.5
At least some graduate study	0.0	0.0[e]	7.7	7.3	8.8	53.9	7.7
Income (%)							
Under $20,000	66.7		58.3		41.7	—[f]	
Over $30,000	33.3		0.0		23.5	30.8	23.1
Employment (%)							
Full-time	100.0	25.0	61.5	23.1	20.6	46.2	15.4
Unemployed	0.0	—[g]	23.1	—[g]	0.0	7.7	0.0
Homemakers	0.0	58.3	0.0	46.2	44.1	0.0	69.2
Retired	—[g]	—[g]	—[g]	—[g]	26.5	38.5	—

[a] Mean value followed in parentheses by the standard deviation.
[b] One husband reported 44 years whereas his wife reported 46 years, which accounts for the difference.
[c] Standard deviations were not available for these data due to way in which data were coded.
[d] Item referred only to children living *at home* (1981 study only).
[e] One of the wives in this group had even a college degree.
[f] The category of less than $20,000 was not used.
[g] Data not available.

Analysis

SPSS (Nie, 1983) routines were used to perform one-way analyses of variance, predicting mean values of our dependent variables (marital satisfaction, regard, congruence, and empathy) from duration of marriage, grouped into four categories of 0–9, 10–19, 20–29, and 30 or more years of marriage. Tests for polynominal trends were conducted in order to permit detection of significant quadratic effects, as hypothesized. We wished to determine if duration of marriage interacted with each independent variable (empathy, regard, and congruence) in predicting marital satisfaction, as well as the main effect of each independent variable. Significant interaction effects would possibly support our second hypothesis, depending upon the relative slopes of the regression lines for those couples married less than 30 years and those married 30 years or more. Scatterplots in which the regression lines for younger couples were steeper than those of older couples would support our hypothesis that positive regard, empathy, and congruence would be more important predictors of marital satisfaction for younger couples.

Results

Hypothesis 1

For our first hypothesis concerning the curvilinear relationship between marital satisfaction, empathy, regard, and congruence with duration of marriage, we investigated those four dependent variables in seven groups of husbands and wives (excepting empathy for husbands and wives in the 1981 study) for a total of 26 tests as shown in Table 3.2. Of the 26 tests analyzed, 14 showed evidence of the U-shaped pattern of curvilinearity we had hypothesized, whereas another six showed only a positive linear trend with duration of marriage. However, the overall F tests in our analyses of variance were significant only for four variables in the sample from the 1979 study, as had been found by Anderson et al., (1983). For the four variables, significant ($p < .05$) quadratic trends were found: $F(1, 206) = 10.56$, regard; $F(1, 206) = 6.38$, empathy; $F(1, 206) = 7.14$, congruence; and $F(1, 207) = 13.6$, marital satisfaction. Significant linear trends were found in some cases as well: $F(1, 206) = 8.32$, regard; and $F(1, 206) = 4.74$, congruence. In each of those cases, post hoc LSD tests found significant differences between the marriages of longest duration and the next cohort (20 to 29 years), and between the youngest

Table 3.2
Marital Satisfaction, Regard, Empathy, and Congruence
and Duration of Marriage[a]

Sample (N)[b]	Variable	Duration of marriage (years)			
		0-9	10-19	20-29	30 or more[c]
1977					
Husbands	Marital satisfaction	17.60	18.46	18.94	19.55 (.88)
(N = 76)	Regard	20.43	20.70	20.19	21.42 (.81)
	Empathy	16.14	18.76	17.66	18.58 (.89)
	Congruence	11.57	11.60	10.69	11.75 (.31)
Wives	Marital satisfaction	16.86	17.19	19.51	20.08 (.13)
(N = 79)	Regard	20.86	20.60	21.00	20.91 (.72)
	Empathy	17.86	17.03	18.22	18.00 (.73)
	Congruence	11.14	10.67	11.53	11.55 (.63)
1978					
Husbands	Marital satisfaction	19.00	17.86	18.45	19.22 (.05)
(N = 76)	Regard	20.00	20.58	20.38	19.77 (.90)
	Empathy	14.33	17.10	17.89	19.00 (.52)
	Congruence	9.67	10.90	11.18	11.25 (.92)
Wives	Marital satisfaction	19.00	18.47	18.20	19.31 (.99)
(N = 92)	Regard	22.00	21.74	20.13	20.46 (.95)
	Empathy	14.33	16.65	17.00	17.31 (.94)
	Congruence	11.67	11.35	10.85	11.92 (.88)
1979					
Wives	Marital satisfaction	17.92	16.21	15.75	18.35 (.96)
(N = 210)	Regard	22.81	21.15	19.88	21.73 (.94)
	Empathy	18.75	17.49	15.67	18.18 (.92)
	Congruence	20.36	18.95	17.46	19.55 (.75)
1981					
Husbands	Marital satisfaction	17.58	17.78	18.75	18.92 (.83)
(N = 72)	Regard	23.00	21.80	22.38	22.85 (.84)
	Empathy[d]	—	—	—	—
	Congruence	20.85	20.24	20.25	22.15 (.83)
Wives	Marital satisfaction	17.46	16.82	17.25	18.23 (.94)
(N = 70)	Regard	22.66	23.06	22.25	23.45 (.81)
	Empathy[d]	—	—	—	—
	Congruence	20.83	19.94	21.67	22.27 (.86)

[a] Scores represent mean values for each variable for subjects within each year group.
[b] Sample size reported reflects smallest N after elimination of maximum number of cases because of missing data.
[c] Cronbach's (1951) alpha for each variable for only those subjects in last group is reported in parentheses after last mean score.
[d] Data on empathy not collected for these samples.

cohorts and the 20 to 29 cohort. The above results and the five other significant effects that were scattered among the other groups could have been due largely to chance, given the large number of tests involved, although quite a few trends ($p < .20$) toward a significant quadratic effect were also obtained. Because only a few patterns actually reached acceptable levels of statistical significance, we must conclude that only weak support was obtained for hypothesis 1.

Hypothesis 2

For hypothesis 2, concerning the relative importance of empathy, regard, and congruence in predicting marital satisfaction among older couples, we found that of the 19 possible significant interaction terms (between duration of marriage and our independent variables in the four samples), only one reached significance, $t(68) = -2.61$ ($p < .02$) between duration of marriage and empathy for rural wives in the 1978 sample. Because one of the 20 such tests might be statistically significant by chance alone, we must reject hypothesis 2. As indicated in Table 3.3, in spite of very small numbers of subjects and low reliabilities in some cases for our variables (Table 3.2), most of the correlations between marital satisfaction and the three independent variables remained at least moderately substantial, often statistically significant. Thus, it is apparent that even for couples who have been married for many years, what we believe to be intrinsic measures of communication quality have remained (or perhaps, have become) very important in their self-reported evaluations of marital quality, as assessed by our marital satisfaction scale. These results assume even more significance in view of the rather high mean values found for marital satisfaction, because ceiling effects might be expected to limit the variance in the dependent variable, and thus limit the maximum possible correlations of the dependent variable with other measures.

Discussion

In spite of popular opinions to the contrary (Rice, 1983; Mace, 1972; Mace & Mace, 1974), it does not appear that couples who have been married over 30 years value any less those aspects of their relationship that would seem to be more intrinsic than utilitarian. It may be that couples who married in the late 1940s or early 1950s had already adopted more intrinsic attitudes about the needs that might be fulfilled in marriage, and it would take research with much older cohorts to find very many truly utilitarian marriages. It is also possible that couples in our samples *changed* their views about marriage to fit the times, becoming more intrinsically oriented through the years. In any case, it would be hazardous, we believe, to assume that older marriages are any less intrinsic than younger marriages, given the result of our research. It might even be true that the assumption that most marriages were less intrinsic years ago is stereotypical.

While it is possible that our failure to control for marital/social desirability might have affected our results, it must be remembered that Anderson (Anderson et al., 1983) found minimal effects due to that

Table 3.3
Bivariate Relationships between Marital Satisfaction and Independent Variables for Husbands and Wives Married 30 Years or More from Four Samples

	Independent variables								
	Regard			Empathy			Congruence		
Sample	r[a]	B[b]	N[c]	r	B	N	r	B	N
1977									
Husbands	.62*	.47	11	.66*	.32	11	-.07	-.13	11
Wives	.69†	.38	11	.79†	.28	11	.57*	.31	11
1978									
Husbands	.52	.44	9	.17	.15	9	.74*	.71	8
Wives	.48*	.28	13	.75‡	.31	13	.18	.16	13
1979									
Wives	.70‡	.64	33	.63‡	.56	33	.64‡	.60	33
1981									
Husbands	.80‡	.66	12	—[d]	—[d]	—[d]	.49	.51	12
Wives	.63*	.78	11	—[d]	—[d]	—[d]	.67*	.73	11

[a] Pearson zero-order correlation coefficient. Because of small sample size, some moderate-size correlations do not quite reach statistical significance.
[b] Unstandardized regression coefficient, the slope of the linear relationships.
[c] The number of subjects analyzed for the group of respondents married 30 years or more within each sample.
[d] Data not available.
* $p < .05$.
† $p < .01$.
‡ $p < .001$.

variable other than possible masking of the depth of the u-shaped patterns. (That is, the patterns were stronger for subjects responding in less socially desirable ways.) Future research in this area should involve larger samples than those used in this report; however, the consistency obtained with four samples and seven sets of spouses would seem, in our opinion, to offset, in many respects, the sample-size limitations of the present study.

Chapter 4

Quality of Marriage
A Comparison between Golden Wedding Couples and Couples Married Less Than 50 Years

Linda Ade-Ridder
Department of Home Economics and Consumer Sciences
and
Family and Child Studies Center
Miami University
Oxford, Ohio 45056

Survival of a marriage beyond the Golden Wedding Anniversary occurs for no more than 3% of all American marriages (Parron & Troll, 1978). Although relatively little is known about marriages of 50 or more years' duration, it might be anticipated that as the life expectancy increases so will the number of long-term marital relationships. Glick and Norton (1977) estimate that one in five marriages will achieve a 50-year milestone. These marriages no doubt reflect a high degree of stability, luck, and survival of the fittest. However, the mere survival of a relationship does not address the quality of that marriage. Significant changes such as retirement, declining health, and reduced income impact upon many older marriages. The burden of providing assistance to older people with special needs often falls to their children or other family members. Alternatives are needed that allow older couples and individuals to grow old gracefully, to maintain as much independence as possible, and to stay together as long as they can. Retirement communities can be a bridge between totally independent living and the nursing home environment necessitated by extreme physical and/or emotional impairment.

Marriage has been found to be central to the "good life" for happily married older couples (Parron & Troll, 1978). One major advantage of comprehensive retirement communities is that they can allow married couples to remain together even if one person's health is poorer than the other's, or enable a couple to move back to a more independent level of care as health improves. Such communities provide much-needed options for older couples. Knowledge is needed about the impact these communities have on their residents. In this study, the marital relationships of couples are examined for a group of married men and women living independently within one midwestern retirement community. What levels of marital quality are evidenced among married couples in a retirement community setting? In particular, are there differences between couples married for 50 years or more when compared with their counterparts married for shorter durations within a retirement community? Better understanding of couples married to the same person for 50 or more years can provide "an excellent opportunity to view a rare design for living" according to Parron and Troll (1978). Because Golden Wedding couples are older, they are especially vulnerable to the ravages of time, and retirement community residency is an important alternative to community living.

Literature Review

Only a small quantity of literature deals specifically with marriages of fifty or more years duration or on retirement community residency; for a review see Brubaker (1985b). Three variables thought to be important to married life were included for study: marital quality, morale, and sexual interest.

Marital quality is defined as the subjective evaluation of the process of dyadic adjustment, including evaluation of: troublesome differences, interpersonal tensions and personal anxiety, satisfaction, cohesion, and consensus on matters of importance (Spanier, 1976). Other aspects also thought to be important in the maintenance of high quality marriage include sexuality. Links between marital quality and sexual behavior have been found to exist for younger couples (Clark & Wallin, 1965). And a positive relationship has been found for elderly couples between marital quality and morale (Gubrium, 1974).

Retirement Community Residency

Retirement communities provide a transitional link for individuals and couples who need some assistance but do not need total institutional care. For some couples, age-segregated living is a functional alternative to the family or community in meeting the needs of persons in their last stages of life. Lawton (1970) reported that even though the amount of direct contact time with family declined following a move into a retirement community, there was no increase in feelings of abandonment or estrangement from the family. In a comparative study of 600 members of six different retirement communities with 600 control subjects living in the community-at-large, Sherman (1975) concluded that living either in the community-at-large or in a retirement community can be satisfactory as long as the older persons freely choose where to live. Sherman (1975) also claimed that members of the retirement communities had more friends and visited more frequently with them than did their counterparts living in the community-at-large. Lawton and Cohen (1974) found that newly re-housed senior citizens demonstrated significantly higher morale and life satisfaction and were more involved with activities than were applicants for senior housing.

Marital Quality

The multiplicity of studies of marital quality over the life cycle presents widely varied and inconsistent findings. Nearly all of the studies were cross-sectional in nature. Some studies looked for correlates with marital quality. Others looked at marital quality over the life cycle to see how it changes with time. The impact of retirement upon marital quality has been addressed more recently. Unfortunately, nearly all studies have been cross-sectional. Only a few have followed the same couples over more than one stage in the family cycle.

Health has been found to correlate strongly with marital maladjustment (Medley, 1977). Sexual behavior was also found to relate positively with marital quality for young to middle-aged couples (Clark & Wallin, 1965; Glass & Wright, 1977). Lee (1978) correlated morale with marital satisfaction for men and for women.

A review of the findings about older couples' marriages reveals conflicting findings (Ade-Ridder & Brubaker, 1983a). Most earlier studies (pre-1970) that reported a decline in marital quality over the marital cycle did not study older men and women; or if they did, the samples were too small for reliable inferences (Hicks & Platt, 1970). Many of the recent studies support a curvilinear pattern, from an initial period of happiness in very early marriage to a low during the early child-rearing years followed by an increase in marital happiness during the later years (Anderson, Russell, & Schumm, 1983; Miller, 1976; Orthner, 1975; Smart & Smart, 1975). A third pattern did not support either the model of decline or the curvilinear pattern. Clark and Wallin (1965) found that couples who previously had high levels of marital satisfaction tended to stay high, supporting a continuous pattern of marital quality over the life cycle, a finding supported by Spanier, Lewis, and Cole (1975).

The impact of retirement on the quality of married life is not conclusive. Atchley and Miller (1983) in a study of 208 married, middle-class older couples, found no significant relationship between retirement and marital quality. On the other hand, an increase in marital quality among retired men and women was reported after a dip around the actual retirement time (Rollins & Feldman, 1970). Support has been found for the notion that postretirement marital quality is related to the level of preretirement marital quality experienced (Fengler, 1975; Medley, 1977).

Marriages of 50 Years or Longer

Most couples married 50 years or longer are retired, and most tend to say they are very satisfied with their relationships (Brubaker, 1985a, 1985b; Brubaker & Ade-Ridder, 1986; Roberts, 1980; Parron & Troll, 1978; Sporakowski & Hughston, 1978). Brubaker's (1985a) sample of 32 Golden Wedding men and women were very happily married (mean = 124.3 for men and 127.1 for women on Spanier's Dyadic Adjustment Scale, 1976). This study looked at sex role expectations and behaviors and found that these couples had expectations that closely matched actual behaviors. In sum, husbands were responsible for primarily masculine activities, and husbands and wives tended to share feminine activities.

The high levels of marital happiness claimed by these Golden Wedding couples probably results from the types of marriages they have developed over the years (Brubaker, 1985b). Companionship seems to be a key element, as these couples demonstrate "give and take" and sharing in their relationships (Brubaker, 1985a; Roberts, 1980; Parron & Troll, 1978; Sporakowski & Hughston, 1978).

Only one study looked at marriages of couples in a retirement community setting. Peterson (1968) reported that of the 500 residents of this particular retirement community, those still married were happiest and demonstrated a great deal of mutual dependence and stability.

Morale

Positive correlations have also been found between marital quality and morale, at least for persons above the poverty line (Gubrium, 1974;

Hutchison, 1975; Lee, 1978). Lee's 1978 study of 439 older married men and women found that the higher marital satisfaction scores were obtained by the persons with the higher morale scores, especially for women. For men, simply having a spouse present seems to be the primary factor in the level of morale. Gubrium's 1974 study of 210 older men and women found that married persons were more satisfied with daily life than were divorced or widowed persons. Hutchison (1975) reported that low-income married elderly claimed higher morale than did unmarried low income persons. However, for poverty-level individuals, morale did not vary by marital status.

Sexual Interest

Sexual behavior correlates with marital quality for young couples (Glass & Wright, 1977), but little work has been done with older couples. In spite of the societal myth that sex is only for the young, sexual interest and behavior is a concern of older people. Although the literature is sparse and somewhat inconclusive, some trends have been noted. Most studies have been cross-sectional; however, the Duke Longitudinal Study, started in 1955 to study the aging of 256 normal men and women, also has gathered data on sexuality. This ongoing study of older Americans has contributed greatly to the literature gap in sexuality (Newman & Nichols, 1970; Pfeiffer & Davis, 1972). Although there is some decline in sexual activity and interest with age (Cameron & Biber, 1963; Pfeiffer & Davis, 1972), the patterns established during the middle years are likely to persist into old age (Huyck, 1977; Masters & Johnson, 1964; Pfeiffer & Davis, 1972).

Sexual behavior is likely to persist for older couples as long as the husband is capable; one or more health problems are the most likely reasons to cease sexual activity for a married couple (Garza & Dressel, 1983; Kinsey, Pomeroy, Martin, & Gebhard, 1953; Robinson, P., 1983). Even so, more than 50% of older married couples claim to continue having a sexually active relationship (Newman and Nicholas, 1970; Roberts, 1980). The frequency of nonintercourse sexual behaviors has largely been unmeasured because most instruments used to date are at a very cursory level (Huyck, 1977).

Sexual interest is an important dimension of sexuality with different meanings to different people (Comfort, 1980). Sexual interest has also been found to decline with age (Huyck, 1977; Parron & Troll, 1978), although interest seems to remain higher than actual activity levels for most older couples (Huyck, 1977; Levinger, 1966; Newman & Nichols,

1970). Although declines are noted, present interest rates, like present sexual behavior rates, tend to reflect past experiences, especially for women (Pfeiffer & Davis, 1972).

Sample

Questionnaires were mailed to both the husband and wife of 103 couples living in a Protestant, comprehensive retirement community located in southwestern Ohio. All subjects were housed in independent living environments, that is, all were capable of caring for themselves completely. Only 12% said that health restricted their activities most of the time or always. And most said that, compared with five years ago, their health was pretty much the same. Either the husband or the wife was at least 65 years of age. Usable responses were received from 79 couples (158 men and women) or 76.7% of the sample polled. These subjects ranged in age from 61 to 92 years and averaged 74.8 years. Sixty percent of the men and 47% of the women were 75 years or older. Well educated, most had completed at least some college or technical school; 40% of the men and 19% of the women had done graduate work or received a graduate degree. Prior to retirement, 52% of the men were professionals or managers by occupation. Another 20% were employed in the service sector, including ministers without advanced degrees and teachers. Forty-three percent of the wives were homemakers, 29% were employed in the service sector, and another 24% worked in clerical or sales positions prior to retirement. All but two of the respondents were retired at the time of data collection. On average, these individuals retired at 64.2 years of age, although four men retired prior to age 60 years. Overwhelmingly, these people retired because they chose to; 76.4% of the men but only 31% of the women cited that reason. Only six people said they were forced to retire unwillingly. Seven retired due to declining health. And, 33% of the women retired because their spouses had, but no men claimed that reason for retirement. Family income the year prior to retirement averaged $10,000 to $14,999 and ranged from less than $4,999 to more than $45,000 per year. The average length of marriage was 41 years with a range from less than one year to 63 years for these couples; however, 11 men and women had been married for two years or less, an added benefit of retirement community living! Marriages of 50 years or more were reported by 34.8% (N = 55) of the respondents. The average length of residence in the retirement community was 4.1 years and ranged from two months to 25 years. Due to the recent expansion of the retirement community's independent housing, one-third of the respondents had lived in the community less than one year at the time of testing. An additional one-fourth had lived there between one and two years, and almost 42% had lived there for three or more years. The large influx of new residents lowered the average length of residence for the sample. All but four of the residents said they would choose to live in this particular community again if they had it to do over. Because of the United Methodist religious affiliation of this particular community, it is not surprising that 96% of the respondents said they attend church once per week or more often. Only one person said they never attended church or only attended on special days. For the most part, this is a sample of middle-class, well-educated Protestant men and women.

Measures

Marital quality was measured using Spanier's Dyadic Adjustment Scale (1976), with one modification because of the age of these respondents. Spanier (1976) claimed content, criterion, and construct validity. Reliability was determined using Cronbach's Coefficient Alpha and the Spearman-Brown formula; total scale reliability was found to be .92 for this sample, compared with .96 in Spanier's first study (1976) and .91 in his second study (Spanier & Thompson, 1982). This scale has a theoretical range from zero to 151 and an actual range from 38 to 146, with a high score indicating a positive or high level of dyadic adjustment. The total sample mean was 117.1 (n = 87; SD = 14.4), compared with 114.8 (n = 218; SD = 17.8) for Spanier's "happily married" group (1976). The men and women married less than 50 years had a mean of 117.1 (n = 50; SD = 13.7), and the respondents married for 50 years or longer had a mean of 116.1 (n = 35; SD = 15.2).

Sexual interest and behavior were measured using the Sexual Behavior Scale devised for use in the Duke Longitudinal Study on Aging (Pfeiffer, Verwoerdt, & Davis, 1972). Only frequencies of incidence of response to individual items were reported by the Duke researchers; validity and reliability were not addressed. However, the repeated use of the scale suggests face validity and reliability (Newman & Nichols, 1970; Pfeiffer et al., 1972). The three behavioral items about sexual frequency are simply reported in Table 4.1; the items about sexual interest are ordinal and are summed with a theoretical range from five to 21 and an actual range from eight to 16, with a high score indicating high amounts of sexual interest and enjoyment. The mean sexual interest score for the total group is 13.7 (n = 113; SD = 2.6).

Morale was measured using Lee's (1978) six-item morale scale. Lee defined morale as "a feeling of overall well-being and personal satisfac-

Table 4.1
Sexual Behavior Responses by Marital Length

	Married 49 years or less		Married 50 years or more		Total	
	n	%	n	%	n	%
Frequency of sexual intercourse during the first years of marriage						
Never	0	0.0	0	0.0	0	0.0
Once a month or less	4	4.9	2	4.0	6	4.6
Two-four times/month	26	32.1	23	46.0	49	37.4
Two-three times/week	43	53.1	20	40.0	63	48.1
More than three times/ week	8	9.9	5	10.0	13	9.9
Totals	81	61.8	50	38.2	131	100.0
Missing cases = 27						
Frequency of sexual intercourse now						
Never	28	35.0	23	46.9	51	39.5
Once a month or less	24	30.0	16	32.7	40	31.0
Two-four times/month	25	31.3	8	16.3	33	25.6
Two-three times/week	0	0.0	1	2.0	1	0.8
More than three times/ week	3	3.8	1	2.0	4	3.1
Totals	80	62.0	49	38.0	129	100.0
Missing cases = 29						
Noticed any change in sexual activity over the years						
Decrease	53	74.6	44	91.7	97	81.5
Increase	14	19.7	3	6.3	17	14.3
No change	4	5.6	1	2.1	5	4.2
Totals	71	59.7	48	40.3	119	100.0
Missing cases = 39						

tion" (1978, p. 134). Although, he did not make a case for validity, repeated use of the scale suggests face validity. The reliability was measured to be .81 using Cronbach's Coefficient Alpha, which compared with Lee's reported .85 for males and .87 for females (1978). The theoretical range is from six to 24 with high scores denoting high levels of morale. The mean for this sample is 20.4 (n = 141; SD = 3.5); Lee (1978) reported a mean of 18.7 for men and 18.9 for women (SD = 2.3 for men and 2.6 for women) in his study of older people.

Findings

Using the Student's t, there is no significant different in marital quality between Golden Wedding couples and those married for shorter time periods, as shown in Table 4.2. Comparing the means indicates that all of these men and women are happily married.

Declines in frequency of sexual intercourse from early marriage to the present time were noted in both groups of the men and women. During the early years of marriage, most claimed a sexual intercourse rate of two to three times per week. At the time of testing, 37.2% of the total sample said they no longer engaged in sexual intercourse; 32.5% of those married less than 50 years had stopped having sexual intercourse (n = 26), and 44.9% of the Golden Wedding couples no longer engaged in coitus (n = 22), a difference that is not significant. For those who were

Table 4.2
Student's t-Values of Scale Variables by Marital Length

Scale	Married 49 years or less			Married 50 years or more			
	n	M	SD	n	M	SD	t-Value
Dyadic adjustment scale	50	117.1	13.7	35	116.1	15.2	0.31
Sexual interest	67	14.3	2.5	43	12.6	2.2	0.00*
Morale	80	20.7	3.5	46	20.4	3.4	0.67

* $p < .001$.

still active, almost all engage in coitus between once a month or less and two to four times per month (see Table 4.1). Most respondents noticed the change in sexual behavior prior to the age of 65 (65% of the combined sample); there was no significant difference between the Golden Wedding couples and the people married less than 50 years. However, when sexual interest was examined using Student's t, men and women married for less than 50 years reported significantly higher levels of interest than did the Golden Wedding men and women (see Table 4.2).

Morale did not differ significantly between those married for 50 years or more and those married for shorter durations when the means were compared using Student's t, as shown in Table 4.2. Both groups appear to have very high levels of morale.

Only two other variables, prior marriage and friendship interaction, differed significantly between the Golden Wedding couples and those married for 49 years or less. Health was not significantly different for these two groups. None of the Golden Wedding couples had been married previously, whereas 36% ($n = 31$) of the couples married for 49 years or less had had a prior marriage, as shown in Table 4.3. Applying a Yates correction to chi-square, this difference is significant, although not surprising. While the amount of time the individual spends with friends each week does not differ significantly between the two groups, the hours per week the couple spends interacting with friends is significantly different, also shown in Table 4.3. The Golden Wedding couples tend to spend less time with friends than do the couples married for shorter lengths of time.

Discussion

The high levels of marital quality reported by these retired couples supports previous literature findings (Anderson et al., 1983). The couples married 50 years or longer are not significantly different from the couples married for shorter times except in levels of sexual interest and in previous marital history. The entire sample is very homogenous in that all are in intact marriages, all are relatively healthy, and all live in the same retirement community, thereby somewhat controlling for standard of living. The lack of sufficient differences in marital quality, morale, and sexual behavior lends support to the previously reported theories of continuity; that is, that patterns established during the middle years are likely to persist into the later years (Brubaker, 1985b; Medley, 1977; Spanier, Lewis & Cole, 1975). Consistent with previous literature, these retirement community older men and women exhibit high levels of marital quality (Peterson, 1968) and high levels of morale (Lee, 1978). Although sexual intercourse frequency declined over the years, 63% were still active sexually. Sexual interest differed significantly by length of marriage. Men and women married shorter times claimed higher levels of sexual interest. Interaction with friends also differed significantly for Golden Wedding couples when compared with couples married fewer years. Golden Wedding couples spend less time interacting

Table 4.3
Significant Chi-Square Values of Scale Variables for
Golden Wedding Couples and Couples Married Less Than 50 Years

	Married 49 years or less		Married 50 years or more		Total	
	n	%	n	%	n	%
The number of hours you spend with friends each week						
None	26	30.2	19	36.5	45	32.6
1-4	48	55.8	21	40.4	69	50.0
5-9	9	10.5	6	11.5	15	10.9
10 or more	3	3.5	6	11.5	9	6.5
Totals	86	62.3	52	37.7	138	100.0

Chi-square = 5.192; degrees of freedom = 3

The number of hours you and your spouse spend with friends each week						
None	0	0	4	7.7	4	2.9
1-4	31	36.9	24	46.2	55	40.4
5-9	32	38.1	14	26.9	46	33.8
10 or more	21	25.0	10	19.2	31	22.8
Totals	84	61.8	52	38.2	136	100.0

Chi-square = 8.795*; degrees of freedom = 3

History of previous marriage						
No	55	64.0	55	100.0	110	78.0
Yes	31	36.0	0	0.0	31	31.0
Totals	86	61.0	55	39.0	31	100.0

Chi-square = 23.355†; [a] degrees of freedom = 1

[a] Yates Correction applied (before Yates Correction: Chi-Square = 25.413†; degrees of freedom = 1)
* $p < .05$.
† $p < .001$.

with friends than do couples married for shorter times. This supports Brubaker's (1985b) findings that companionship and mutual sharing are high for couples married 50 years or more.

In general, the findings about marital quality, morale, and sexual interest and behavior for this sample of 79 older married couples residing in a retirement community are similar to findings from previous studies. They claim to be happily married, have high morale, and exhibit high levels of sexual interest and behavior. Marriage does seem to enhance the quality of life for those fortunate enough to survive to enjoy it. Needed are comparisons between husbands and wives to see if they agree on their levels of happiness. Most studies ask only one spouse or only treat the sample groups as unrelated men and women; closer inspection of these relationships could teach us more about marriage in the later years.

Chapter 5

Family Strengths in Long-Term Marriages

Robert F. MacKinnon and Carol E. MacKinnon
Department of Child Development and Family Relations
University of North Carolina at Greensboro
Greensboro, North Carolina 27412

Mary L. Franken
Department of Home Economics
University of Northern Iowa
Cedar Falls, Iowa 50613

Although focus upon family strengths is relatively new, considerable interest exists in identifying the characteristics of families that exhibit a high level of functioning. This is a change from the orientation toward investigating dysfunctional family characteristics, typically motivated by an interest in providing a prescription for remedying family problems. The departure from the remedial approach is a significant contribution to efforts to strengthen all families, not only those in distress.

The examination of qualities in strong, long-term marriages (more than 40 years) could help find answers as to whether strong families in later stages of the family life cycle continue to develop new areas of strength or basically resemble families in earlier stages.

Research on Family Strengths

Stimulated by the early work of Otto on family strengths (Otto, 1962, 1964), several studies have investigated characteristics of strong families. Stinnett and Sauer (1977) identified six characteristics typical of strong families: appreciation of family members, sharing of quality time, good patterns of communication, commitment to family, religious orientation, and the ability to successfully negotiate family crises. In a study of college students' perceptions of their families' strengths, Beam (1979) found that religious orientation, togetherness, recreational activities, satisfactory communication with parents, and the value placed on strong families by other groups, to be salient concepts. Although these two studies agree on the importance of religion, communication, and shared time, each included unique characteristics of strong families.

Utilizing national sampling, Stinnett, Sanders, and DeFrain (1981) and Stinnett, Sanders, DeFrain, and Parkhurst (1982) identified love, religion, respect, communication, and individuality as characteristics of strong families. The majority of the respondents also reported that their husband-wife and parent-child relationships were both close and happy.

Identification of Strong Families

Strong families have been identified for study in various ways. Stinnett et al. (1981) and Stinnett et al. (1982) used a self-selection process of strength based on self perceptions, assuming that those families who perceived themselves as being strong families acted upon that perception. However, even though a family perceives itself as strong, it may not function as such. Because there is also little agreement about the specific traits of strong families (Stinnett et al., 1981), researchers are faced with a dilemma.

It may be possible to avoid this dilemma by looking at families that have demonstrated their ability to function effectively. It can be argued that families who have negotiated life events and have remained intact are successful and stable. The primary determinant of the stability of a marriage is its quality (Lewis & Spanier, 1979). As Spanier and Lewis (1980, p. 826) argue, "marital quality is inexorably related to marital stability."

Although marital quality is a primary determinant of stability, the converse does not necessarily hold. Some marriages persist despite relatively low quality. Spanier and Lewis (1980, p. 836) stress the "need to pay more attention to low quality, high stability marriages." The configuration of factors that combine to enable low-quality marriages to endure is still a matter of speculation, as is the question of how high-quality versus low-quality marriages differ in how they remain intact.

In the present investigation, an empirical measure of family strengths was used to dichotomize the couples in long-term relationships into two groups, rather than relying solely on stability as the determinant of family strengths. By examining characteristics of strong, long-term marriages, the qualities inherent in stable relationships can be identified and compared with the strengths identified in previous studies.

Previous studies have not addressed gender differences in spouses' perceptions of family strengths. Bernard (1972, 1982) suggests that there are really two marriages in every marital union. According to Bernard (1982, p. 5):

> there is usually agreement in the number of children they have and a few other such verifiable items, although not, for example, on length of premarital acquaintance and of engagement, on age at marriage, and interval between marriage and birth of first child. Indeed, with respect to even such basic components of the marriage as frequency of sexual relations, social interaction, household tasks, and decision-making, they seem to be reporting on different marriages.

The present study, therefore, investigates differences in the perceptions of husbands and wives in long-term marital relationships.

Method

Subjects

The sample consisted of 116 couples, 232 respondents, residing in Iowa. The couples are identified through (a) church organizations, (b) senior citizen organizations, (c) newspaper announcements of anniversaries, and (d) referrals from participants. The subjects were each placed into one of two groups based on their Family Strengths (FSTR) scores. Individuals scoring above the median score (48.8) were assigned to a high family strengths group ($n = 114$), those below to the low family strengths group ($n = 118$). All couples (a) had been married in excess of 40 years, (b) lived in the same household, and (c) had at least one child. Subjects ranged in age from 57 to 88 years, with a mean of 69.0 years. The number of years married ranged from 40 to 62, with an average of 46.1 years; 25.9% had been married over 50 years. The families had a mean of 3.13 children. Education attainment ranged from grade school (22.8%) to college or postgraduate degree (13.4%). (See Table 5.1).

Procedure and Instruments

Couples were contacted by phone and asked to participate; approximately 70% agreed to complete the questionnaires. The couples completed the questionnaires in the presence of an experimenter to ensure independent responses by the husbands and wives. The instruments included in this study were selected because they assess areas previously identified as being characteristic of strong families.

Family Strengths (FSTR).   The FSTR (Olson, Larsen, & McCubbin, 1982) is an instrument to measure family strengths. It identifies a family's level of pride, loyalty, trust, and respect attributes, in addition to its sense of competency. This instrument has been shown to be both a valid and reliable measure of family strengths.

Family Satisfaction (FSS).   The FSS (Olson & Wilson, 1982) is a 14-item measure of family satisfaction. The FSS focuses on family cohesion and adaptability. The areas of cohesion assessed are emotional family boundaries, coalitions, time, space, friends, decision making, and interests and recreation. The aspects of adaptability measured are assertiveness, control, discipline, negotiation, roles, and rules.

Quality of Life (QOL).   The QOL (Olson & Barnes, 1982) questionnaire was designed to investigate the relationship between overall life

Table 5.1
Description of the Two Family Strengths Groups

Variables	High family strengths	Low family strengths
Age	69.15	68.74
Years married	46.13	46.08
Mean number of children	2.95	3.31
Education		
Grade school	18.5%	27.4%
High school degree	30.3%	34.5%
Post-high school (no college degree)	23.5%	23.9%
College degree Graduate degree	27.7%	14.2%
Employment status		
Never employed	7.6%	9.7%
Part time	9.2%	15.9%
Full time	20.1%	7.1%
Retired	63.0%	67.3%
Mean family income	22,474	17,463

satisfaction and an individual's satisfaction with specific domains of life experience. The domains included were marriage and family life, friends, extended family, home, education, time, religion, employment, financial well-being, neighborhood and community, health, and impact of mass media. The parent form, consisting of 40 questions, was utilized in the present study.

Family Coping Strategies (F-COPES). The F-COPES (McCubbin, Larsen, & Olson, 1982) was designed to identify problem-solving approaches and behaviors used by families in response to problems or difficulties. It assesses the family's use of social support networks, such as extended family members, friends, and neighbors, as well as the family's perception of the meaning of the stressful situation. F-COPES identifies two major dimensions of family interactions: internal family strategies and external family strategies. Internal family strategies are those utilizing resources within the nuclear system, whereas external family strategies are those that employ resources outside the nuclear system. The instrument consists of five subscales: acquiring social support, reframing, seeking spiritual support, mobilizing of family to acquire and accept help, and passive appraisal.

ENRICH. The ENRICH inventory (Olson, Fournier, & Druckman, 1982) consists of 125 items designed to describe marital dynamics. The instrument consists of 12 subscales assessing personal issues (values, background differences, commitment, expectations, and personality issues), interpersonal issues (power and role strategies, communication), and external issues (time priorities, friends, work).

Results

Group x (low family strengths, high family strengths) gender (wife, husband) analyses of variance (ANOVA) were performed on the FSS, QOL subscales and total score, F-COPES subscales, and ENRICH subscales. These analyses revealed a significant main effect for group on the FSS, five QOL subscales, QOL total score, three F-COPES subscales, and eleven of the twelve ENRICH subscales. The statistically significant F and p values, group means, and standard deviations for the total and subscale scores by group can be found in Table 5.2. A significant main effect was found for gender on the health, mass media, and marital satisfaction subscales. The group by gender interactions did not attain significance.

An examination of the means revealed that the high-family-strengths group reported greater satisfaction with their family and with their quality of life as measured by the marriage and family, health, home, time, and financial well-being subscales and the overall quality-of-life score. The high-family-strengths group reported a greater tendency to cope by reframing problems and were less likely to acquire social support and resort to passive appraisal. The high-family-strengths group was also found to display higher scores on the idealistic distortion, marital satisfaction, personality issues, communication, conflict resolution, financial management, leisure activities, sexual relationship, children and marriage, family and friends, and religious orientation subscales.

The gender main effect attained significance on the health ($F(1,228)$ = 7.02, $p < .01$) and mass media ($F(1,228)$ = 6.02, $p < .02$) subscales of the quality-of-life instrument. It was found that wives reported less satisfaction than their husbands with their own and other family members' health (M = 6.71 and 7.27, respectively) and mass media (M = 9.86 and 10.60, respectively). A main effect for gender was also found on the marital satisfaction subscale of ENRICH, $F(1,228)$ = 3.86, $p < .05$. Husbands (M = 40.63) reported higher perceived marital satisfaction than their wives (M = 39.25).

Discussion

Inspection of the overall means revealed a pattern for couples in long-term relationships, irrespective of their level of family strengths: to score consistently higher than the normative samples associated with the various instruments. This suggests that stability may be a molar indicator of family strengths, but this warrants further study.

Findings That Replicate Previous Studies

People in strong, long-term relationships report high levels of family and marital satisfaction. They are aware of the impact of children on the marital relationship and are satisfied with their parenting and household roles and responsibilities. They have a compatible philosophy toward child rearing and share desired goals and values for the children. They view, positively, the cohesiveness and adaptability mechanisms of the family. Strong families report that their use of time for work and interaction with family members is a source of satisfaction. Furthermore, they tend to reserve time for themselves. This is consistent with Stinnett's (1979) assertion that strong families exert control over the use of their time so that rewarding activities can be incorporated.

Individuals involved in long-term relationships view open communication as a necessary component in the maintenance of a relationship. They enjoy greater comfort because of their ability to share their emotions and beliefs with their partners. They are comfortable with the manner in which information is openly communicated and reflect an awareness of the level and type of communication in the relationship.

The choice of leisure activities in strong families reflects a higher level of compatibility and flexibility; whereas, families with lower levels of family strengths express less consensus about leisure-time activities. Characterized by a more traditional view that religion is an essential component in successful marriages, strong families show greater involvement in church activities.

This description of qualities found in strong, long-term relationships is consistent with those identified in previous studies of family strengths (Beam, 1979; Stinnett & Sauer, 1977; Stinnett et al., 1982). Another characteristic of strong families identified by Stinnett and Sauer (1977) was the capacity to deal with crises in a positive manner. They suggested that a family's ability to deal positively with crises stemmed from trust developed by relying on themselves. In this study, individuals in strong, long-term relationships tended to engage in reframing and to eschew passive appraisal and the acquiring of social support. The strong families redefined stressful events to make them more manageable. They were unlikely to react passively, waiting for outside agents to resolve a problem. They held idealistic attitudes about the probability of relationship conflicts and were confident of their successful resolution.

Qualities Unique to Strong Long-Term Families

A number of characteristics not identified in previous studies were found to discriminate between strong and less-strong families in this study. These were: satisfaction with health, sexual relations, financial management and well-being, and personality issues.

Persons in the high-strengths group reported greater satisfaction with their own health as well as that of other family members. They perceived that their sexual relationship with their partner was healthier than that reported by the lower-strengths group, both in terms of affectional expression and sexual behavior.

Table 5.2
F Ratios, Means, and Standard Deviations by Group

	High family strengths			Low family strengths	
	F	M	SD	M	SD
Family satisfaction	29.55 $p < .001$	52.95	7.19	49.00	7.68
Quality of life subscales					
Marriage and family	28.37 $p < .001$	17.94	2.09	16.22	2.79
Friends	3.297 $p < .07$	3.88	.76	3.70	.78
Extended family	.435 $p < .51$	3.90	.80	3.84	.74
Health	8.35 $p < .005$	7.29	1.68	6.67	1.68
Home	8.41 $p < .005$	19.79	3.40	18.54	3.15
Education	1.97 $p < .16$	6.48	1.47	6.23	1.22
Time	7.07 $p < .01$	19.09	3.31	17.96	3.14
Religion	3.39 $p < .06$	3.83	.87	3.62	.91
Employment	2.03 $p < .16$	7.95	.99	7.75	1.12
Mass media	.875 $p < .35$	10.09	2.36	10.38	2.33
Financial well-being	13.27 $p < .001$	22.03	4.27	20.05	3.96
Neighborhood and community	1.94 $p < .17$	20.65	3.46	20.01	3.51
Quality of life total	13.74 $p < .001$	146.76	17.33	138.59	16.46
Family coping subscales					
Acquiring social support	3.71 $p < .05$	24.56	7.08	26.35	6.95
Reframing	5.46 $p < .02$	32.89	3.74	31.82	3.22

Table 5.2 *(Continued)*

	High family strengths			Low family strengths	
	F	M	SD	M	SD
Seeking spiritual support	2.19 $p < .14$	16.31	3.24	15.69	3.09
Mobilizing family to acquire and accept help	.104 $p < .75$	13.29	3.24	13.42	2.90
Passive appraisal	46.36 $p < .001$	8.40	2.93	11.13	3.13
ENRICH subscales					
Idealistic distortion	50.36 $p < .001$	50.60	4.02	45.98	5.80
Marital satisfaction	83.71 $p < .001$	43.21	9.98	36.49	6.96
Personality issues	98.58 $p < .001$	41.56	5.54	32.87	7.71
Communication	78.95 $p < .001$	40.03	5.77	32.41	7.24
Conflict resolution	88.04 $p < .001$	38.33	3.74	32.01	5.49
Financial management	65.09 $p < .09$	42.59	5.13	36.68	5.99
Leisure activities	65.72 $p < .001$	41.50	4.86	36.24	5.01
Sexual relations	53.52 $p < .001$	43.05	5.32	39.97	7.27
Children and marriage	69.47 $p < .001$	50.79	4.39	44.66	6.65
Family and friends	63.46 $p < .001$	48.19	4.95	42.30	6.22
Egalitarian roles	3.57 $p < .06$	30.31	6.40	28.77	6.03
Religious orientation	33.27 $p < .001$	44.23	6.00	39.32	6.93

Members of strong families reported greater satisfaction with their financial well-being than the lesser strong families. They reported satisfaction with their level of savings, indebtedness, income, and ability to deal with financial emergencies. In general, they possessed a more positive attitude about the management of economic issues within their families.

The high-strengths group differed from the low-strengths group on personality issues, that is, perceived traits of the marital partner, such as tardiness, moodiness, stubbornness, jealousy, and possessiveness. People in the high-strengths group reflected better adjustment to their partners and greater satisfaction with their partners' behavior.

Gender Differences

Based on Bernard's work, differences in the perceptions of husbands and wives would be predicted. However, this study provides, at best, qualified support for this position, because only three differences were detected. Women were found to be less satisfied with mass media, including the quality of television programs, movies, and magazines, and the amount of time the family watches television. Women also reported lower satisfaction with their own health and the health of other family members. The most interesting gender differences was that husbands reported greater marital satisfaction than wives. Although studies on marital satisfaction have produced inconsistent findings, in general, husbands tend to report that they are more satisfied with their marriages than wives (Bernard, 1972; Campbell, Converse, & Rodgers, 1976; Rhyne, 1981).

A possible explanation for the overall, relative similarity of perceptions of husbands and wives is offered by symbolic-interaction theorists (Berger & Kellner, 1964). They suggest that through repeated interactions, spouses construct shared perspectives of reality. Long-term couples have had a longer period of interaction, which may result in greater similarity.

Implications

This study has interesting implications about family strengths in long-term relationships. Individuals in such relationships differ markedly in their perceptions when level of family strength is considered. Overall, the traits identified in strong, long-term relationships are consistent with the findings of other studies of family strengths that have not considered this stage of the family life cycle. The strengths found in self-selected younger families are essentially found in strong long-term marriages. The similarity also suggests that the self-selection technique used in previous studies compares favorably with empirically based identification of strong families.

Long-term relationships did display some unique areas discriminating between levels of family strength. Though further research is required, the differences raise the possibility that some family strengths may have a developmental character or that strong families in later stages of the family life cycle acquire a large configuration of strengths. Research that examines families' strengths in different developmental stages is clearly needed. This approach would also address the possible convergence of spouses' perceptions of the relationship over time.

Finally, care should be taken in generalizing the results of this exploratory study. It is questionable whether findings from a sample of Iowa couples can be generalized to other regions. It is likely that interactional patterns do differ between rural Midwestern families and metropolitan ones.

Future studies should examine the qualities of families across the life cycle. Emerging family forms (e.g., single-parent, remarried, special needs) should also be examined. It is important that positive models of family functioning be generated for these family forms, as well as the more traditional married family.

Chapter 6

Relationship Quality in Long-Term Marriages
A Comparison of High-Quality and Low-Quality Marriages

Charles Lee Cole
Department of Family Environment
Iowa State University
Ames, Iowa 50011

Marital quality has been systematically studied for over 50 years, and, based upon reviews of family research (Spanier & Lewis, 1980), adjustment, happiness, and satisfaction (all of which are concepts related to marital quality) have perhaps been the most frequently studied variables in family research. Despite this proliferation of research on marital quality, only a handful of studies have examined long-term marriages (Cole, 1984). The purpose of this chapter is to examine marital quality in long-term marriages, specifically, how couples in long-term marriages who have participated in marriage enrichment differ from troubled couples in long-term marriages who have sought marital and family therapy.

Conceptual Model

This research is guided by Lewis and Spanier's (1979) theory of marital quality and stability. Marital quality is defined as the subjective evaluation of the marriage on a number of interpersonal relationship styles and dyadic-interaction dimensions that range along a continuum differentiating levels of marital functioning and vitality. According to Lewis and

The author would like to express appreciation to Anna L. Cole, M.S., who is a Marital and Family Therapist in private practice in Ames, Iowa, for her helpful comments. This research was supported in part by the Iowa State University Home Economics Research Institute during the writing of this paper.

Spanier (1979) it is heuristic to conceptualize the marital relationship in terms of typology that differentiates both the quality and stability of the relationship. They suggest that marital quality is a function of intradyadic factors that define the relationship in terms of: (1) sources of attraction to dyadic interactions that are rewarding and thus move the couple in the direction of high-quality marital functioning and (2) sources of marital tensions perceived as costly dyadic interactions that propel the couple in the direction of low-quality marital functioning.

Marital stability is defined in terms of the durability and permanence of the relationship remaining intact. Lewis and Spanier (1979, p. 269) note that: "a stable marriage is one that is terminated only by the death of one spouse." They go on to define unstable marriages as relationships "which are willfully terminated by one or both spouses," (Lewis & Spanier, 1979, p. 269).

Marital stability is conceptualized as being a function of: (1) external pressures, such as expectations of significant others (family and friends) for the marriage to succeed or fail; and (2) sources of alternative attractions, such as friendships and extramarital affairs. The external pressures can take the form of normative inputs (Reiss, 1976) that provide support for the couple and thus serve to reinforce the marital bond remaining intact. External pressures can also take the form of structural constraints (Nye, White, & Frideres, 1973) such as economic and occupational demands and parental duties, which can serve both to increase the level of marital stress and reduce choices available to the couple in making lifestyle decisions. Thus the external pressures can either insulate the marital bond from divorce, or it can increase the burdens to the point of driving a wedge between the spouses that push them further apart.

Lewis and Spanier (1979) note that all marriages can be placed into one of four quadrants defined in terms of the dimensions of high quality, low quality, high stability, or low stability. Because this chapter is concerned with long-term marriages, we will only examine the two high-stability quadrants. Quadrant I are those marriages with high quality and stability. Quadrant IV are marriages with low quality but high stability. According to Lewis and Spanier (1979, p. 287):

> The extradyadic factors associated with high marital stability are those external pressures and social and psychological forces which prevent an individual from crossing the threshold to separation. Strict divorce laws, strong social stigma, strict adherence to or influence from restrictive religious doctrine, low evaluation of nonmarital alternatives, high degree of commitment to marriage, and high tolerance for marital conflict and

tensions are factors which are likely to influence the dyad in the direction of high marital stability.

Because the marital relationship is evaluated in terms of the balance of attractions (rewards) and tensions (costs) with regard to the level of quality present at any given point in time as well as the balance of alternative attractions (pulling one or both spouses away from dyadic interactions) and external pressures (pushing the couple together and/or driving them apart), it is necessary to consider all four vectors simultaneously.

In the case of long-term marriages it seems possible for alternative attractions to serve as safety valves in low-quality marriages that may actually help to keep them intact. For couples with grown children who have children of their own, it is possible for the grandparenting role to serve as a "safe" alternative attraction that provides both spouses with a socially legitimized caregiving relationship where they can be affirmed by their grandchild's love and acceptance. This seems to be easier for grandparents of preschool grandchildren than for grandparents of teenagers.

It is also likely that continued involvement in their adult children's lives can provide couples in low-quality marriages with alternative sources of meeting interpersonal needs not met within the marriage. Friends and hobbies can play a similar role in the lives of low-quality couples. Friendships involving other couples where both partners benefit will have higher reward value and less cost than a friendship where only one spouse benefits.

And because these types of alternative attraction relationships frequently serve as normative inputs that build extradyadic expectations for the couple to make their marriage succeed, they serve a dual function. This would likely occur in terms of the grandparenting relationship in the sense that grandchildren might serve as a strong alternative attraction that would take the pressure off of the couple having to face each other as intimate others. At the same time, the children and grandchildren would serve as normative inputs to insure the continuity of the "couple front," because parenting and grandparenting roles are normatively patterned as being part of a couple's role-set (Merton, 1969).

Criteria for Differentiating High-Quality and Low-Quality Marriages

An earlier paper outlined criteria that have been used in the marital quality literature to differentiate high-quality and low-quality relationships (Cole, 1984). Lewis and Spanier (1979) suggest that marital quality is a generic construct incorporating conceptual properties that have frequently been treated as the dependent variables in marriage research. These include subjective evaluations of the marital relationship in terms of degree of satisfaction, happiness, adjustment, role strain, conflict, communication, cohesion, integration, adaptability, potential, commitment, and so forth. They view marital quality as varying along a continuum that would differentiate levels of marital functioning. "High marital quality, therefore, is associated with good judgement, adequate communication, a high level of marital happiness, integration, and a high degree of satisfaction with the relationship" (Lewis & Spanier, 1979, p. 269).

Borrowing from Rosow's (1967) life continuity theory of interpersonal relationships in aging, Cole (1984) argued that the best predictor of marital quality in the retirement years would be the level of marital quality at earlier points in the family life cycle. In terms of Lewis and Spanier's (1979) criteria, we would expect that couples who had satisfying marital relationships in which they were happy, had an effective communication system, enjoyed each other's company, had established cohesive bonds, exercised good judgment in making life decisions, and successfully solved problems in the middle and earlier years of their marriage would be expected to continue to function well and receive a great deal of satisfaction from their marital relationship in the later years. Conversely, couples who were unhappy with their marriage in the earlier years of their marriage would be expected to continue being unsatisfied in the middle and later years.

In essence, high-quality marriages facilitate both partners in getting their needs met. Low-quality marriages, on the other hand, frequently fail to facilitate either partner in getting their needs met. In part, this is a function of the expectations that each partner brings into the relationship in terms of what they expect from their spouse and how they expect their needs to be met. Low-quality marriages are likely to result when the expectations are unrealistic and inflexible. In high-quality marriages, the expectations are tempered by reality and are reshaped in light of the partners' abilities and interests as well as situational factors. High-quality marriages are able to work out a healthy balance of independence, dependence, and interdependence. There is a respect for boundaries and the autonomy of each spouse is valued. In a low-quality marriage, this is not the case, because the spouses frequently view autonomy as threatening to the marital cohesion and thus boundaries are blurred. Consequently, low-quality marriages frequently have power struggles and fail to understand how anger and conflict can be used creatively to facilitate growth and change as a couple to meet each others' needs more effectively.

In their classic study of healthy families, Lewis, Beavers, Gossett, and Phillips (1976) found that the quality of the marital relationship and the degree of autonomy and emotional well-being of each member were key factors that differentiated the level of family functioning. In a later book, Lewis (1979) argued that true intimacy in a marriage can only be achieved if the couple share power and treat each other with respect, so that a working partnership based upon cooperation and trust can be established. Mace (1982) made a similar point, arguing that power and manipulation have no place in a loving relationship because they erode trust and create barriers to establishing the relationship depth and intimacy that is possible in an intentional companionship marriage (Hof & Miller, 1981) committed to marital growth.

It is beyond the scope of this chapter to provide a detailed review of the marital quality literature. (See Cole, 1984; Cole & Cole, 1985; Lewis, 1979; Lewis & Spanier, 1979; Mace, 1982; Spanier & Lewis, 1980 for a more complete discussion.)

The Case Study Method

This paper draws upon data from case studies of long-term marriages (40 or more years) observed in marriage-enrichment events and in marital and family therapy by the author. A composite picture of a high-quality, long-term marriage will be constructed that typifies characteristics of each of the 16 couples married over 40 years whom I have observed in marriage-enrichment events that my wife and I have participated in over the past ten years. A second composite picture characterizes 12 long-term, troubled marriages I have worked with in marital and family therapy.

Case I: John and Mary Smith[1]

John, who just turned 76 years old, is still employed on a part-time basis. He is in the process of trying to gradually phase out his work. Mary, 64 years old, has been looking forward to the time when John will be fully retired. She retired a year ago after working on and off for 45 years. Although she and John have maintained a healthy balance of work and play throughout their nearly 45 years of marriage, she is looking forward to the time when they can enjoy a more relaxed pace.

They have grown children, two of whom are married and have children of their own, whom they visit two or three times a year. Their youngest daughter is in the Peace Corps and has been out of the country for nearly two years. Their oldest daughter and her husband and children live in another state; their son, oldest of the three children, is married and lives several miles away. Although their children and grandchildren are important to them, John and Mary realize that their children and grandchildren have their own lives and should be encouraged to develop autonomous and independent lives of their own. As Mary puts it, "we tried to teach our children to speak their own mind and pursue their interests, and although we love our children and grandchildren very much, we are glad that we have more time alone as a couple to enjoy each other."

Mary and John have had their share of hard times and marital quarrels over the years but have grown stronger as a couple as a result of their ability to meet the challenge of marital conflict. John readily acknowledges that their 45 years have been filled with a few disappointments and frustrations along the way, "Like the time that I lost my job when the kids were all under 10 years old. Boy was that tough! I really got down on myself and felt like a real failure, but Mary would have none of that and helped me to keep it in perspective. Together we worked it out and I eventually got another job."

Both John and Mary remember many good times when things were going right for them as a couple. Mary openly tells of how kind and considerate John has always been of her. "Our sex life has always been pretty good, but I must say that it has gotten really good in the ten years since we took that course on sexual enrichment."

John and Mary have always been comfortable being open with each other and sharing their deepest fears and disappointments as well as hopes and dreams. They have a great deal of respect and appreciation for each other and they are not reluctant to express it to each other in a manner that affirms the uniqueness each of them brings to the marriage. They are able to express the full range of human emotions. I have seen them cry together and express their pain, and I have seen them laugh together and beam with excitement as they share the simple joys of life.

John and Mary have worked out a good balance of separateness and togetherness, with each having their own space. They have many interests in common and basically value the same things in life but also have separate interests each pursues with the encouragement of the other. They have many couple friends with whom they share their marriage, mutually providing and receiving support and encouragement for continued marital growth. They have always had a high degree of commitment to make their marriage a growing relationship responsive to the needs of both partners. In short, they have kept the electricity that characterizes their marriage alive and well over the years. They both view marriage as a relationship that is important enough to take the time to continually work on making it better and to have periodical checks along the way to see if it is going the way they want. By doing so, they never allow fate to rule, but rather retain control of their own destiny with an intentional direction that keeps them on course. As they discover their needs have changed and that a change in course is in order, they reevaluate their current plan and make the necessary adjustments to ensure that they continue to be sensitive to each other's needs.

Case II: Betty and Bob Jones

Betty, a 63-year-old homemaker, has been married to Bob, for the past 43 years. Bob, 69 years old, has been retired for nearly four years. They have two grown children and are raising a grandchild who was born out of wedlock to their daughter 17 years ago. They have essentially lived what Cuber and Haroff (1969) call an empty-shell marriage. They came to me for therapy because they were afraid their granddaughter would run off and get pregnant and repeat the family pattern. Bob had gotten Betty pregnant, been forced to marry her, and had only stayed with her over the years out of a sense of duty. Betty has lived with a great deal of unspoken pain. Over the years she has grown resentful of Bob. And Bob has grown indifferent to her. He expressed that he too had felt some resentment about being tricked into marrying a woman that he really did not respect, much less love.

On the surface Bob and Betty were always polite to each other. Underneath their facade of politeness, both were receiving messages from the other that they were at fault for the marital problems. Their conversations were stilted and guarded, neither trusted the other, and their indifference reflected a masking of the real pain that each silently carried but was afraid to openly share. It became evident to me that they had never really established much of a marriage and were cast into parental roles before they were ready. I asked them why they had stayed married for this many years when they didn't seem to care for each other. What they told me painted a vivid picture of how their marriage had been the product of both sets of parents forcing them into it and keeping the guilt and sense of obligation dangled in front of them to hold them together in a marriage that neither had ever wanted. Bob and Betty had both been raised to be obedient children and to follow the wishes of their parents.

They had not learned to be autonomous human beings, with minds of their own, capable of standing up to their intrusive parents. The forced togetherness simply increased their anger, but because they could not express the anger openly and directly they pretended that everything was fine. This pretense led each to withdraw emotionally more and more over the years and not to expect much from the other. Their communications with each other were indirect and incomplete, serving to reify the images that each held of the other as being insensitive and indifferent. But because they were not able to express these feelings openly and directly, each was led to believe that the partner was getting along quite well and did not need or want anything. In their lives of quiet desperation, each privately longed for love and support from the other.

Unlike the Smiths, the Joneses had never learned how to develop an intimate relationship with each other. They kept their feelings bottled up and were afraid to take risks, partially as a result of what had happened when they had taken risks in their families of origin where their individual needs were always ignored or denied, and they were expected to do as they were told. The Joneses had steadily become alienated from each other and had begun to feel isolated, estranged, powerless, and meaningless. They had given up hope of ever having the marriage provide for needs which they kept private but secretly hoped that their partner would miraculously understand. When they did not receive this understanding, each became disillusioned and grew more intolerant of irritating differences. In turn, this led to increased attempts to manipulate each other covertly, and because this only led to more rejection and feelings of despair, they felt even more frustrated and hopeless of ever getting anything they really wanted. The Joneses were constantly afraid of facing their differences and saw no way that their differences could ever be peaceably resolved in a way that respected and satisfied both. They gradually became fatalistic about their inability to solve problems together.

Toward a Typology of Marital Quality in Long-Term Relationships

Lewis and Spanier (1979) propose that marriages can be classified and typed in terms of the level of quality and stability present in a relationship at any point in time. They suggest that an individual couple can move within the same quadrant as well as between quadrants over the life course of the marriage.

According to Lewis and Spanier (1979), it is possible to differentiate high-stability marriages into high and low quality by using the concepts of attractions and tensions. An earlier section of this chapter delineated a number of factors that can be used to differentiate levels of marital quality. Attractions would include such things as trust, respect, comfort being around each other, self-other disclosure, need fulfillment, sexual satisfaction, intimacy, communication effectiveness, empathy, appreciation, affirmation, value consensus, interaction, climate, autonomy, self-other-marriage esteem, and commitment. Tensions would include variables such as the amount of separateness and togetherness, power, conflict, anger, rejection, disillusionment, alienation, threats, problem solving, rules, adaptability, stress, change, division of labor, division of responsibility, orientation toward their future destiny. Table 6.1 illustrates how high- and low-quality long-term marriages would differ with regard to these variables.

Summary and Conclusions

The qualitative data presented in the form of the composite case studies is illustrative of the differences in high-quality and low-quality long-term marriages. The results of the case studies are integrated with marital quality theory (Lewis & Spanier, 1979) and used to construct a typology of long-term marriages that differentiates high-quality and low-quality relationships. More research needs to be done to further test the utility of the typology. The richness of qualitative data has promise of providing a more detailed understanding of the relationship dynamics operating in the marital dyad.

Table 6.1
Marital Quality in Long-Term Relations

Criteria	High-quality	Low-quality
Attraction factors		
Trust	Confide/believe	Possessive/secretive/doubt
Respect	Value/admire	Disrespect
Comfort	At ease together	Awkward
Self-other disclosure	Balanced/open	Skewed/guarded
Intimacy	Closeness	Distant
Need fulfillment	Satisfied	Unmet-partial
Sexual satisfaction	Mutual	Partial/unilateral/none
Communication	Open/effective	Closed/incomplete
Empathy	Understanding/support/ identification	Insensitive/lacks awareness & skill
Acceptance of unique differences	Acknowledged-respected/ appreciated	Denied-not respected/ intolerant
Integration	Differentiated-cohesive	Undifferentiated-enmeshed/ atomic/isolated
Values	Consensual-existential/ compatible	Conflictual-egocentric/ incompatible
Affirmation	Intrinsic	Extrinsic
Emotional climate	Warm/friendly	Cool-indifferent/hostile
Autonomy	Encouraged	Discouraged
Self-other-marriage esteem	Valued	Discounted
Commitment	Intrinsic/volitional/growth orientated to achieve full marital potential	Utilitarian/obligation-duty/ stability orientated
Satisfaction criteria	Partner/relationship specific in terms of affective/ emotional well-being of self/ partner/relationship	Nonmarital specific, usually in terms of utilitarian roles/children/friends/job
Happiness	Contentment and appreciation	Discontent/disillusionment
Tension factors		
Power	Respectfully shared	Covert power struggles
Anger	Respectfully processed	Overtly denied-covertly acted out/suppressed/ hostility

(continued)

Table 6.1 *(Continued)*

Criteria	High-quality	Low-quality
Conflict	Constructively managed/ resolved	Destructively managed/use of strategic threats/ unresolved
Rules	Jointly established through consensus/clearly understood	Unilaterally and covertly established/ambiguous
Roles	Flexibly interchangeable with a high degree of role competence	Rigidly fixed with moderate to low role competence
Adaptability	Flexible with ability to successfully integrate life changes	Limited ability to make life changes successfully/ fragmented
Problem-solving effectiveness	Good problem-solving skills and full use of resources	Limited problem-solving skills with restricted use of resources
Ability to handle stress	Views stress as a challenge/ excellent coping skills	Views stress as a crisis/ some dysfunctional coping skills
Division of labor	Equitable/flexibly negotiated	Skewed/rigid
Division of responsibility	Balanced with each sharing responsibility for maintenance of their relationship and lifestyle	Asymmetrical with one partner being over-responsible and the other partner being under-responsible for maintenance of their relationship and lifestyle
Destiny orientation	Intentional	Fatalistic

Note

1. The names and personal identification information of the couples in the case studies have been changed to protect the anonymity of the couples participating in this study.

Chapter 7

Five Factors in Long-Term Marriages

Clifford H. Swensen
Department of Psychological Sciences
Purdue University
Lafayette, Indiana 47907

Ron W. Eskew
Department of Psychology
Buffalo Psychiatric Center
Buffalo, New York 14213-1298

Karen A. Kohlhepp
Kennebec Valley Mental Health Center
Augusta, Maine 04330

Because of the increase in life expectancy, new stages of marriage are emerging (Swensen, 1983). They are the following: (1) postchildbearing, preretirement; (2) postchildrearing, early retirement years; and (3) postchildrearing, late-retirement years. The big difference between stages (2) and (3) is the health and physical vigor of the couple. In stage (2), both are fairly healthy and active. In stage (3), problems of health and energy have begun to constrict the activities of the couple.

The emergence of these new stages of marriage is a challenge to research: the obvious challenge to obtain data from this previously unstudied group, as well as the challenge to discover the underlying factors involved in long-term, intimate relationships. It seems clear that data obtained in early studies of long-term married couples are likely to differ from later data as a function of changes from one cohort to another.

Older married couples are different from other married couples. They have had an intimate relationship for a longer period of time. They are

---

This research was supported in part by NIMH Grant No. RO1 MH26933.

past the pressures of raising children and of earning a living, so that they have more time available to devote to activities of choice and personal preference rather than of necessity. However, eventually they face the problems of accumulating losses. Friends and siblings die, and the marriage itself may be stressed, first by serious illness, and finally by death.

Thus, research on this group of married couples will probably produce results and reveal problems that are different from those of other groups. Furthermore, results obtained from one cohort of older couples may not necessarily apply to following cohorts.

Variables Considered in This Study

Most of the research on this group has focused on the quality of marriage among older people. The earliest studies (e.g., Birren, Butler, Greenhouse, Sokoloff, & Varrow, 1963; Cuber & Harroff, 1965; Pineo, 1961) suggested that marriage satisfaction declined with length of marriage. Others (e.g., Feldman, cited in Troll, 1971; Rollins & Cannon, 1974; Spanier, Lewis, & Cole, 1975; Stinnett, Carter, & Montgomery, 1972) produced data that suggested that the quality of marriage declines until the children leave home, and then improves.

A second area of concern for this group is retirement. Retirement has been observed to be a stressful time, especially for men (Reichard, Livson, & Peterson, 1962; Rollins & Feldman, 1970). Others have found that retirement has little impact on marriage (Dressler, 1973).

Children are clearly important to older people. Contact with children is maintained over the years, and relationships with children do not appear to be replaceable by other relationships (Brown, 1974; Rosow, 1967; Towsend, 1963). However, the relationship between interaction with children and well-being in later life may be positive (Stinnett et al., 1970) or may not (Glenn & McLanahan, 1981).

There is substantial ground for belief that marriage is different for husband and wife (Bernard, 1972), and this may hold true for older couples as well as for younger couples (Stinnett, Carter, & Montgomery, 1970). However, some studies have failed to find differences in marital satisfaction (Gilford & Bengtson, 1979) between husbands and wives among older married couples.

Commitment appears to be important to the maintenance of a long-term relationship. Commitment to client welfare, for example, is one characteristic shared by successful therapists of various persuasions

(Swensen, 1971). Commitment in marriage has been described as an important but often-ignored factor in marriage (Rosenblatt, 1977).

Ego development is conceived to be the master personality trait that organizes the personality (Loevinger, 1976). Two factors related to marriage in older people may be aspects of ego development. One longitudinal study found that mentally healthy older men shared the capacity to form and maintain satisfactory marriage relationships (Vaillant, 1977). Couples who had maintained satisfactory marriages over extensive periods of time used active, rather than passive, methods of coping with their problems (Meneghan, 1983; Perlin & Schooler, 1978). The capacity to form mutually satisfying relationships and the use of active methods of coping with problems are found in people at more complex levels of ego development (Swensen, 1977; Michaelson, Michaelson, & Swensen, 1982).

Ego development includes stages that range from the simplicity and total dependency of the newborn infant, to the complexity, independence, and active coping capacity of a mature, creative adult. It ranges from the inability to differentiate between one's self and other people, to the ability to empathize and relate with deep intimacy to other people.

Research Design

This study was one of a series of studies based on a model for interpersonal relationships derived from Lewin's (1951) model for behavior. A relationship is a function of the people involved in the relationship and of the situation within which the relationship exists (Swensen, 1977), or: Relationship = f(Person 1, Person 2) Situation.

For the purposes of this research, three person variables (sex, commitment, and ego-development) and two situation variables (retirement, closeness to children) were assessed. Four variables were used in the main part of the study: sex, commitment, interaction with children, and retirement status. The basic design was a posttest-only control group design (Campbell & Stanley, 1963) with a 2 x 2 x 2 x 2 analysis of variance. The independent variables for the 2 x 2 x 2 x 2 design were sex (husband, wife), commitment (low commitment, high commitment), interaction with children (high interaction, low interaction), and retirement status (retired, not retired). The inclusion of a nonretired group provided another postchildrearing group with whom the older, retired group could be compared. This also provided some data on a group that has scarcely been studied at all: the preretired, postchildrearing group.

Ego development was assessed separately in conjunction with retirement status from separate groups selected out of the larger groups. A problem with using a factorial design with ego development is that older people are predominantly at the Conformist Stage of ego development. Therefore, to include ego development as a part of a larger analysis of variance design would result in great difficulty in finding enough subjects to fill certain cells.

The Variables

Scale for Measuring Feelings and Behavior of Love (Love Scale).   The scale is composed of 120 items describing ways in which love is expressed (Swensen, 1973). It contains six subscales: (a) verbal expression of affection; (b) self-disclosure; (c) toleration of less plesant aspects of the loved person to maintain the relationship; (d) moral support, encouragement, attention, and concern; (e) feelings that are not verbally expressed; (f) material support, chores, and instrumental help. The Love Index is an algebraic sum of the subscale scores. This scale reveals different patterns of love expression for different kinds of relationships (Swensen, 1972) and differentiates between functional and troubled married couples (Fiore & Swensen, 1977).

Marriage Problems Scale.   This is a 43-item scale (Swensen & Fiore, 1982) that contains six subscales derived by factor analysis: (a) problem solving, decision making, goal setting; (b) childrearing and home labor; (c) relatives and in-laws; (d) personal care and appearance; (e) money management; and (f) expression of affection and relationships with people outside marriage. These are summed to produce a Total Marriage Problems Score.

Commitment.   The assessment of commitment was based upon the answers to two questions: (a) Why did you marry your husband (wife) when you did instead of marrying someone else or remaining single? (b) Why do you think your marriage has lasted as long as it has? These questions were chosen out of a set of open-ended questions as a measure of commitment, because they elicited answers that differentiated among the older, married couples in the content of the answers. The answers were scored on a five-point scale, which ranged from one pole in which the answers had nothing to do with the spouse (e.g., "I was tired of eating my own cooking") to answers that indicated awareness of, and concern for, the spouse as a person ("I felt he was a person I could believe in and trust."). Basically, this scale differentiated between those who got married and stayed married because it was the convenient and appropriate thing to do, and those who married and stayed married because of their concern for, and relationship with, the spouse. The sample was split into two groups at the median.

Interaction with Children.   The sample was divided into two groups: a group who interacted with the nearest child more than once per week, and a group that interacted less frequently.

Ego Development.   Ego development was assessed with the Sentence Completion Test developed by Loevinger (Loevinger & Wessler, 1970). The group was divided into two groups, Conformist and Post-Conformist. The Conformist Stage people are "conventional." They perceive life as governed by rules. They are concerned with what other people think, and refrain from doing things they think that other people would disapprove of. Their relationships tend to be governed by the conventions of the time and place in which they live. Conformist Stage people tend to deal with conflict by passive methods such as avoidance, denial, and repression. The Post-Conformist Stage people in this study were mostly at the Conscientious Stage, which is the next more complex stage above the Conformist Stage. The Conscientious Stage person is aware of his or her internal needs, fears, and wishes, and is sensitive to the internal processes of those with whom he or she relates. The relationships of people at this stage are characterized by a greater sensitivity to the other person. People at this and more complex stages of ego development are more likely to cope with problems through active means such as probing, questioning, trying alternative behavior, and so on.

Subjects

The total sample consisted of 448 married people, 212 retired, post-childrearing, and 236 preretired, postchildrearing. The subjects were obtained from Indiana (302), Florida (122), Oklahoma (12), Pennsylvania (8) and two other locations (4). The subjects were obtained through various organizations for older people, including retirement and senior citizens organizations, churches, and so on. They were all white with high school education modal for the group. Demographic statistics are shown in Table 7.1. From this, it can be seen that the preretirement group was not only younger and married fewer years, but also had more children.

The retired group had been married in the predepression and depression years, whereas the preretired group had been married primarily in World War II or the immediate postwar years.

Results

The retired, postchildrearing group of married people express less love to each other than couples who are younger and have been married for shorter periods of time. However, they express more love to each other than couples in troubled, dysfunctional marriages. The older married couples have fewer marriage problems than any other group of married people. For comparison, Table 7.2 includes data from dysfunctional married couples, from an earlier study (Fiore & Swensen, 1977).

The decline in love expression from the earlier married years affects all areas of love expression, but is particularly noteworthy in the decline of self-disclosure and tolerance, and the increase in feelings that are not verbally expressed. Other research (Swensen, Eskew, & Kohlhepp, 1981) indicates that these declines are continuous over the whole length of the average marriage. Other studies also report less "passionate and companionate" love (Traupman & Hatfield, 1982) and less positive interaction (Gilford & Bengtson, 1979) among older married couples than among younger married couples.

The significantly lower number of marriage problems is in agreement with the findings of others (Gilford & Bengtson, 1979): There is significantly less negative sentiment in the marriages of older people when compared with those married for shorter periods of time.

These results might be attributed to length of time married, because retired couples have also been married longer than preretired couples. Research (e.g., Spanier, Sauer, & Larzelere, 1979) suggests that it makes no difference whether stage of family life cycle or length of marriage is used as the variable. With this data, we obtained the same results using both stage of family life cycle and length of marriage; the two were so highly correlated (.92) that it was impossible to separate the effects of stage from length of marriage.

Commitment appears to be related primarily to marriage problems. Those subjects who were committed to the spouse, as a person, had significantly fewer problems making decisions and setting goals in their marriage, fewer conflicts over relatives, fewer disagreements about personal care, and less dissatisfaction with the expression of affection. In the area of love expression, they had less to tolerate from the spouse.

Table 7.1

Demographic Statistics for the Total Sample

Statistic	Preretired	Retired
n	236	212
Mean age	54.94	67.50*
Mean years married	31.54	40.13*
Age at marriage	23.19	27.49*
Years education	14.13	13.58*
Number children	2.78	1.89*

* $p < .01$.

Table 7.2

Comparison of Retired, Postchildrearing Group with Other Married Couples Who Have No Children, and with Dysfunctional Married Couples on Expression of Love and Marriage Problems

	Preretirement/ postchild	Retired/ postchild	Dysfunctional marriages
Mean age (years)	54.9*	67.5	32.8*
Mean years married	31.5*	40.1	9.4*
Love scale			
1. Expression affection	39.6	38.6	31.8*
2. Self-disclosure	42.4*	38.6	41.1*
3. Tolerance	35.3*	33.6	36.0*
4. Moral support	62.6	61.5	53.3*
5. Unexpressed feelings	27.8*	33.5	31.6*
6. Material support	35.0	34.7	32.6*
Love scale index	187.1*	173.5	163.2*
Marriage problems scale			
1. Decision making	13.5*	13.0	14.6*
2. Childrearing	9.4*	9.0	13.3*
3. Relatives	8.2*	7.6	10.1*
4. Health, personal care	7.3*	7.2	10.6*
5. Money management	7.4*	6.8	8.8*
6. Expression affection	6.8*	6.6	9.4*
Total	52.7*	50.3	66.8*

* Difference from retired, postchildrearing group significant at $p < .01$ level.

These results, presented in Table 7.3, are in agreement with the result of a separate study of retired people in Norway (Swensen & Trahaug, 1979), which also found that spouses committed to each other as persons had significantly fewer marriage problems.

Stage of ego development seems to be related to the expression of love. Those who are at Post-Conformist stages of ego development express more love to each other than do those at the Conformist Stage of ego development. The Post-Conformists express more affection to each other verbally and give each other more encouragement and moral support than do couples at the Conformist Stage. These data are presented in Table 7.4. There were no significant differences between the Conformists and the Post-Conformists on any of the Marriage Problems Scales, so these are omitted.

No significant relationships were found between the expression of love and marriage problems and the variables of retirement, sex of the subject, or the frequency of interaction with children. Therefore, data for these factors are not presented.

Discussion and Conclusions

This group of retired, postchildrearing couples expressed less love for each other and had fewer marriage problems when compared with younger married couples. The picture that emerges is that of a relationship that is devitalized (e.g., Cuber & Harroff, 1965), and has less going on within it for either good or ill.

However, this picture is an average which fails to reflect individual differences among couples within the group, as well as factors of which these differences are a function. The data on stage of ego development suggests that some couples—those who are able to perceive the factors that create barriers within their relationship and are able to cope actively with those barriers—are able to be more open and expressive to each other. The commitment of partners to one another as persons provides the basis for the resolution of problems. One might hypothesize that commitment provides the security in the relationship that makes it possible for a couple to take the risk of actively grappling with problems.

One could speculate that people at the more complex stages of ego development would be more likely to be committed to each other, but in fact, these two measures do not correlate. Ego development is the measure of a person's own stage of development, while commitment is the measure of a commitment to another person. They are two independent

Table 7.3
Love Scale and Marriage Problems Scale Scores for
High-Commitment and Low-Commitment Subjects

Scale	High-commitment	Low-commitment
Love scale		
1. Expression affection	38.26	37.59
2. Self-disclosure	37.52	38.04
3. Tolerance	31.82	33.78*
4. Moral support	59.37	61.32
5. Unexpressed feelings	30.71	33.73
6. Material support	33.29	33.36
Love scale index	168.99	167.73
Marriage problems scale		
1. Decision making	12.52	13.18**
2. Childrearing	8.81	9.03
3. Relatives	7.43	7.58**
4. Health, personal care	6.86	7.30**
5. Money management	6.64	6.68*
6. Expression affection	6.20	6.78*
Marriage problems total	48.28	50.59*

* $p < .01$.
** $p < .05$.

Table 7.4
Love Scale Scores for Conformist and Postconformist Groups

Scale	Conformist	Postconformist
Love scale		
1. Expression affection	34.7	43.7*
2. Self-disclosure	37.6	43.6
3. Tolerance	32.1	35.9
4. Moral support	61.1	63.9*
5. Unexpressed feelings	32.7	29.8
6. Material support	35.1	34.7
Love scale index	168.2	192.1*

* $p < .05$.

measures and within this group, have a low correlation (.15) with each other. However, these results would suggest the hypothesis that a marriage relationship between older people that has the highest expression of love and the fewest number of problems would be one in which the couple is at the postconformist stage of ego development and is highly committed.

The finding that there was no relationship between the husband-wife relationship and the relationship with children is in keeping with other studies that have found little relationship between children and well-being in older people (Glenn & McLanahan, 1981).

These results were obtained from a wide variety of white, basically middle-class Americans from several different sections of the country. The results would appear to be general in that population. However, almost identical results were obtained following the same design (Swensen & Trahaug, 1979) in a study conducted in Norway with subjects who had, on the average, less than a high school education and who worked mostly in skilled labor and clerical occupations. This suggests that these results may be general in a fairly broad segment of the older population.

Of the variables studied (retirement, closeness of children, commitment, ego development, and sex), significant results were obtained for three; one situational variable (retirement) and two person variables (commitment and ego development). However, the results clearly imply that in circumstances that are not extreme, the person variables overcome, or have stronger influence than the situation variables. Although love expression is lower for those who are retired, it is greater for retired couples who are at the more complex levels of ego development. Marriage problems are lower for those who are retired, but they are significantly lower for those retired married couples who are highly committed to each other.

Although marriage changes from one stage of the family life cycle to another with increasing duration, the results of situational effects are not the same for all married couples. Each married couple reacts to and copes with these changes in different ways. For the average couple, changes over time lead to devitalization of the relationship. However, those who are at the more complex stages of ego development, who cope actively with problems and conflicts in the relationship, and who have created security in their relationship by a personal commitment to each other, create a vital, stimulating, and satisfying intimate relationship that does not deteriorate. Perhaps good relationships, like good wine, improve with age, while the others, the majority, go flat.

Chapter 8

Effects of Work and Retirement
within Long-Term Marital Relationships

Georgeanna M. Tryban
Department of Sociology
Case Western Reserve University
Cleveland, Ohio 44106

An increasing number of people are living to old age. Because of this, the length of those marriages that remain intact is also increasing. Gerontologists who study these individuals note the marital status of their subjects, usually married or widowed, but only infrequently has this been the focus of study. Recently this area has attracted the interest of researchers concerned primarily with work, retirement and the marital relationship.

This chapter explores the marriages of 21 couples who have been married 30 to 50 years. Demographics, age, age at retirement, length of retirement, number and living arrangements of children, education and income, are examined. Couples' involvement in employment is also investigated by comparing the ten couples following the traditional male-breadwinner pattern, with the 11 couples who were two-paycheck earners. These two groups will be contrasted on demographic variables as well as the main variables of interest: social integration, happiness, involvement and satisfaction.

Long-Term Marriages

Roberts' (1980) study of long-married couples emphasized happiness and adjustment together with the preferences for expressive role behavior from each spouse. He concluded that among the long-married, "findings suggest a companionship marriage with little struggle for dominance." Sporakowski and Hughston's (1978) work contributes to our understanding of companionship as a form of a common perception of situations. They found marital satisfaction in 50-year or more marriages related to the couple's congruence of perception.

With respect to the actual everyday behaviors, however, a somewhat different picture emerges. Keith and Brubaker (1979) conclude that "despite evidence of greater androgyny in old age, the tasks that men are most involved in during retirement seem to remain highly sex-linked." In contrast, they go on to say that "in general, correlations between household involvement and well-being in old age tended to be positive." Tagnoli (1979) found an interesting parallel between activity and perception. He concluded that when household tasks were shared in a less stereotypic manner, husbands and wives tended to hold more similar views; perhaps the congruence of perception that Sporakowski and Hughston reported. Tagnoli reports Hayward's findings that when men worked in jobs outside the home and women were homemakers, and when there was little sharing of the housework, as is common in these situations, the men's view of the home was the "physical structure" of the house, while women tended to see it in terms of "self-identity" and "personalized space."

The situation that men with this view face at retirement is illustrated by Szinovacz (1980) and confirmed by Keating and Cole (1980) and Brubaker and Hennon (1982). Szinovacz found that among a small pilot sample of retired university employees and their husbands, 36% of the women maintained their preretirement (basically traditional) division of labor whereas 28% increased their housework (mainly through more extensive cooking and cleaning). In the 20% of the couples with increased husband participation she found it only partially due to the desire of husbands for more sharing; other husbands were responding to their wives' illness-related physical limitations. Although she found that spouses' marital adjustment was affected by the wife's retirement, the underlying reasons had more to do with a reduction in tension and stress due to the demands of work and that retired women did more housework, which pleased the husband and reduced discord. In short, often the sharing that might lead to greater perceptual congruence and companionship are not present, and women's expectations for greater sharing are not met (Brubaker & Hennon, 1982), with a concomitant lowering of life satisfaction likely (Seleen, 1982). Szinovacz points out that women who have chosen to work in their later years may have done so partly out of dissatisfaction with the housewife role, though work does not ensure escape and may add stress because, as Lovell-Troy (1983) notes, comparisons of housewives and employed women often neglect to acknowledge that employed women are housewives in addition to being working women.

Employment

The most significant economic change for women in the past 30 years has been their increased labor force participation (Bianchi & Spain, 1983). This economic change has implications for the domestic arrangements of families (Moore & Sawhill, 1978). As more women participate in the work force, more will experience the work force exit of retirement that is concomitant with aging. In spite of this, most research has focused on the meaning of retirement for the white collar male and, occasionally, his homemaking wife. Very little is known about blue-collar retirees, both male and female, or the situation of families that have one retiree and one homemaker or two retirees composing the marital dyad (Maddox, 1968; Prentis, 1980; Szinovacz, 1982).

The effect of retirement on employed women has previously been assumed to be minimal, because women were thought to be only marginally interested in the work role and primarily committed to the roles of wife and mother (Cumming & Henry, 1961; Kline, 1975). Subsequent research has shown that work may hold even greater meaning for women than men (Jaslow, 1976), with role relinquishment being more difficult (Atchley, 1976) and retirement being experienced differently by retired women than by retired men (Atchley, 1982).

When nonemployed women are studied, it is usually as housewives and, as such, as reacters to their husbands' retirement (Szinovacz, 1982). In a rare study comparing retired women and homemakers, Keith (1982) concluded that these two groups manage their lives differently with formal organizational involvement and informal relationships with others (nonfamily contacts) more important to the well-being of retired women, with close friends important to both groups. Very few studies have looked at the marital dyad as a whole, composed of two retirees or a retiree married to a homemaker. This chapter examines the postretirement effects of one or both members of the marital dyad's employment on the long-term marriage's social integration, happiness, involvement, and satisfaction.

Methodology

Sample

Subjects in the study were United Auto Worker retirees or spouses of retirees. Retired members of a large Midwest local, living within a 25-mile radius of the researcher's university, and retired between one and five years, were randomly selected and screened on six criteria (marital status and length, retirement status of individual and spouse, age, and health) via telephone interviews. The initial phone interview was not able to be completed for 18% of the retirees, and 49% were disqualified by not meeting one or more of the screening criteria. Sixteen percent declined to participate either by refusing the first request for an interview or refusing to make an appointment for the interview.

Data Collection

Data were collected from the remaining 27 married couples, currently members of the United Auto Workers local retirement division. A one-time cross-sectional data-gathering procedure used questionnaires and in-depth interviews. Each individual was interviewed in his or her home, alone if possible, with open-ended questions tape recorded. The findings here are based on the analysis of a subsample of 21 of the couples who were in long-term marriages of 30 years or more.

Variables

The demographic variables were current age, age at retirement, length of retirement, length of marriage, number of children, their presence in the home or the number of years since they began living away, the household income, and the level of education.

In addition to demographics, the major variables of interest were social integration with family (children and siblings), preretirement and postretirement happiness and satisfaction, and involvement with home and family, groups and clubs, and friends. Social integration was measured by the amount of reported contact with children and siblings. Subjects were asked to recall their preretirement happiness and to report their current level of happiness. In addition, they estimated subjective preretirement involvement with work, home and family, clubs and friends and also reported their current involvement using a ten-point scale that ranged from "completely involved" at 10 to "not at all

Table 8.1

Characteristics of a Sample of Long-Term Married Couples[a]

Characteristics	M	SD	Range	%
Age	65.0	4.3	54–78	
Age at retirement	61.9	3.0	55–67	
Length of retirement (months)	44.1	22.4	15–99	
Length of marriage	41.6	4.5	32–50	
Number of children	2.9	1.3	1–6	
Years since children left home	9.0	10.0	2–30	
Couples with children residing with parents				57
	n	%		
Household income				
$ 5,000– 9,999	8	19		
$10,000–14,999	29	69		
$15,000–19,999	2	5		
$20,000–24,999	2	5		
Education				
College, business, or tech school	12	29		
High school graduate	18	43		
Attended high school	8	19		
Elementary school graduate	4	10		

[a] $N = 42$.

involved" at 1. Satisfaction with the same areas was estimated and reported in the same way as was involvement. Occupation and employment history were measured by ascertaining whether the female had been a homemaker, or if she had worked outside the home for pay, at least at a half-time status, for five years or more since the age of 45. This was used to classify couples as either "traditional" in which the female was/had been a homemaker, or "dual paycheck" in which the female had a job from which she was currently retired.

Characteristics of the Sample

As can be seen in Table 8.1, these were couples who had been married between 32 and 50 years with an average length of 42 years. They ranged in age from 54 to 74 and had been retired an average of 44 months or $3\frac{1}{3}$

years. The males and females who had been previously employed retired at a fairly young age, the average being 62 with some retiring as young as 55. Youthful retirement typically occurred for two reasons. Many women chose to retire at the same time as their husbands. Families with two-paycheck incomes often seemed to feel that in some ways the wife had done something "extra" by working and "deserved the reward" of retiring, and enjoying retirement, with her husband. Several women reported that they had planned to continue working, but their husbands seemed to enjoy retirement so much that they either retired earlier than they had planned to originally or that they "could hardly wait" to reach the planned-for age. Another reason that many are likely to have chosen to retire prior to reaching 65 is that factory work is often not only tedious, but the repetition and working conditions combine to make it also physically demanding. The increased demands of hours and factory conditions on the aging body combined with a "30 and out"[1] contract agreement won by the UAW enabled workers to retire in economic security with their health still relatively good.

All couples had children, with the average family size being three children. A surprising finding was that 12 couples (57%) had their offspring currently living with them. Children living away from home had been doing so an average of 9 years. Household income ranged from $5,000 to $25,000 per year with the majority of couples in the $10,000 to $14,999 income bracket. There was also a fairly high level of education with the majority having at least graduated from high school (70%). Work history showed that 11 of the women were retired from full-time or part-time jobs, in most cases held for a number of years. These women and their husbands were classified as dual-paycheck couples. The ten women who were homemakers were classified, with their husbands, as traditional couples.

Results

Differences between Dual-Paycheck and Traditional Couples

Dual-paycheck couples differed little from traditional couples and those differences that did exist were not significant (see Table 8.2). Both groups were similar in age, marriage length, and age at retirement. Because dual-paycheck husbands were a bit older than traditional husbands, they had been retired longer on the average (52 months compared with 36) but for about the same length of time relative to age, because

Table 8.2
Comparison of Characteristics of Dual-Paycheck and Traditional Couples[a]

	Dual-paycheck couples			Traditional couples		
Characteristics	Husbands (n = 11)	Wives (n = 11)	Total (n = 22)	Husbands (n = 10)	Wives (n = 10)	Total (n = 20)
Mean age	68	63	65	65	64	65
Mean age at retirement	63	60	61	63	[b]	—
Mean length of retirement (months)	52	44	48	36	[b]	—
Mean length of marriage			41			42
Mean number of children			2.73			3.00
Mean years since children left home			9.1			8.9
Couples with children residing with parents			55%			60%
Education						
College, business, tech school	27%	18%		50%	20%	
High school graduate	46	64		20	40	
Attended high school	27	18		10	20	
Elementary graduate	—	—		20	20	
Household income						
$ 5,000- 9,999			18%			20%
$10,000-14,999			64			80
$15,000-19,999			9			—
$20,000-24,999			9			—

[a] N = 42.
[b] Not applicable or calculable since traditional wives were homemakers.

both groups of men retired at the average age of 63 years. Traditional couples had a slightly higher average number of children (3.00 compared with 2.73) and slightly more had children living with them (60% compared with 55%) but these differences were not significant. A more detailed examination of education showed that dual-paycheck and traditional husbands differed in the highest category with over 20% more of the traditional husbands having attended college, business, or technical school. There was a difference between the wives, as well. Though the percentage of wives in the highest educational category was about equal, the second highest category, high school graduate, contained almost 40%

more dual-paycheck women than traditional women. In combination this indicates less disparity of education between dual-paycheck couples and greater for traditional couples. Household income was slightly higher for dual-paycheck couples but this, too, was not significant.

Social Integration. Home and family are important components of daily life and interaction with one's family comprises a substantial part of daily living. Retirees showed high amounts of contact with their families, with 80% of both dual-paycheck and traditional couples in contact with their children at least once a month (see Table 8.3). There was a difference, though not significant, in levels of contact, however, with a higher percentage of traditional couples seeing their children the most frequently (40% compared with 20%). This situation is reversed in levels of contact with siblings where 53% of the dual-paycheck couples fall in the highest levels compared to only 34% of the traditional couples. When looking at contact on a category by category basis, dual-paycheck couples have somewhat lower levels of contact with their children and somewhat higher contact with siblings when compared with traditional couples. Residential propinquity was not considered to be a possible intervening variable because 80% of both groups had their children living within 50 miles and almost 65% of both groups had their siblings that same distance from them.

Table 8.3
Levels of Family Interaction by Marital Type[a]

Marital type	No contact (%)	Once to several times a year (%)	One to three times a month (%)	Once a week or more (%)	Total (%)
Amount of contact					
Contact with children					
Dual-paycheck	10	10	60	20	100
Traditional	—	20	40	40	100
Contact with siblings					
Dual-paycheck	11	37	32	21	101
Traditional	11	56	28	6	101

[a] $N = 42$.

In spite of their age and retiree status, over half of the sample had their children living at home with them. In most cases the offspring was divorced and was temporarily living at the parent's home. In some other cases a child was "house-sitting" when parents traveled and provided peace of mind and welcome freedom; sometimes it simply reduced housing costs. In two cases the parents were waiting for their somewhat "slow" child to leave the nest for the first time.

Obviously there are implications for the levels of integration that parents experience with children. Table 8.3 shows the level of contact, including all those couples whose children are residing with them, although parents answered the question of contact by describing their contact with children *not* residing at home. Even so, parents with children in residence may see their other children less often because of the satisfactory level of interaction already present with the one child who is living there, or conversely, see them more frequently as they "drop in" to visit not only their parents but the also-resident-sibling. Unfortunately this sample size is too small to make a meaningful comparison of couples with and without children in residence.

Happiness. The long-term married couples in the sample reported and presented themselves as very happy people, though in answering the open-ended questions later, their statements sometimes contradicted this impression. Table 8.4 shows their responses to questions about

Table 8.4
Percent Reporting Preretirement and Postretirement Happiness by Marital Type and Gender[a]

	Percent of couples reporting		
Marital type	Preretirement happiness	Postretirement happiness	Change (%)
Dual-paycheck			
Husbands	100	100	0
Wives	55	91	+36
Traditional			
Husbands	80	90	+10
Wives	70	60	-10

[a] $N = 42$.

remembered and current happiness. Husbands (particularly traditional husbands) had a marked tendency to report themselves happy and were the group especially likely to contradict this report in later statements to the interviewer. Conventionality may have accounted for these initial responses while more detailed questions, in conjunction with developing subject-interviewer rapport, later yielded a more complete picture.

Women reported themselves as less happy, though there is a sharp distinction over time between dual-paycheck women and homemakers. A sizable percentage of dual-paycheck wives showed an increase in happiness (36%) while in contrast the postretirement situation caused 10% of the homemakers to report that their happiness decreased.

Involvement. The area of greatest involvement for all long-term marriage couples was home and family (Table 8.5). The average for both traditional and dual-paycheck couples was about 8 points on a 10-point scale of involvement indicating a self-assessment of very high involvement. The next greatest area of involvement was friends followed by groups or clubs. Both dual-paycheck and traditional husbands report the same patterns of involvement, though dual-paycheck husbands have higher levels (not statistically significant, however). It is the dual-paycheck wife who stands out, both in comparison with traditional wives

Table 8.5
Current Mean Involvement Scores in Three Areas
by Marital Type and Gender[a]

Marital type	Area of involvement		
	Home and family	Groups and clubs	Friend
Dual-paycheck			
Total	8.96	6.14	7.27
Husbands	8.91	6.09	6.45
Wives	9.00	6.18	8.09
Traditional			
Total	8.40	5.00	6.55
Husbands	8.40	4.80	6.20
Wives	8.40	5.20	6.90

[a] $N = 42$.

Table 8.6
Current Mean Satisfaction Scores in Three Areas
by Marital Type and Gender[a]

| | Area of satisfaction | | |
Marital type	Home and family	Groups and clubs	Friend
Dual-paycheck			
Total	8.78	6.32	7.91
Husbands	8.82	5.91	6.82
Wives	8.73	6.73	9.00
Traditional			
Total	8.85	5.70	7.60
Husbands	8.90	6.00	7.70
Wives	8.80	5.40	7.50

[a] $N = 42$.

and with all husbands, as the most involved in all areas, though this difference did not achieve statistical significance.

Satisfaction. As was true of happiness and involvement, couples tended to rate themselves as very satisfied (Table 8.6). The patterns of self-reported satisfaction are similar to the patterns of involvement reported above. As with involvement, the ranking of areas was home and family, followed by friends, and then groups and clubs. Again traditional and dual-paycheck husbands showed similar patterns, with dual-paycheck wives about equal in home and family satisfaction but quite high in satisfaction with friends and slightly higher in satisfaction with groups and clubs, again similar to their pattern of high involvement. In contrast to the always-high dual-paycheck wife, the traditional home-maker seems consistently to be the lowest in all but one of the satisfaction and involvement areas.

Changes in Involvement and Satisfaction

Because self-reported involvement and satisfaction was very high, and therefore more difficult to analyze in terms of variance, it is helpful to

Table 8.7
Change in Mean Involvement Scores in Three Areas
After Retirement by Marital Type and Gender[a]

| | Area of involvement change | | | |
Marital type	Home and family	Groups and clubs	Friends	Total
Dual-paycheck				
Husbands	-.36	-.27	-.91	-1.54
Wives	+.73	+.54	+.64	+1.91
Traditional				
Husbands	-.60	-.20	-.90	-1.70
Wives	-.70	-.20	-.10	-1.00

[a] $N = 42$; $\bar{x}_2 - \bar{x}_1$.

Table 8.8
Change in Mean Satisfaction Scores in Three Areas
After Retirement by Marital Type and Gender[a]

| | Area of satisfaction change | | | |
Marital type	Home and family	Groups and clubs	Friends	Total
Dual-paycheck				
Husbands	[b]	-.82	-.82	-1.64
Wives	+.37	+.73	+.73	+1.83
Traditional				
Husbands	-.20	+.10	—[b]	- .10
Wives	-.10	-.30	—[b]	- .40

[a] $N = 42$; $\bar{x}_2 - \bar{x}_1$.
[b] No change.

look at the mean change between retrospective satisfaction and involvement and current levels of these variables (Table 8.7 and 8.8). The most
striking fact emerging from these tables is that dual-paycheck women
show consistent increases in all areas; in fact they are the only group to

do so. With the exception of a very minute increase in traditional husbands' satisfaction with groups and clubs, the three other groups—dual-paycheck and traditional husbands and traditional wives all decline in satisfaction and involvement in all three areas after retirement.

Discussion

This study suggests there is a cumulative effect associated with employment that not only extends from work to family (Houseknecht & Macke, 1981; Piotrowski & Crits-Christoph, 1981), but also from work into retirement. Patterns evolved in response to the work situation over the course of time result in somewhat different types of relationships in dual-paycheck compared with traditional couples. The two patterns, termed egalitarian and hierarchical, are evidenced by the relationship of the couples within the marital dyad, in interactions with relatives, and in their reaction to retirement.

Dual-paycheck couples show a lower disparity of education than do traditional couples because the husbands have slightly less education and the wives slightly more than do their traditional counterparts. Less disparity on an important variable like education may create an environment conducive to the development of equality while greater disparity between people is more conducive to the evolution of a hierarchy. Education could be the first in a chain of differentiating factors whose outcome can be seen in these long-term marriages.

In interactions with relatives there is also evidence of differentiation between egalitarian and hierarchical patterns. Although all retirees have a fairly high level of contact with their children, the traditional couples have greater contact. In contrast, the dual-paycheck couples have higher levels of contact with siblings. Thus traditional couples give slightly more emphasis to hierarchical relationships (parent-child), whereas dual-paycheck couples emphasized lateral, egalitarian ones with siblings.

It is important to recognize that women serve to define the two groups. In traditional couples, women who used to work as homemakers *still* work as homemakers, while dual-paycheck women are now *formerly* employed. Women who were previously employed experienced the stress of discontinuity both at their entry to the job market (typically as their children grew and left home) and their exit from it at retirement. But these entrances and exits are essentially their own choices. In contrast, homemakers experience discontinuity not as a result of their initiatives but as a result of the actions of children and husbands. Homemakers' lives are changed as children leave home for school and, later, marriage, and as husbands retire from employment. One way of combating discontinuity and the shrinkage of their role may be to emphasize continuing contact with children. However, this does not seem consistent with the reduced levels of happiness, satisfaction and involvement with home and family that we find among homemakers after their husbands have retired. Keating and Cole (1980) found wives happier than their retired husbands because, while husbands were leaving their area of expertise, homemakers who had been "laid off" since their children had grown and gone were now being "called back" to the domestic arena, which was their area of expertise. However, there are a number of factors that point in the opposite direction. Retired men are not children, and disharmony may well result if their wives attempt to mother them. Additionally, men may not wish or even notice the help that homemakers offer as part of enacting that role. Keating and Cole report that while 96% of their sample of housewives said they had been actively or passively supportive of their newly retired spouses, only 44% of those husbands reported that support.

Why do homemakers appear to be less happy, satisfied, and involved with home and family at just the time that Keating and Cole suggest their role is expanding? The answer lies in the same dissatisfactions that Keating and Cole's sample reported. A lack of autonomy since their husband's retirement was a recurrent complaint of homemakers, many of whom thought of themselves as generally happy people. Work often increased with more meals to prepare and someone to keep company as well, allowing women less discretionary time. In the present sample, most of the women had husbands who worked in the auto industry during its peak production period putting in seven-day weeks. These women were used to considerable autonomy. They had already made the adjustment to their husband's absence and lack of involvement[2] in the family. Retirement brought them a person who was not used to free time, did not "know how to play anymore," as one husband put it, and often seemed envious of the women's inner directedness.[3]

As one women put it, "What free time I do have I still have to monkey around with things he wants to do." Another said she resented her husband's attitude that she should be ready to go with him anywhere and anytime "at the drop of a hat." One particularly unhappy woman described things since her husband's retirement as sitting around and doing nothing because her husband often sat around with nothing to do. Women who overcame this type of problem seemed to have done so by distancing themselves from their husband's needs. They decided that it was "silly," to use one woman's word, to stay home and take care of all their husband's needs.

When their husband's retirement was given an overall positive evaluation, the reasons seemed primarily to do with the husband's autonomy. Wives reported that their husbands did things for themselves, especially in fixing meals for themselves or keeping themselves occupied with activities that they found meaningful. Outdoor work or a ham radio in the basement seemed to be the most frequent and most appreciated activities that gave privacy and autonomy to both husband and wife. In addition, these husbands often actually helped with the housework or took over certain household tasks, most frequently cooking, doing dishes, and cleaning, as well as lawn and garden work that some women had previously done by themselves.

In summary, homemakers who lost large amounts of privacy and autonomy without the compensations of greater sharing and reduced work demands seemed to express the greatest dissatisfaction and unhappiness over the changes brought about by their husband's retirement. In contrast to the lowered happiness, satisfaction, and involvement of the homemakers, the dual-paycheck wives found retirement a time of improvement in all three areas. Husbands were very important to these women who had relationships characterized by long-standing patterns of sharing. They had had to work hard in the home as well as have their husbands' cooperation. Many reported that their husbands had regularly shared household tasks when both were working. In some cases this seemed to have created a feeling of togetherness that influenced the wives to retire earlier than planned so as to share their husband's retirement. The benefits of retirement that these women mentioned were many. For themselves, they enjoyed staying up later at night and being able to sleep late (since the day shift typically began at 6 a.m.) and to do the household chores at a more flexible pace. But most of the activities that these women were happy to see increased were activities they shared with their husbands such as camping, travel, dancing, golf, attending a health club, or participating in church work. In startling contrast to homemakers, none of the retired women suffered from too much togetherness or an inactive husband.

Hiller and Philliber (1982) have suggested that women may readjust their work commitment if it conflicts with husband, home, and marriage. The lives of these women suggest an alternative possibility. Some women enlisted and received their husband's support; in essence their husbands readjusted their commitment to the home. Other women allowed a low-level dissonance to exist during their working years. Both these situations, but especially the latter, put the women in a position to reduce the negatives associated with work while retaining the positive, sharing relationship with their spouse that they had achieved because of it.

Participation in employment and the type of work done appears to be related to later life patterns (Simpson, Bach, & McKinney, 1966; Karp & Yoels, 1982), and although this conclusion is supported by the data presented here, the relationship is complex. Work means different things to different workers (Simpson et al., 1966). The situation of the long-term marriage is both complex and heterogeneous and is certainly ripe for future inquiry.

Notes

1. This historic agreement specified that workers could retire with full pension benefits, regardless of their age, after completing 30 years of employment.
2. Although traditional husbands express great satisfaction and involvement in home and family both before and after retirement, the researcher suspects this is a conventionality phenomenon. Interviews indicated that, in contrast to dual-paycheck husbands and wives, traditional husbands' involvement and satisfaction seemed more often to be psychological and sustained through their economic support of the home and family, than mundane, sustained through day-to-day involvement in household routines.
3. These are the very reasons behind the declines in satisfaction and involvement exhibited by traditional husbands.

Chapter 9

Who Is Responsible for Household Tasks in Long-Term Marriages of the "Young-Old" Elderly?

Timothy H. Brubaker and Beth I. Kinsel
Family and Child Studies Center
Miami University
Oxford, Ohio 45056

Within the past 30 years, the research spotlight has been focused on the study of marriages of young persons. Adjustment to marriage, the birth of a child, and other topics have received considerable attention. Occasionally the beam of the research light has been broadened to include couples who have raised and launched their children. However, the dynamics of long-term marriages have seldom been illuminated. Couples who have achieved 50 years or more of marriage are survivors (Brubaker, 1985a). First, they have outlived many other people and, second, they have stayed married to one person for a long time. The experiences and patterns of behavior established by these husbands and wives may provide clues for younger couples regarding the complexities of the marital relationship.

The way in which married couples divide the responsibility for household tasks has received some attention from family researchers. For example, Brubaker and Hennon (1982) compared the divisions of household responsibility of dual-earner and dual-retired wives. Szinovacz (1980) interviewed retired women, while Keating and Cole (1980) studied retired teachers and their wives concerning the impact of retirement on the divisions of household tasks within their marriages. One study (Brubaker, 1985b) considered the divisions of household responsibility in the marriage of elderly aged 75 years or older.

This chapter is concerned with the way in which responsibility is divided between the husbands and wives in the marriages of 18 couples in which one partner is aged 74 years or younger. In gerontological literature, a distinction between the "young-old" (74 years and younger) and "old-old" (75 years and older) elderly has been made. Generally, the "young-old" are more active and have fewer health difficulties than the "old-old." Because the physical ability to perform household work may alter the division of household responsibility (Szinovacz, 1980), a look at the marriages of the "young-old" is warranted. This chapter is primarily descriptive and the findings will be compared with those reported in Brubaker (1985b).

The description of household responsibility includes *expected* as well as *actual* divisions as reported by the husbands and wives. These long-married couples were asked what responsibility they expected and actually had for 12 household tasks. Do they expect to share responsibility with their spouses? Or, do they expect their spouses to be responsible for activities which have been traditionally associated with their spouses' gender? Answers to these questions provide some insight into the sex role orientations of these older people.

Previous Research and Theory

Research on Household Tasks

Research focusing on the division of household tasks indicates that there is a continuation of task assignment rather than a change in the later years. For example, Szinovacz (1980) studied 24 retired wives to determine if their retirements had an effect on the way in which they divided household chores. Prior to retirement the wives had a gender-differentiated division of household tasks. The husbands did the "outside" activities and the wives completed the "inside" chores. After the wives retired, these patterns continued. Husbands became more involved in the "inside" work if their wives had health problems that precluded their involvement in the household tasks. Thus, health difficulties, not retirement, altered the way in which the household chores were divided.

Two other studies reported similar findings. Keating and Cole (1980) queried 400 retired teachers and found that retirement did not significantly alter the traditional divisions of household labor. Brubaker and Hennon (1982) examined 62 dual-retired and 145 dual-earner women. Both groups were traditionally oriented in their divisions of household labor and the dual-retired group continued patterns established before they retired. However, both the dual-earner and dual-retired women expected more sharing of household responsibility than actually occurred after retirement.

An analysis of 32 "old-old" couples who have been married 50 or more years indicates that traditional divisions of household responsibility are prevalent but, at the same time, there is some sharing of activities (Brubaker, 1985b). These couples expected husbands to share responsibility for feminine-oriented tasks and they actually shared responsibility for many of these activities. Also, the husbands were expected to have, and actually had, responsibility for the masculine-oriented tasks. Seldom were husbands expected to be responsible for feminine tasks and wives for masculine tasks. In short, these couples seemed to share more responsibility than the other studies indicated, but their expectations approximated the traditional divisions of household tasks.

Theory and Research on Sex-Role Orientations of Older People

The division of household responsibility is one indicator of the sex-role orientations of older people. Theories about sex-role orientations suggest that older people become less gender specific and may take on the characteristics of the opposite gender (Brim, 1976; Gutmann, 1975; Livson, 1983). Thus, men may become less aggressive and women more so. Even if there is no "cross-over" of sex role orientation, it is suggested that there is a tendency to become more androgynous. In terms of household responsibility, these theories expect older husbands and wives to be less gender specific. They should be sharing many activities. Further, husbands should be responsible for some of the tasks traditionally assigned to the wife and the wife may be responsible for some of the tasks traditionally assigned to the husband.

Several studies have focused on the sex-role orientation of older people, and the findings do not clearly support the theories. For example, three studies found less-differentiated gender orientations (Cameron, 1968, 1976; Minnigrode & Lee, 1978). Two other studies reported that gender differentiation continued with older people (Puglisi, 1983; Puglisi & Jackson, 1980–1981). A third study suggested that both men and women tend to be expressive in later life. In short, the research findings are not definitive in terms of sex-role orientations in later life.

Present Study

This study provides a description of the way in which "young-old" older people divide the responsibility for household tasks. Their division of household tasks is one indicator of the sex-role orientations of these older people. The theory suggests that they may have switched responsibility for household tasks or, in the least, they may be sharing the responsibility for gender-specific tasks.

Sample

The sample for this analysis was derived from in-depth interviews with persons married 50 years or more. The 18 couples each includes a partner who is 74 years of age or younger. As described in another paper (Brubaker, 1985b), this is a nonprobability, purposive sample. A list of couples married 50 years or more was developed from senior center memberships, newspaper announcements, and referrals made by knowledgeable community people and other golden anniversary couples. Most of the couples on the list agreed to complete a questionnaire and participate in a tape-recorded in-depth interview. In most instances, the interviews were conducted in the couple's primary place of residence. A questionnaire was completed by each husband and wife separately, and then they were interviewed jointly.

The couples resided in small rural communities or in medium-sized industrial towns. While various occupations were represented, most of the couples were retired from factory positions. Other occupational categories included professional, business, and farming. One-half (9) of the couples have an average yearly income of $10,000 and over. Six of the couples reported an annual income of $8,000–$9,999 and the remainder stated that their income was $6,000–$7,999. In general, the sample is representative of middle-class or working-class individuals.

The average age of the husbands is 72 years with a range of 70–74 years. For the wives, the average is 70.5 years with a range of 66–74 years. Two couples had been married 52 years, and an equal number stated that they were married 50 and 51 years. On the average, the wives had 11 years of education and the husbands had 10.5 years. One-half (9) of the husbands and wives rated their health as good, 7 as fair and 2 as excellent.

To measure marital satisfaction, the couples were given the Spanier Dyadic Adjustment Scale (Spanier, 1976). The average score for the husbands was 118, while the wives scored 114. Although there is no significant difference between the husbands' and wives' marital satisfaction scores, these average scores are less than those reported for couples who had a partner 75 years of age or older (Brubaker, 1985b). On the whole, these couples are quite satisfied with their marriages.

Measure of Household Responsibility

As described in Brubaker (1985b), the division-of-household-responsibility measure focused on who *should* and who *actually* does have responsibility for 12 different household tasks. The tasks are presented in Table 9.1. This is similar to a measure used in other studies of household responsibility (Brubaker & Hennon, 1982; Keith & Brubaker, 1977, 1980). When the twelve tasks are combined to form an index of traditional-nontraditional division of household responsibility, the higher score indicates a less traditional orientation and the lower score represents a traditional division of household responsibility.

Results

The *expected* division of responsibility for the 12 household tasks is presented in Table 9.1. These data indicate that these "young-old" cou-

Table 9.1
Percentage of *Expected* Division of Responsibility for Household Tasks by Golden Wedding Husbands and Wives[a]

	Husbands			Wives		
Tasks	Husband	Wife	Shared	Husband	Wife	Shared
Cooking meals	—	78%	22%	—	100%	—
Washing dishes	—	33%	67%	—	44%	56%
Yardwork	82%	6%	12%	61%	6%	33%
Washing clothes	—	100%	—	—	94%	6%
Car maintenance	100%	—	—	100%	—	—
Writing letters	22%	72%	6%	6%	67%	27%
Family social events	—	11%	89%	—	11%	89%
Earning money	84%	—	16%	67%	—	33%
Cleaning house	—	50%	50%	—	61%	39%
Shopping	—	44%	56%	—	28%	72%
House repairs	94%	—	6%	100%	—	—
Family decisions	6%	—	94%	6%	—	94%

[a] $n = 18$.

ples expect to share some household tasks but they tend to be traditional in the way they assign responsibility for many tasks. For example, the husbands assign responsibility to their wives for the meal preparation, laundry, and letter writing. Also, they assign responsibility to themselves for yardwork, car maintenance, earning of money, and house repairs. Areas in which husbands expect to share responsibility include washing dishes, arranging family social events, cleaning the house and making family decisions. Although the husbands expect to be responsible for the "masculine"-oriented tasks, they expect to share responsibility for some "feminine" tasks.

A majority of the wives expect to have responsibility for cooking the meals, washing clothes, writing letters, and cleaning the house. They expect their husbands to be responsible for the yardwork, car maintenance, earning money, and house repairs. For the most part, these women expect traditional divisions of responsibility for all areas except four. The four exceptions are washing the dishes, arranging family social events, shopping, and making family decisions. For these tasks, the wives expect to share responsibility.

There are few differences in husbands' and wive's expectations for household tasks. Only in earning money, yardwork, and writing letters are there discrepancies between whom the husbands and wives assigned responsibility. Most of this discrepancy relates to the tendency for more wives to expect to share responsibility, whereas the husbands expect the "traditional" spouse to perform the tasks.

The husbands' and wives' *actual* divisions of responsibility for household tasks is presented in Table 9.2. Husbands report that their wives actually have more responsibility for some of the tasks than they expect. For example two-thirds of the wives are responsible for washing the dishes when only one-third are expected to do so. At the same time, the husbands participate in other activities more than they are expected. One-third of the husbands state that they are responsible for cleaning the house. However, husbands expect more sharing than actually occurs and their wives are more responsible for some "feminine" tasks than they expected.

The wives report that they are responsible for cooking the meals, washing the dishes and clothes, writing letters, and cleaning the house. Their husbands are responsible for yardwork, car maintenance and house repairs. Although the majority (56%) of wives assign the responsibility for earning money to their husbands, a large percentage (44%) stated that they shared responsibility for this task. The wives assign responsibility to themselves for many of the "feminine" tasks and perceive more sharing than they expect in other tasks.

Table 9.2

Percentage of *Actual* Division of Responsibility for Household
Tasks by Golden Wedding Husbands and Wives[a]

Tasks	Husbands			Wives		
	Husband	Wife	Shared	Husband	Wife	Shared
Cooking meals	—	89%	11%	—	83%	17%
Washing dishes	—	67%	33%	—	72%	28%
Yardwork	78%	6%	16%	71%	12%	17%
Washing clothes	—	94%	6%	—	100%	—
Car maintenance	100%	—	—	100%	—	—
Writing letters	6%	82%	12%	6%	67%	27%
Family social events	—	17%	83%	—	11%	89%
Earning money	72%	—	28%	56%	—	44%
Cleaning house	33%	67%	—	39%	61%	—
Shopping	—	39%	61%	6%	27%	67%
House repairs	89%	11%	—	100%	—	—
Family decisions	—	—	100%	6%	—	94%

[a] n = 18.

The spouses' assignments of expected and actual responsibility for household tasks were compared. Comparison of the husbands' average (M = 16.18) and the wives' average (M = 16.72) on the Expected Household Responsibility Index indicates that there is no significant difference between the spouses' scores (t = .78, p = .44). Similarly, there is no significant differences between the husbands (M = 16.65) and wives' (M = 16.94) averages on the Actual Household Responsibility Index (t = .38, p = .71). These findings of congruency are similar to findings reported by Brubaker (1985b). As couples live together for many years, their expectations and actual participation in household tasks tend to be similar.

Previous research on the division of household responsibility indicates that there is a discrepancy between what is expected and what actually occurs (Brubaker & Hennon, 1982). In this sample of "young-old", golden anniversary sample, there is congruency between the expectations and actual assignment of responsibility. The correlation coefficient for the husbands' expected and actual assignment of responsibility is .83 (p = .001), and the correlation coefficient for the wives' expected and actual scores is .61 (p = .005). This congruency between expected and actual assignments of responsibility was also found in a sample of "old-old," golden wedding couples (Brubaker, 1985b). This finding suggests that long married couples' expectations for household tasks correspond with what they actually do around the house.

Research on sex role orientation suggests that age, education, income, and marital satisfaction may be related to the division of responsibility in households (Brubaker & Hennon, 1982; Ericksen, Yancy, & Ericksen, 1979; Farkas, 1976). Also, Brubaker (1985b) found that the number of years married was related to less traditional expectations for husbands, and health was related to wives' expectations for less traditional divisions of responsibility. Analysis of these 18 couples indicates that none of these factors is significantly related to the expected or actual division of household responsibility. This finding is contrary to the analysis of "old-old," golden anniversary couples (Brubaker, 1985b).

Discussion and Conclusions

This analysis suggests that "young-old," golden anniversary couples divide responsibility for household tasks in a traditional manner. Generally, husbands expect to be, and actually are, responsible for "masculine" tasks, and wives expect to be, and actually are, responsible for "feminine" tasks. This finding is similar to the results of a study of "old-old," golden anniversary couples (Brubaker, 1985b). At the same time, the "young-old," golden anniversary couples share more responsibility than has been found in studies of younger aged persons (Brubaker & Hennon, 1982; Keith & Brubaker, 1977, 1980). In many ways, these golden anniversary couples have developed an interdependent, gender-specific division of household tasks. Even though they follow gender-differentiated divisions of household tasks, they do share several tasks.

A unique finding of this group of married couples is the congruency between what is expected and what actually occurs. For the most part, these couples are responsible for tasks they expect to be within their domains. Contrary to younger-aged groups (Brubaker & Hennon, 1982), they are doing what they expect to be doing (or are expecting what they are doing).

This analysis of "young-old" and a previous study of "old-old" golden anniversary couples suggests that long-married couples may be unusual in that they share more than other aged couples and they do what they expect to do. These long-married couples have developed ways to accomplish tasks around the house in which they are responsible for gender-specific tasks *and* they share responsibility. In many ways, golden anniversary couples have negotiated elaborate, interdependent relationships.

Additional research on long-married couples is needed to determine if they shared activities throughout their marriages. Or, do they gradually share more activities after their golden anniversary? Based on this research, golden anniversary couples may be unique in their divisions of responsibility. Future research is needed to determine how unique they may be.

Part II

Family and Friends

Chapter 10

Life Satisfaction and Family Strengths of Older Couples

Gregory F. Sanders
Department of Child Development and Family Relations
North Dakota State University
Fargo, North Dakota 58105

James Walters
Child and Family Development Department
University of Georgia
Athens, Georgia 30605

The myth of family abandonment of older members has been largely discredited in recent years. Several studies have demonstrated a high rate of contact between older persons and their children. For example, findings of studies by Shanas (1973) and Watson and Kivett (1976) suggested that over half of older persons see at least one of their children daily and over 70% visit with one or more of their children weekly. Rather than abandoning aging parents, many children try to delay their parents' institutionalization at considerable costs to themselves (Robinson & Thurnher, 1979). The percentage of older persons living with their children increases with age: 14% of the men and 26% of the women over 85 years of age live with one of their children (Glick, 1979), demonstrating that older persons are not abandoned by their family. Although the family is often not needed for support of older members, the support network is in place and set into motion when needed. Especially in times of crisis, children have been found to be important sources of aid for older parents (Shanas, 1973).

A high rate of contact and support, however, gives little insight into the quality of family interaction of older persons with their children, or the influence that interaction with offspring has on meeting the daily social, psychological, and physical needs of older persons. Indications of how well these needs are being met can be gained from research on life satisfaction. Overall, such research has demonstrated that significant relations exist between life satisfaction and such factors as: health status, with those in better health reflecting greater satisfaction (Bull & Aucoin, 1975; Edwards & Klemmack, 1973; Fengler & Jensen, 1981; Palmore & Luikart, 1972); socioeconomic status (Edwards & Klemmack, 1973; Fengler & Jensen, 1981; Markides & Martin, 1979; Spreitzer & Snyder, 1974); and age (Cavan, Burgess, Havighurst, & Goldhamer, 1949; Edwards & Kelmmack, 1973), but *not* when health and SES were controlled. Most past research has demonstrated a lack of relationship between life satisfaction and gender (Cavan et al., 1949; Liang, Dvorkin, Kahana & Mazian, 1980; Neugarten, Havighurst, & Tobin, 1961).

Although these studies have focused on the relation of a variety of demographic variables to life satisfaction, little work has been done investigating the relative importance of family characteristics. When family variables have been considered, researchers have relied heavily on measures of quantity, such as frequency of contact (Edwards & Klemmack, 1973; Kerckhoff, 1966; Lee & Tallmann, 1980; Martin, 1973), yet *frequency* of family contact has not been found to contribute significantly to an understanding of life satisfaction. Other studies, however, have shown that satisfaction with the family is related to life satisfaction in general (Medley, 1976; Quinn, 1983). Obviously, these two variables are not independent of each other, yet their precise relationship is unknown (Markides & Martin, 1979).

The measure of family interaction quality used in this study, family strengths, has been defined as: Those relationship patterns, interpersonal skills and competencies, and social and psychological characteristics that create a sense of positive family identity, promote satisfying and fulfilling interaction among family members, encourage the development of the potential of the family group and individual family members, and contribute to the family's ability to deal effectively with stress and crises (Stinnett, 1979).

In one of the earlier studies of this area, Otto (1962) found the characteristics listed most often as strengths included: (a) shared faith, religious and moral values; (b) consideration and understanding; (c) common interests, goals, and purpose; (d) love, happiness of children; (e) working and playing together; and (f) sharing specific recreational activities. These characteristics of strong families were similar to those found in a national study of adults (Stinnett, Sanders, & DeFrain, 1981) and with a group of college students (Beam, 1979).

An Exchange Theory Perspective

Family involvement may be considered a resource of the older person. From an exchange perspective, it would be expected that those elderly with more resources would come out better in social exchanges and thus have greater satisfaction (Dowd, 1975; 1980). Such resources might include financial capacity, health, personality and family characteristics, and general independence. The basic premise of exchange theory as stated by Nye (1979) is that "humans avoid costly and seek rewarding statuses, relationships, and interaction and feeling states to the end that their profits are maximized . . . or minimize their losses, since at times no alternative viewed as desirable in a positive sense is open to the individual group or organization" (p. 5). Nye lists some of the general sources of rewards, such as social approval, autonomy, security, money, agreement on values and opinions, and equality.

Once obtained, these and other rewards might become resources that can be used to gain further rewards in social exchanges. From this perspective, it could be predicted that some older persons would have less control over what they receive because they have fewer resources to bargain with, including physical, financial, personal, and ecucational resources. Life satisfaction would thus tend to be lower in situations where the older person could not achieve a satisfactory exchange due to lack of resources.

Often, however, even those older persons who lack resources receive many "rewards," especially those necessary for survival. Such exchanges, although they may satisfy many essential needs of older persons, may seem unequal to the older person and, thus, lower life satisfaction due to feelings of guilt or dependency. In exchange theory, feelings of dependency may be viewed as a cost, that is, older family members receiving aid may not be satisfied because they may believe they are overbenefiting from the help given by their children.

Some family members may instill a sense of dependency and role loss in older parents by doing too much to help their parents and not allowing or encouraging them to perform significant family and community roles. In such cases, lesser amounts of contact might serve to enhance rather than lower life satisfaction. Thus, it seems reasonable that the quality of family interaction may have a greater impact on life satisfaction than the quantity of interaction.

Purposes

The present study was designed to assess what one measure of family interaction quality, (i.e., family strengths) contributes to an understanding of life satisfaction of older persons. This variable, along with other individual and familial characteristics (i.e., job prestige, health, education, age, gender, and family exchanges) are viewed here as resources that enable the elderly to foster positive social exchanges and thus have greater satisfaction. Because particular roles have been identified as more important for one gender than the other (e.g., the role of provider has traditionally been of greater importance to men; Dowd & LaRossa, 1982), in the present study analyses were done of the responses on males and females separately, as well as for the total group. Specifically, the study focused on the following research questions: (a) What is the relative importance of family strengths, satisfaction with interaction quality, family exchange, occupational prestige, education, health, age, and gender in explaining variance in life satisfaction? and (b) What are the differences between males and females concerning the relative importance of these factors in explaining variability in life satisfaction?

Procedure

The Sample

The sample was comprised of 68 elderly couples living in Georgia and North Carolina. Sources of the participants included older couples living in their home, a rented home or apartment, or congregate housing units. The older married couples were identified through: (a) senior citizen groups, (b) church organizations, (c) congregate housing units, and (d) contacts made with other participants. Couples were included if they met the following criteria: (a) The couple had been married at least three years, (b) both the husband and wife were retired, (c) the couple were parents or stepparents to an adult child age 20 or older. The adult offspring about whom the couple responded was the son or daughter with whom they interacted the most. All older persons included in this study were married. Persons aged 60-69 represent 46% of the total sample, and the mean age was 69.8 years. Wives were somewhat younger (M = 65.5) than their spouses (M = 71.6). Overall, the group was well educated with 39.4% having college or postgraduate degrees; yet 37% had less than a high school education. Most (62.5%) of the respondents rated their health as "Good" or "Excellent," only 8.8% stated that they were in "Poor" or "Very Poor" health. The men rated their health slightly less favorably than the women with 57.4% of the men rating their health as "Good" or "Excellent" compared with 67.4% of the woman. The couples were married an average of 45.3 years with 56% of the group being married between 40 and 49 years; 26% had been married for over 50 years. These families had a mean of 2.6 offspring; 54.5% had 2 or 3 offspring.

Categories of job prestige were determined using categories of the National Data Program for the Social Sciences (1976) job prestige score listing. The higher the score on this listing, the higher the job prestige of an occupation. Job prestige was defined as earned respect determined by one's occupational status. Husbands and wives were markedly different on preretirement job prestrige. Forty percent of the wives had prestige scores under 20; none of the husbands had scores in this category. A total of 29% of the men and only 6% of the women had job prestige scores above 60.

Administration of Instruments

Questionnaires were distributed to various church groups, senior citizen organizations and to persons identified as willing to participate in the study. Sixty-eight husband-wife sets of questionnaires were returned. The precise number of questionnaires that were received by older couples who fit the criteria is not known because of the use made of organizations and personal contacts. Thus an accurate assessment of the return rate cannot be made.

Description of the Instruments

The Family Relations Questionnaire. The Family Relations Questionnaire is a paper-and-pencil instrument consisting of 21 separate items and two scales to which the participants were asked to respond independently. The scales used in this questionnaire were the Family Strengths Scale designed for this study and the Life Satisfaction Inventory-A (Adams, 1969).

Family Strengths Scale. A Family Strengths Scale (FSS) was constructed so that persons rated their families in terms of their perceived behavioral characteristics. The 47 Likert-type items had response categories ranging from "Very Frequently" to "Never." Characteristics were included that were discovered in other research to be descriptive of strong families (Beam, 1979; Stinnett et al., 1981). Items reflected either positive "Appreciates me" or negative "Uses sarcasm" behavior. The validity of these characteristics was originally assessed by means of rating by expert judges (Stinnett & Sauer, 1978). The scale was further evaluated and shortened to 30 items by the use of a factor analysis. The factor analysis revealed that 30 of the 47 items were moderately to highly correlated on one of six factors. These six factors each had an underlying characteristic described by the titles "Support," "Treatment of the Older Person," "Love," "Feelings of Significance," "Support in Need," "Trusts my Decisions." For the total 30-item scale a Spearman-Brown split-half coefficient of .86 was obtained.

Participants were also asked the global question, "How satisfying is the time spent with your child?" This question is similar to how quality of family interaction has been measured in previous studies (Medley, 1976; Quinn, 1983).

Life Satisfaction Inventory-A.   The measure of life satisfaction of this sample was Adam's (1969) short version of Neugarten et al.'s (1961) Life Satisfaction Inventory (LSI-A). This version was chosen for brevity and high correlation with other measures of life satisfaction ($r = .75$ or greater). Reliability of this test is moderately high ($r = .79$) and validity has been estimated at .57 (correlation with interviews ratings) (Lohmann, 1977).

Results

Multiple Regression Analysis on Life Satisfaction

In order to understand the relation between family and demographic variables and life satisfaction of the elderly, multiple regression equations were calculated. The first analysis included life satisfaction as the criterion variable and individual and familial circumstances (i.e., family strengths, family exchange, satisfaction with interaction quality, occupational prestige, education, health, age, and gender) as predictor variables. Regression analyses for the whole sample were first calculated using the total family strengths score as an independent variable and then using the separate factors of family strengths as independent variables. The second round of analyses compare factors related to life satisfaction for men and women, also using the total family strengths score and the factors of family strengths in separate equations.

Multiple Regression Using the Total Family Strengths Scores. Six of
the predictor variables were included in the multiple regression equation (see Table 10.1). These six predictor variables accounted for 26.7%
of the variance in life satisfaction scores. The older person's health rating
explained 11.4% of the variance in life satisfaction and the family
strengths score accounted for an additional 4.2% of the variability. Job
prestige of the older person's spouse and job prestige of the older person
were the third and fourth variable entered in the regression equation.
The finding that the fourth variable entered accounted for a greater
amount of variance (4.4%) than the third (3.9%) may indicate some
interaction between these two variables. This issue was explored by
further analyses (to be discussed later).

Table 10.1
**Results of Multiple Regression Analyses of Individual
and Family Circumstances with Life Satisfaction**

Predictors	Increase in R	R^2	R	F	p	Beta	Pearson r
Analysis with total family strengths score							
Total		.267	.516	7.81	.000		
Health rating	.114					.207	.397**
Family strengths	.042					.205	.276*
Job prestige of spouse	.039					.165	.268**
Job prestige	.044					.278	.208*
Gender	.019					.180	.190*
Financial help given	.008					-.097	-.256**
Analysis with family strengths subscale scores							
Total		.278	.528	7.06	.000		
Health rating	.114					.209	.397**
Treatment of older person	.057					.141	.258**
Job prestige of spouse	.033					.180	.268**
Job prestige	.035					.280	.208*
Gender	.016					.157	.190*
Love	.014					.137	.174
Financial help given	.008					-.098	-.256

* $p < .05$.
** $p < .01$.

Multiple Regression with the Family Strengths Subscale Scores. Using the family strengths subscale scores as separate independent variables (rather than the total family strengths scores) yielded a slightly higher percentage of variance accounted for in life satisfaction scores. Six variables accounted for 27.8% of the variance in life satisfaction. Life satisfaction was best explained by the older person's health rating (11.4%), "treatment of the older person" (5.7%), job prestige of the older person's spouse (3.3%), job prestige (3.5%), gender (1.6%), and "love" (1.4%). As shown in Table 10.1, two of the family strengths subscale scores, "treatment of the older person" and "love" were entered in the equation.

Gender Differences in Characteristics Related to Life Satisfaction

Gender Differences Using the Total Family Strengths Score. The total sample was divided into subsamples of husbands and wives in order to assess gender differences in the relation between individual and familial circumstances and life satisfaction. It can be seen in Table 10.2 that the predictor variables accounted for a greater amount of the variance in life satisfaction scores of females than of males when the total family strengths score was used as one of the predictors. Three variables accounted for 20.5% of the variance in males, whereas four variables accounted for 31.8% of the variance in life satisfaction of females. The greatest amount of variance in the satisfaction scores of the males was accounted for by job prestige (16.6%); this predictor was entered third in the regression equation for females and accounted for 5.4% of the variance. Job prestige explained a greater amount of variance for both males and females than job prestige of spouse. Thus, because of the potential for job prestige of spouse to act as a suppressor variable, this precictor was dropped from the analysis.

Health rating explained 16.6% of the variance of the female sample, but was not entered as a predictor in the male sample. The family strengths score was entered second in both equations but accounted for a greater amount of variance in satisfaction of the female sample (8.7% vs. 2.4%). The third predictor entered in the equation for males, financial help given, explained 1.4% of the variance in life satisfaction but was not entered for the female sample. Another family exchange variable, goods provided, accounted for 1.2% of the variance for females and was not entered for males.

Gender Differences Using the Family Strengths Subscale Scores. Separate multiple regression equations were computed for the male and female subsamples using the family strengths subscale scores as predictors. As seen in Table 10.2, "love" and "support in need" were the

Table 10.2
Results of Multiple Regression Analyses of Individual and Familial Circumstances with Life Satisfaction by Gender

Predictors	Increase in R^2	R^2	R	F	p	Beta	Pearson r
Results of analysis for males using the total family strengths score							
Total		.205	.453	5.49	.002		
Job prestige	.166					.378	.434**
Family strengths	.024					.139	.183
Financial help given	.014					-.125	-.254*
Results of analysis for females using the total family strengths score							
Total		.318	.564	7.36	.000		
Health rating	.166					.391	.493**
Family strengths	.087					.290	.440**
Job prestige	.054					.237	.289*
Goods provided	.012					.115	.007
Results of analysis for males using family strengths subscale scores							
Total		.295	.543	3.08	.006		
Job prestige	.166					.466	.434**
Love	.026					.263	.129
Goods received	.025					.175	.193
Financial help given	.015					-.148	-.254*
Support in need	.014					-.182	.094
Education	.015					-.212	.306*
Number of health problems	.018					-.153	.319*
Phone visits	.014					-.123	.046
Results of analysis for females using family strengths subscale scores							
Total		.347	.589	6.61	.000		
Health rating	.166					.421	.493**
Treatment of older person	.105					.228	.341*
Job prestige	.048					.250	.288*
Love	.015					.160	.207
Goods provided	.013					.124	.007

* $p < .05$.
** $p < .01$.

subscale scores entered in the equation for males. These predictors explained 2.6% and 1.4% of the variance in life satisfaction respectively. In this equation, life satisfaction was best explained by job prestige (16.6%), "love" (2.6%), goods provided (2.5%), financial help given (2.5%), "support in need" (1.4%), education (1.5%), number of heatlh problems (1.8%), and phone visits (1.4%). These eight variables accounted for 29.5% of the variance in male life satisfaction.

Five predictors were entered for the female subsample and explained 34.7% of the variance in life satisfaction. Life satisfaction of the females was best explained by health rating (16.6%), "treatment of the older person" (10.5%), job prestige (4.8%), "love" (1.5%), and goods provided by the older person (1.3%).

Discussion

The present study revealed that family strengths were related to life satisfaction of older persons but accounted for only a small amount of variance. Job prestige was the strongest predictor of life satisfaction for the husbands, and health accounted for the most variance in life satisfaction of wives. The component of family strengths, "treatment of the older person," accounted for more variance in life satisfaction than either the total score or the scores of the other components of family strengths. This aspect of family quality was more important as a predictor of life satisfaction for wives. "Treatment of the older person" may have been the best indicator of life satisfaction variance among the family strengths components because the items in this subscale reflect mostly a lack of negative responses (i.e., complaining, controlling, disrespect) by the offspring. Such negative responses, if present, would reflect a cost of interacting with the offspring, causing such interactions to be less profitable.

Satisfaction with interaction quality was not found to be a significant predictor of life satisfaction. Whereas great variability was found in family strengths scores, respondents almost exclusively replied that the time spent with their child was satisfying or very satisfying. Beyond the problem of a satisfaction measure of quality not being an independent variable from life satisfaction, such global measures of variables tend to elicit responses not highly correlated to more precise measures (Lohmann, 1977).

The finding that strengths were more highly related to life satisfaction for females than for males has been supported indirectly in research showing that the role of father was less important in determining life satisfaction of males than factors such as income and health (Watson & Kivett, 1976). Dowd and LaRossa (1982) have noted that the roles of breadwinner and head of the household are of greater importance as resources for males.

Receiving financial help had no effect on the life satisfaction of males or females, a finding that seems inconsistent with exchange theory and previous findings by Dowd and LaRossa (1982). Perhaps ascertaining the extent of financial help received by older parents would better assess the importance of this variable.

None of the family exchanges were strong predictors of life satisfaction and should be considered only suggestive indicators of support for exchange theory. Giving and receiving appeared to occur as a mutual trade between older couples and their children. The correlation between giving and receiving goods and services was significant ($r = 28, p < .001$) as was the correlation between giving and receiving personal help ($r = .35, p < .001$). Perhaps those elderly persons whose exchanges with their children were imbalanced would be more affected by them. The fact that these elderly persons were not in need of great physical or financial support and were married possibly related to the relative balance of exchanges and thus the minimal effect of exchanges on life satisfaction. Even when an elderly person is in need, if they are married, it is often the spouse who provides the most care (Koopman-Boyden & Well, 1979).

Health was the greatest single predictor of life satisfaction for the total sample, accounting for 11% of the variability and supporting the exchange perspective that more-dependent persons would be less satisfied. The findings presented in this study indicated that perceived health was of greater importance for females than for males as a predictor of life satisfaction and, in fact, was not a significant predictor of life satisfaction for males. In contrast, both Medley (1976) and Palmore and Luikart (1972) found perceived health to be slightly more important for males than females. Perhaps, because of the relative good health of the sample used in the present study, the feelings of dependence and loss of power discussed by other researchers (Dowd & LaRossa, 1982; Lemert, 1963) were not of primary concern.

Job prestige was found to be a significant predictor of life satisfaction in the total sample (approximately 4% variance explained). For males, job prestige was the strongest predictor of life satisfaction (approximately 17% variance explained) and was also an important predictor life satisfaction for females (approximately 5% variance explained). Job prestige may be an important source of social respect and an indicator of financial status, both resources from an exchange theory perspective. These results are also consistent with the belief of the greater value placed on the work role by men.

In sum, one measure of family quality, family strengths, was found to be only minimally related to life satisfaction of older married persons. This does not, however, negate the potential importance of family quality for life satisfaction of all older persons. Among those who are more dependent on offspring or those who have no spouse, quality of interaction with offspring may be more important. On the flip side of this relationship, quality of interaction has been related to the offspring's perceived caregiver burden (Robinson, B., 1983). In the present study, the strengths of the husband-wife relationship may have been a better predictor of life satisfaction.

The current study reemphasizes the need to research subgroups of the elderly population. In this study, husbands and wives differed concerning which variables best predicted their satisfaction in life. Other subgroups of elderly would be expected to be affected differently by family members. As suggested above, widowed persons may vary greatly from their married counterparts in regard to the quality of the relationships with their children and the importance of those relationships for life satisfaction may be greater due to the lack of spousal interaction. Future research should investigate the quality of a variety of family relationships and should study elderly persons of varied marital status and health.

Chapter 11

Relationships between Marital Quality and Social and Familial Interactions by Residential Location
Implications for Human Service Professionals

Ellie Brubaker
Department of Sociology and Anthropology
Miami University
Oxford, Ohio 45056

Linda Ade-Ridder
Department of Home Economics and Consumer Sciences
and
Family and Child Studies Center
Miami University
Oxford, Ohio 45056

Researchers have become interested in the quality of married life over the family life cycle, particularly during the later years (Hicks & Platt, 1970). Information concerning the quality of older couples' marriages can contribute to research as well as to the provision of services to older families.

Various factors are related to the quality of marriages of older couples; however, little is known about the relationships between marital quality and the social and physical environments in which older couples function. Do the social interactions of older couples with individuals external to the marriage influence the quality of marriage for those couples? Are living arrangements related to marital quality for the elderly?

All individuals function within the limitations and supports of their environments. Their behavior is influenced by and influences those to whom they relate. Information about the relationships between marital quality, living arrangements and social interactions of older couples are relevant to researchers examining the marital quality of older couples as well as to service providers working with older couples.

Within this chapter, the marital quality of older couples living in a retirement community and of couples living in the community-at-large is examined. The following questions are investigated:

1. Is the frequency of interaction with friends by elderly couples, as a couple, related to the quality of their marriages? If a relationship exists, does this differ for the retirement facility couples and the community-at-large couples?
2. Is the frequency of interaction with children by elderly couples related to the quality of their marriages? If a relationship exists, does this differ between retirement facility couples and community-at-large couples?

Review of the Literature

Marital quality, for the purposes of this study, is determined by the subjective evaluation of the process of dyadic adjustment, including evaluation of the couples: (1) troublesome differences, (2) interpersonal tensions and personal anxiety, (3) satisfaction, (4) cohesion, and (5) consensus on matters of importance (Spanier, 1976). Research in the area of marital quality of the elderly indicates that the marital quality of older couples is often satisfactory (Ade-Ridder & Brubaker, 1983a).

Studies concerning marital quality of the elderly present conflicting results (Ade-Ridder & Brubaker, 1983a), suggesting that marital quality may be related to the passage of time and subsequent life experiences. For example, a number of earlier studies reveal that the longer the marriage continues, the less satisfactory it is to the spouses (Blood & Wolfe, 1960; Glass & wright, 1977; Yarrow, Black, Quinn, Youmans, & Stein, 1971). Other research indicates that marital quality increases with the passing of time, particularly after children have left the home, following an initial decline while the children were young (Anderson, Russell, & Shumm, 1983; Smart & Smart, 1975).

Factors found to relate to the marital quality of older couples include sex role orientation, health, leisure interests, and morale. Schram (1979) reported that marital quality is positively related to egalitarian sex role orientation patterns of behavior. Poor health has been related to marital maladjustment of older couples (Harry, 1976; Medley, 1977). Literature also reveals positive relationships between marital quality of older couples and several other variables, including shared leisure interests (Harry, 1976; Orthner, 1975) and morale (Gubrium, 1974; Lee, 1978).

Research concerning marital quality of older couples has primarily focused on relationships between marital quality and factors internal to the marriage. Additional information concerning the relationship between marital quality and external factors would provide the applied gerontologist with valuable knowledge. Elderly couples are not only influenced by the relationships with their spouses. In addition, older couples have relationships with other individuals, groups, and organizations that may have an impact on the couples relationship. Although their social circle may have narrowed due to deaths of friends, they continue to be involved in reciprocal relationships with others. The literature substantiates that older individuals have relationships with family and friends (Shanas, 1979a). This is the case for individuals in the community-at-large as well as for those in retirement facilities (Brubaker & Brubaker, 1984).

However, there is a dearth of literature concerning relationships of residence and social interactions to older couples' marital quality. A comparison of the social interactions of older couples living in an institutional setting with older couples living in a community setting provides information not previously available. The uniqueness of this sample controls for residence and provides information about the relationship of residence to variable potentially influencing marital quality.

Methodology

Sample

Older subjects have long lives full of varied experiences, which are difficult to examine separately. Consequently, two very similar groups of married men and women were studied in order to control for as many extraneous events and variables as possible. The primary difference between these groups of older individuals is the location of their residence. One group is living in a retirement community, whereas the other is composed of those on the waiting list for the same facility while living in the community-at-large. The retirement facility is nonprofit and church-affiliated. The sample is composed of 232 older couples who live in the community-at-large and 103 couples who reside in the retirement facility. In all cases, respondents are married couples and at least one spouse is over age 65. All couples, even those within the retirement facility, live in independent living environments.

For retirement facility couples, the length of time in their current residence averages 4.1 years, while the average community-at-large couple has resided in their residence for almost 19 years. The retirement facility couples are slightly older than are the community-at-large respondents, and had lower incomes prior to retirement. In both samples, men tend to be older than women, are better educated, have had higher-status careers, and are more likely to consider themselves retired. In each of the above areas, their is no significant difference between the two samples.

In both groups, most subjects are Protestant and attend church regularly (96% of the retirement facility couples and 84% of the community-at-large couples attend church once a week or more). The subjects in both groups feel that their health has not changed much during the past five years, but that health occasionally restricts their activities.

Data Collection

The administrators of the facility furnished a list of: (1) all married couples currently residing in independent housing in the retirement facility (n = 103), and (2) the couples waiting for future admission to similar housing (n = 232). All of the men and women on these lists were asked to complete questionnaires. Letters were sent to all 103 married couples living in independent housing units at the retirement facility, inviting them to attend an informational meeting. At the meeting, questionnaires were distributed and inquiries were answered. Questionnaires were mailed to all couples not in attendance and to the 232 married couples on the waiting list. Both husbands and wives were asked to complete separate questionnaires in order to gain information about each spouse.

Measures

Spanier's Dyadic Adjustment Scale (Spanier, 1976) was utilized to determine the quality of marital relationships of the respondents. Spanier's Dyadic Adjustment Scale is composed of 32 items: 13 items on the Dyadic Consensus Subscale, ten on the Dyadic Satisfaction, five on the Dyadic Cohesion, and four on the Affectional Expression Subscales. One item on the scale was modified from "Ways of dealing with parents or in-laws" to read "Ways of dealing with children" in order to make the scale relevant to the age of the sample. The theoretical range for the marital quality scale is 0 to 151. The actual range for all couples is 38 to

146. Spanier (1976) has claimed content validity, criterion-related validity, and construct validity for the Dyadic Adjustment Scale. Total scale reliability was shown to be .96 in Spanier's (1976) first testing and .91 in his second study (Spanier & Thompson, 1982).

Hours in which couples spend weekly with friends or relatives was measured by asking both husbands and wives how many hours in a typical week they spent as a couple together with friends or relatives. Respondents could choose from the following categories: none, 1-4, 5-9, 10-14, or 15+. The theoretical range for hours spent per week, as a couple, with friends or relatives is 0 to 15 or more. The actual range for all couples is 1 to 15 or more hours per week.

The frequency with which the respondents see their children was measured by the question, "How often do you see any of your children?" The subjects could choose from the following categories: once a day or more, one to six times a week, one to three times a month, less than once a month, or I have no living children. For those respondents with living children, the theoretical and actual ranges for frequency children are seen: once a day or more, to less than once a month.

Results

Overall, the quality of marriage of the couples in both the retirement facility and the community-at-large is high. The mean score for the retirement facility couples is 117.1 compared to 115.4 for the community-at-large couples, an insignificant difference as measured by the t-test.

The *hours couples spend weekly with friends* ranges from none to ten or more. The mean for the retirement facility elderly is 2.87 hours and the mean for the community-at-large subjects is 2.95 hours (see Table 11.1). Respondents in both groups interact with friends and relatives as a couple more than they do as individuals, although women spend more time with friends and relatives without their husbands than do men without their wives. The hours spent weekly with friends as a couple is found to be significantly related to marital quality when partial correlation (controlling for group) is applied to these two variables ($r = .17$; $p = .01$).

Couples living in the retirement facility spend significantly less time with friends per week as a couple than do couples residing in the community-at-large. The marital quality of retirement couples is higher than the marital quality of community-at-large couples. This relationship might suggest that those couples who see friends less frequently as a couple report greater happiness with their marriages.

Table 11.1
Interaction with Friends

Frequency of interaction with children by location	f	%
Retirement facility respondents		
Once a day or more	5	3.7
One to six times per week	17	12.7
One to three times per month	44	32.9
Less than once a month	44	32.8
Have no living children	24	17.9
Totals	134	100.0
Community-at-large respondents		
Once a day or more	11	3.5
One to six times per week	92	29.0
One to three times per month	77	24.3
Less than once a month	112	35.3
Having no living children	25	7.9
Totals	317	100.0

Hours spent weekly as a couple with friends by location	f	%
Retirement facility respondents		
None	4	2.8
One to four	59	41.3
Five to nine	48	33.6
Ten or more	32	22.4
Totals	143	100.1
Community-at-large respondents		
None	3	1.0
One to four	105	33.7
Five to nine	126	40.5
Ten or more	77	24.8
Totals	311	100.0

The respondents range from *seeing their children* once a day or more to less than once a month. Forty-nine of the respondents report having no living children. The average retirement facility couple sees their children slightly less than once a month while community-at-large residents see their children slightly more often (see Table 11.1). However, this difference is not statistically significant. Correlation was utilized to examine the findings in terms of a relationship between the respondents' marital quality and their interactions with their children. When controlling for group, no significant relationship is indicated (r = .08; p = .175). This finding indicates that a significant relationship does not exist between the frequency of seeing children and marital quality.

Although the retirement facility couples see their children slightly less often than do couples residing in the community-at-large, the difference between the two groups is not statistically significant. In addition, the frequency with which each group sees their children is not related to the marital quality of either group.

Implications

The findings indicate that couples living in the residential community spend significantly less time with friends, but experience slightly higher level of marital quality in their couple relationship. Interaction with children is not significantly related to living environment nor to marital quality of the respondents. These findings have implications for applied gerontologists. The findings indicate that retirement facilities can potentially provide a positive environment for older married couples.

Living in a retirement facility (at least for the facility studied) is an option that can be satisfying and can reinforce the strengths, specifically, marital quality, of older couples. In fact, retirement facilities may have the potential to provide supports to older individuals, which can enhance their ability to function successfully. A relationship must receive positive inputs from its environment that contribute to its support for it to function successfully. A couple relationship is no exception. Although the friendships of those couples living in the community may have been positive, it could be that the respondents required resources beyond that which friendships could provide. For example, some friends may have primarily provided emotional support to couples in need of physical help as well. Those couples residing in the retirement facility were receiving support from the facility staff. Even though they saw their friends less frequently, the combination of resources in the form of friends and facility services may provide the inputs necessary to the successful support of the couple relationship.

In addition to requiring external resources which provide support, the spouse relationship also needs the resources of its members to function successfully. The fact that the retirement facility respondents can, to an extent, choose resources from both formal and informal resource systems may provide them with a greater sense of power over their lives. A facility that contributes to this feeling can help to create the personal satisfaction that frees individuals to give to, rather than take from, their partners.

Summary

The findings reveal that the marital quality of the couples in both groups is high. The mean scores for marital quality of both retirement facility couples (117.1) and community-at-large couples (115.4) is higher than is the mean score of (114.8) for married couples reported originally by Spanier (1976). This finding supports those studies suggesting that marital quality is higher for those couples whose marriages have lasted beyond the time when children leave home.

It would appear that although the retirement facility couples see friends on a less frequent basis, their perception of their marital quality is slightly (although not significantly) higher than that of the couples residing in the community-at-large. In both groups, however, marital quality was significantly related to interactions with friends. Frequency of visits from children was not found to be related to residence or to marital quality for either group of couples.

It is suggested that residence in retirement facilities that provide necessary supports to older clients can enhance later-life marriages. In addition, the retirement facility can provide a valuable support system when appropriately utilized by professionals.

Chapter 12

Friendships in Late Life
A Rural-Urban Comparison

Karen A. Roberto
Gerontology Program
University of Northern Colorado
Greeley, Colorado 80639

Jean Pearson Scott
Department of Human Development and Family Studies
Texas Tech University
Lubbock, Texas 79409

Friendships serve important functions in the life of the older adult. Research indicates that friends provide important psychological and social support for the older adult in the form of companionship, mutual aid, and shared activities. Unlike family ties, in which obligation to older members remain strong, friendship ties may be subject to variation due to personal and environmental conditions. Factors such as gender, marital status, and income level may dictate the type of friends and nature of the relationship. In addition, as older people become more dependent on environmental influences, and perhaps less mobile, geographical location may also have an influence on their friendships.

Much of what we know about friendships in late life comes from studies using urban samples. Very few comparisons of rural-urban patterns of friendship in late life have been made. Youmans (1963) examined selected socioenvironmental factors and behavior patterns of a sample of 627 rural and 609 urban older adults living in Kentucky. The

---

This is a revised version of a paper presented at the Families and Close Relationships: Individuals in Social Interaction Conference, Lubbock, Texas, February, 1982.

This study was supported by a grant from AARP Andrus Foundation and the Institute for University Research, College of Home Economics, Texas Tech University, Lubbock, Texas 79409.

aged rural adults in his study were more likely than urban aged to know people in the community, to engage in more informal visiting, and identify a larger number of persons as close friends. In addition, over half the rural respondents (53%) reported they gave help to their neighbors and friends whereas only about one-third (32%) of the urban older persons reported doing so. Those respondents who said they gave help to their friends named a variety of ways this help was given, such as in case of illness, with work, transportation, and providing food. This study did not control for income level or marital status of the respondents. Therefore, caution needs to be taken in interpreting the differences in friendship patterns as due to differences in geographical location.

A number of other studies also suggest that, for the elderly, friendship relations and neighborhood sociability may be stronger in rural areas as opposed to urban areas. Bultena, Powers, Falkman, and Frederick (1971) found the rural elderly in Iowa to be more satisfied with the neighborliness of their communities than their urban counterparts. Hampe and Blevins (1972) reported that rural elderly living in Wyoming were more likely to say they could rely on friends and neighbors for help in a crisis than urban elderly. Donnenworth, Guy, and Norvell (1978) suggest a residential difference in life satisfaction favoring the rural elderly in Tennessee was attributed to higher level of social contacts with friends and relatives among rural versus urban dwellers.

Past studies have lacked control over several important variables that have been found to influence the older adults' friend networks. For example, gender seems to have an important influence on friendships in late life. Research indicates that friendships are more extensive and meaningful for older women in comparison with older men (Arth, 1980; Hess, 1979; Roberto & Scott, 1986; Strain & Chappell, 1982). In addition, a significant difference in friend interaction has been found according to the marital status of the aged individual (Matthews, 1986; Petrowsky, 1976). The aged widow has been found to have a greater frequency of interaction with friends than aged married individuals. Therefore, the present study is designed to gain a better understanding of rural-urban differences in late life by controlling for several possible intervening variables. Specifically, the central questions addressed in the present study are: What are the differences, if any, in the interaction patterns of older friends in rural and urban areas? How are these patterns affected by differences in gender, marital status, and income?

Method

Sample

A comparison of two data sets collected in western Texas was used for this study. The urban sample, consisting of 132 white adults 65 to 90 years of age, was taken from a larger study. It was randomly selected through a proportionate area sampling technique. Collection of the data took place during the spring and summer of 1980. The rural sample, consisting of 126 white adults age 65 to 89, was collected in the spring and summer of 1981. The respondents were randomly selected using a compact-clustering technique. This sample was drawn from a larger study that dealt with the characteristics and needs of the older rural adult.

Procedure

All respondents were interviewed in their own homes by a trained interviewer. The interview schedule used in both samples contained a set of identical questions regarding present friend relations. Questions regarding helping behaviors and social activities with friends in addition to demographic characteristics of the samples used in this study.

Measures

Types of Helping Behavior. All respondents were asked if they had helped a friend in the past year with transportation, household repairs, housekeeping, shopping, yardwork, illness, car care, important decisions, legal assistance, and financial aid. The respondents were also asked if they had received such help from a friend. Responses were coded as either "yes" or "no."

Social Activities. All respondents were asked if they had participated with a friend in any of the following social activities during the past year: Commercial recreation (movies, sports, plays, etc.), home recreation (picnics, watching TV, card playing, etc.), outdoor recreation (camping, fishing, gardening, etc.), brief drop-in visits for conversation, vacation visits, working at same occupation or in same place, happy occasions such as birthdays or holidays, attending the same church or religious group together, and shopping together. Responses were coded either "yes" or "no."

Income.   For both samples, the respondents were shown a card with monthly income categories in increments of $100 (ranging from 0–$99 to $3,000 and over). Monthly income was measured by asking the respondent to indicate the letter of the category that most nearly described his or her monthly income. Because respondents in the urban sample ranged from lower-middle to upper-middle incomes, only respondents with comparable incomes were drawn from the rural sample. In other words, persons below or hovering above the poverty threshold were excluded from the study. (Based on the 1979 Poverty Index Level for a nonfarm two-person family head, aged 65 or older, $4,200, per year; Shultz, 1980.)

Results

Descriptive Statistics

The urban sample was composed of 89 females and 43 males, ranging in age from 65 to 90 (*M* age = 72.6). The rural sample consisted of 52 females and 74 males, aged 65 to 89 with a mean age of 72.9 years. Of the rural sample, 64.3% were married, 34.1% were widowed, 1.6% were never married. For the urban sample, 72.0% were married, 22.0% widowed, 1.5% never married, and 4.5% divorced or separated.

The rural sample had a mean educational level of 10.3 years. The urban sample had completed an average of 11.6 years of school. The mean monthly income for the rural respondents was between $600 and $699. The urban respondents had a mean monthly income of between $700 and $799.

When asked how much their health troubles stood in the way of doing things they wanted to do, 44.4% of the rural sample said not at all, 33.9% said a little, and 21.8% said a great deal. In response to the same questions, 49.2% of the urban sample reported that health problems did not stand in their way of doing things, 31.1% said a little, and 19.7% said health problems stood in their way a great deal.

In regard to friendships, approximately 84.8% of the urban sample had at least one close friend, while 92.9% of the rural participants named at least one close friend. Only 7.1% of the rural sample and 15.2% of the urban sample reported not having a close friend at the present time. The rural respondents had known their close friend for approximately 32.3 years, while the urban respondents reported knowing their close friend for 27.3 years. When asked how the respondents met their close friend, the three most frequent responses for the rural samples were as neighbors (25.6%), at work (12.8%), and at church (12.8%). The majority of the urban sample met their close friend at work (21.6%), as neighbors (21.6%), and through relatives (18.9%). When respondents were asked how frequently they had contact with their close friend, 26.1% of the urban sample said several times a week, 55.0% said weekly, and 18.9% said monthly. For the older rural adults, 19.0% said they had daily contact with their close friend, 27.6% said several times a week, 21.6% said weekly, and 28.1% said monthly. The most frequent means of contact for the rural sample was through visits and telephone (51.3%), visits (26.5%), and a combination of visits, telephone, and letters (11.1%), while for the urban sample the most frequent means of contact with friends were by telephone (42.3%) and visits (48.6%).

Overall, the two samples were very comparable. Virtually no differences existed in terms of age or health status. The urban elderly were more likely to be married and to report a higher monthly income than their rural counterparts. With regard to friendships, a greater percentage of the rural sample reported having at least one close friend. Frequency of contact between friends was similar, with visits (i.e., face-to-face and/or phone) occurring at least weekly for both groups of elderly.

Social Activities

Because variables such as gender and marital status are factors that seem to influence friend relationships in late life, Table 12.1 indicates the percentage of social participation with friends when these two variables were controlled. Widowed males have been excluded from this comparison due to small number of both urban (n = 5) and rural (n = 14) widowed older men. Urban married males participated in a greater percentage of commercial recreation, drop-in-visits, and happy occasions than rural married men. In contrast, rural married men seemed to be more involved with friends in terms of home recreation and vacation visits. The urban married female participated more in commercial activities, vacation visits, and spending happy occasions with friends than the rural married woman. Areas where the rural married woman participated more with friends include home recreation, outdoor recreation, and work. When looking at the widows, urban widows participated in more commercial activities, drop-in-visits, and happy occasions with friends, whereas the rural widow was more involved with home recreation, outdoor recreation, and working together with friends.

Help Received from Friends

The percentage of respondents receiving help from a friend is given in Table 12.2. When gender and marital status were both controlled a greater percentage of rural married males received help from friends than urban married men in the areas of transportation, shopping, assistance when ill, making important decisions, and financial aid. Rural married females received a substantially higher percentage of help from friends as compared with urban married females in the areas of shopping and assistance when ill. A greater percentage of rural widows received help from friends in virtually all areas with the exception of transportation and household repairs where the urban widow received more help. There were few differences in the areas of comfort and car care between rural widows and urban widowed females.

Table 12.1
Percentage of Respondents Participating in Social Activities with Friends (Controlling for Gender and Marital Status)[a]

Activity	Married males		Married females		Widowed females	
	Urban ($n = 37$)	Rural ($n = 52$)	Urban ($n = 53$)	Rural ($n = 25$)	Urban ($n = 24$)	Rural ($n = 25$)
Commercial recreation	58.3	21.2	58.2	8.0	70.8	32.0
Home recreation	54.1	65.4	50.9	64.0	60.9	68.0
Outdoor recreation	21.6	30.8	11.5	24.0	17.4	8.0
Drop-in-visit	91.9	78.8	85.7	80.0	100.0	76.0
Vacation visit	16.7	26.9	20.0	12.0	21.7	28.0
Work together	8.3	13.5	0.0	12.0	4.3	16.0
Happy occasions	52.8	28.8	57.4	24.0	73.9	52.0
Attend church together	30.6	38.5	45.5	48.0	50.0	48.0
Shopping together	8.3	11.5	37.7	36.0	52.2	52.0

[a] Figures incorporate multiple responses.

Help Given to Friends

The percentage of respondents giving help to friends is shown in Table 12.3. Married urban males gave more help to their friends in the areas of household repairs, and yardwork. In the area of car care, assistance when ill, important decisions, and financial aid, rural married males reported providing a greater percentage of help to their friends. The only areas where the married females seemed to differ greatly were in the areas of shopping and illness, where rural married women gave more help to friends, whereas the urban married provided more transportation for friends. The urban widow provided her friend with more comfort, whereas the rural widow was more active in providing her friend help with transportation, household repairs, car care, housekeeping, shopping, yardwork, illness, and important decisions.

Income

It was felt that income level of the respondent would have an influence on the amount of social contact between friends in late life. In order to

Table 12.2
Percentage of Respondents Receiving Help from a Friend
(Controlling for Gender and Marital Status)[a]

Helping behavior	Married males		Married females		Widowed females	
	Urban ($n = 37$)	Rural ($n = 52$)	Urban ($n = 53$)	Rural ($n = 25$)	Urban ($n = 24$)	Rural ($n = 25$)
Transportation	13.5	23.1	35.2	36.0	58.3	44.0
Household repairs	13.9	3.8	7.4	8.0	26.1	20.0
Housekeeping	2.8	0.0	0.0	12.0	8.7	16.0
Shopping	0.0	5.8	3.8	28.0	17.4	28.0
Yardwork	5.7	9.6	9.4	4.0	13.0	20.0
Car care	11.4	11.5	0.0	0.0	13.0	12.0
Assist when ill	17.1	36.5	17.0	60.0	43.5	60.0
Important decisions	5.7	17.3	9.4	8.0	26.1	36.0
Legal aid	0.0	1.9	0.0	4.0	0.0	8.0
Financial aid	0.0	5.8	0.0	0.0	0.0	0.0
Comfort	52.8	55.8	54.7	60.0	70.8	68.0

[a] Figures incorporate multiple responses.

Table 12.3
Percentage of Respondents Giving Help to a Friend
(Controlling for Gender and Marital Status)[a]

Helping behavior	Married males		Married females		Widowed females	
	Urban (n = 37)	Rural (n = 52)	Urban (n = 53)	Rural (n = 25)	Urban (n = 24)	Rural (n = 25)
Transportation	31.4	26.9	40.7	28.0	41.7	56.0
Household repairs	30.6	11.5	5.8	4.0	4.2	12.0
Housekeeping	2.8	0.0	5.7	0.0	4.2	20.0
Shopping	2.8	7.7	13.0	28.0	12.5	36.0
Yardwork	11.1	3.8	5.7	4.0	4.2	16.0
Car care	2.8	13.5	1.9	0.0	0.0	8.0
Assist when ill	22.2	40.4	43.4	56.0	45.8	76.0
Important decisions	5.6	19.2	7.5	4.0	12.5	36.0
Legal aid	0.0	1.9	0.0	4.0	0.0	0.0
Financial aid	0.0	5.8	1.9	4.0	8.3	4.0
Comfort	52.8	51.9	75.0	68.0	83.3	68.0

[a] Figures incorporate multiple responses.

test this the respondents were divided into two groups, low-middle-class ($5,000–$9,999) and middle-to-upper-class ($10,000+) (Grad & Foster, 1979). Comparisons between the urban and rural respondents falling into each category were then made. Regardless of income category, the urban respondents were more likely to engage in commercial activities and happy occasions with friends than the rural respondents. On the other hand, the rural older adults seemed more involved with home recreation, outdoor recreation, and work situations with friends. Income level did seem to make a difference for the low-middle-class adults in terms of brief drop-in-visits with friends. A greater percentage of urban lower-middle-class adults made drop-in-visits to friends and shopped together than their rural counterparts (Table 12.4).

With regard to helping behavior, the rural respondents in both income groups receive and give more help in the areas of shopping, assistance when ill, and making important decisions (with the exception of the lower-middle-class where there was no difference between groups in helping make important decisions and giving assistance with illness). See Tables 12.5 and 12.6.

Table 12.4
Percentage of Respondents Participating in Joint
Social Activities with Friend[a]

Activity	Yearly income $5,000–$9,999		Yearly income $10,000+	
	Urban (n = 51)	Rural (n = 44)	Urban (n = 64)	Rural (n = 43)
Commercial recreation	52.0	13.6	67.2	32.6
Home recreation	49.0	56.8	54.7	67.4
Outdoor recreation	10.0	18.2	21.0	34.9
Drop-in-visits	92.2	65.9	89.2	83.7
Vacation visits	13.7	22.7	23.8	32.6
Work together	4.0	13.6	4.8	16.3
Happy occasions	56.0	29.5	60.3	46.5
Attend church together	40.0	36.4	42.2	41.9
Shopping together	40.0	29.5	30.6	27.9

[a] Figures incorporate multiple responses.

Discussion

The purpose of this study was to compare rural and urban friendships in late life. How these friendships differ in terms of income, gender, and marital status were examined. These comparisons revealed several differences in the type of social activities and helping behaviors exchanged between the elderly and their friends according to rural-urban residence.

While both groups were involved in joint social activities with friends, there seems to be a distinction in the type of activity according to geographical location. Urban respondents were involved to a much greater extent in commercial recreation, making brief drop-in-visits, and spending happy occasions such as birthdays and holidays with friends than rural residents. On the other hand, the rural respondents seemed more involved in home recreation, work, and with the exception of the rural widow, outdoor recreation with friends. Several plausible explanations for these distinctions can be made. First, the fact that entertainment such as movie theaters, sporting events, restaurants, and so forth, are limited in rural areas may account for such low participation with friends. This would also contribute to the fact that much of the social activities of the rural elderly go on in their own homes. In addition, rural friends live at greater distances from each other. Dropping in on a friend for a brief visit may involve a lot more time for the rural resident than the urban resident, who may have a friend in the same neighborhood. Happy occasions were another area that consistently showed greater participation by the urban versus rural elderly. This finding may also be related to the distance friends live from each other. The fact that the rural elderly are more involved in work situations with friends may be due to joint farming or ranching activities. Farm and ranch land comprise much of the rural area. Because farming is often a lifelong occupation, many of the individuals, although over 65, may still be involved with the farm and ranch land.

Differences in helping behavior are evident in the greater percentage of rural adults who received as well as gave help in making important decisions. These distinctions hold true regardless of gender, marital status, or income level. From this it would seem that the geographical location of the respondents has an impact on the type of help between friends. Because shopping facilities are not as accessible in rural areas,

Table 12.5
Percentage of Respondents Receiving Help from Friends[a]

Helping behavior	Yearly income $5,000-$9,999		Yearly income $10,000+	
	Urban (n = 49)	Rural (n = 44)	Urban (n = 63)	Rural (n = 43)
Transportation	36.0	29.5	28.6	41.9
Household repairs	20.4	11.4	11.3	9.3
Housekeeping	4.2	4.5	1.6	14.0
Shopping	4.2	22.7	4.9	27.9
Yardwork	4.2	13.6	13.1	14.0
Car care	10.4	11.4	3.3	7.0
Assist when ill	31.3	38.6	13.1	51.2
Important decisions	18.8	18.2	3.3	30.2
Legal aid	0.0	6.8	0.0	4.7
Financial aid	0.0	4.5	0.0	7.0
Comfort	60.0	65.9	50.0	55.8

[a] Figures incorporate multiple responses.

friends may be more willing to "pick up something" for each other when they are going into town to shop or run an errand. This type of help may not be as necessary in an urban area where stores are conveniently located throughout the city. The rural elderly may also be more dependent on their friends for help during an illness due to the lack of doctors and hospitals in the rural areas. Friends may not only be providing psychological support during an illness but in the case of the farm family help may be needed in keeping up with the daily farm chores. In addition, the similar problems and concerns of farm life may be one reason for the rural residents' tendency to share in decision-making.

In conclusion, this study revealed differences in the friendship patterns of middle-class urban and rural elderly. Geographical location of the respondents played an important role in the type of activities and helping behaviors they engaged in with friends. The rural respondents, regardless of gender, marital status, or income were more involved in home recreation and work situations with friends, whereas a greater percentage of the urban respondents were involved with commercial recreation, drop-in-visits, and spending happy occasions with friends. In

Table 12.6
Percentage of Respondents Giving Help to a Friend[a]

Helping behavior	Yearly income $5,000–$9,999		Yearly income $10,000+	
	Urban (n = 49)	Rural (n = 44)	Urban (n = 63)	Rural (n = 43)
Transportation	40.8	38.6	38.7	39.5
Household repairs	12.5	11.4	17.7	9.3
Housekeeping	2.1	4.5	6.3	4.7
Shopping	4.2	25.0	14.1	27.9
Yardwork	6.1	9.1	8.1	9.3
Car care	0.0	11.4	3.2	11.6
Assist when ill	43.8	45.5	36.5	51.2
Important decisions	4.2	13.6	9.5	37.2
Legal aid	0.0	4.5	0.0	2.3
Financial aid	2.0	4.5	3.2	11.6
Comfort	70.6	59.1	67.2	60.5

[a] Figures incorporate multiple responses.

terms of helping behaviors, the rural respondents gave and received a greater percentage of help in the areas of shopping, illness, and making important decisions. No other differences in helping behaviors were found between the two groups. This study dealt with descriptive information regarding the differences in urban-rural friendships in late life. Future research is needed to examine the quality of the friend relation in urban and rural locations.

Chapter 13

The Grandparenting Role

Mary S. Link
Department of Home Economics and Consumer Sciences
Miami University
Oxford, Ohio 45056

With the proportion of the population that is elderly, and with longer life spans allowing for more people to participate in grandparent and grandchild roles for longer periods of time, the role of grandparent is an important research topic, as well as a potential target of intervention strategies.

If declining mortality rates continue, particularly at age 65 years and above, the number of people in the older age group may increase even more than current projections. With such increases, there is concern for lifestyles of the elderly, including problems faced as well as the contributions they make.

Of the many components within a person's environment, the family is the single most significant factor for human development. People spend a significant proportion of their lives as part of a nuclear family, and much of their lives as part of an extended family (Goldhaber, 1986).

Society must contend with a number of myths regarding old age. That older people are moving in mass to retirement communities is largely a myth. Over 90% of the elderly are living independently in the community. Most older people live in their own household, near at least one of their children (Schiamberg, 1985). While there are significant numbers of older persons who have poor health, suffer from malnutrition, and who are socially isolated and poor, there are many old people who lead active and vigorous lives and who enjoy good health. Old age is not necessarily debilitating. The sum of a person's experiences and social resources that are available do much to determine how that person ages and how he or she feels about the aging process. Many elderly individuals have vitality and are able to contribute to others' lives, because they have years of experiences to bring to the activities in which they participate. Grandparents are recognized for important contributions to the family and to society (Zigler & Finn-Stevenson, 1987).

The elderly, like individuals in other stages of the life cycle, are able to organize activities in a meaningful way when they perceive themselves as competent, self-regulating human beings and receive that same treatment from others. Because personality factors are unique and differ among individuals, there are a variety of ways to adapt to old age. One such way is how people play the grandparent role.

Importance of Family

In the United States, elderly people typically maintain close contact with younger family members; most old people are not isolated. Brubaker (1983) notes that older people lead lives that are enriched by the presence of people who care about them and to whom they feel close. Schiamberg (1985), using survey data reported by Shanas and Sussman, concludes that the family is the major resource of its older members for emotional and social support, crisis intervention, and bureaucratic linkages. Papalia and Olds (1986) report research indicating that most people feel that their relationships with friends and family make a vital difference in their lives. This is true in old age, as well as in earlier stages of the life cycle.

Not only are they not isolated, most old people have important ties to family. These may be with spouse, siblings, grandchildren, great-grandchildren and possibly their own very old parents. Brubaker (1983) has noted that the family is still the primary source of emotional support for the old person. Most cross-generational relationships are with family members. In older age these relationships tend to be with children, grandchildren, and great-grandchildren.

These relationships can be beneficial for both the older and younger generations. For example, older persons (i.e., grandparents) provide a sense of continuity for their grandchildren and a link with the child or the parent's past, while in general the more older adults are able to find satisfaction within a family or social group, the more enjoyable and rewarding they are likely to find the later years. This satisfaction, according to Dworetzky (1984), is also present when a person has obtained a sense of continuity with the past.

Importance of the Grandparenting Role

According to Schiamberg (1985) about 70% of the older people in the United States are grandparents, while 40% are great-grandparents. Many persons become grandparents 15 to 20 years younger than the 65-year category of old age. Schiamberg (1985) also reports that in the United States the role of grandparents is defined in many ways. The role varies depending on the needs, interest and other individual characteristics of the parties involved. Because there is no specific role assigned to grandparents, there is no such thing as a "typical" grandparent.

Individual differences in grandparent-grandchild relationships vary as a function of sex, health, distance from each other, other roles and activities, personality, age of grandparent(s), age of grandchild(ren), and numerous other factors. Grandparents' levels of education, social class, need for affiliation, and number of extrafamilial relationships are factors thought to determine particular grandparenting styles. Hughes and Noppe (1985) relate that involvement in community activities and family tradition are other considerations.

Researchers are just beginning to ask how grandparents influence their grandchildren. Bengtson (1985) has noted that research on grandparenthood seems to have two major themes. These include the diversity of the grandparent role and the symbolism of grandparenthood reflected in presence, as well as behavior. Grandparents, according to Kalish (1982), tend to view themselves as having centrality, being a valued elder, and achieving immortality through the family. Grandparents also tend to view themselves as "reinvolved" with their own past and as a "spoiler." Schiamberg (1985) cites several reasons why grandparenting is important in the lives of older people. These include:

1. Grandparents may receive special meaning from the grandparent-grandchild relationship as other areas of role performance become closed to them.
2. Grandparents can have meaningful relationships with their grandchildren with minimal obligation and responsibility.
3. The grandparent role provides older adults with a sense of human continuity and biological renewal.

Schiamberg (1985) also notes that while the grandparent role is meaningful and satisfying for some older people, it may not be a significant role for others.

Grandparents over the age of 65 are more apt to be formal and distant. This may reflect cohort differences, indicating that persons who were born earlier may see their roles differently than persons born more recently. Troll (1983) has found that younger grandparents tend to have more diverse styles of grandparenting. People usually become grandparents for the first time in middle age; an average age of 52 for men and 50 for women. The role of grandparent, especially for the "young-old," may often be secondary to other roles in life.

Grandparent-Grandchild Relationships

A study by Robertson (1976) noted that remote grandparents, seemingly indifferent to their grandchildren, were rather unhappy people. They were not involved in many friendships with other people or community activities. In grandparenting, as in parenting, Troll (1983) has noted that sex differences exist. Grandmothers tend to have warmer and closer relationships and serve more often as surrogate parents than grandfathers. Their close involvement in the mother role in relationships with their own children is a determining factor.

Children who see and interact with their grandparents tend to derive a sense of family history and also a sense of security in the knowledge that their grandparents understand and love them. The special relationship often found between an old person and a child is recognized by grandchildren who, as teens and young adults, feel a sense of responsibility toward their grandparents. These children have related that they would have missed something if they had not had a relationship with grandparents when they were growing up (Schiamberg, 1985).

Grandparents often have contact with their grandchildren that involve a minimum of obligations and responsibility. According to Kalish (1982), grandparents often are able to be freer and less guarded in these relationships than parents and their children. Troll (1983) found that grandparents tend to stay on the "fringes" of the lives of their children and grandchildren, although 75% of the grandparents see their grandchildren at least once a week. She maintains that grandparents often perform the role of family "watchdogs." During times of noncrisis, grandparents are not as closely involved. When needed, such as during separation and divorce procedures, financial troubles, or in times of illness, grandparents tend to become more actively involved with their grandchildren.

In a discussion of grandparent-grandchild relationships it is important to note that the relationships change over time. Kalish (1982) has noted that when the grandparent is 51 and the grandchild is seven the relationship is different than when the grandparent is 61 and the grandchild is 17. The relationship between a 43-year-old grandparent and a three-year-old grandchild is different than between a 53-year-old grandparent and a 13-year-old grandchild.

It is noted by Schiamberg (1985) and others that relationships between older and younger family members can take many forms. The people who live close together may visit often. They may also relate during shopping, recreation, and religious activities. If younger and older family members do not live in close proximity, they may telephone one another, engage in letter writing, and celebrate family events such as birthday parties, reunions, and weddings. In their diversity and symbolism contemporary grandparents represent important connections between the past and the future. Today's children and youth have more grandparents and great-grandparents available to them than any cohort in the past. Bengtson and Robertson (1985) relate that hopefully children and youth will appreciate this advantage and utilize the resources of grandparents in developing their own diversity and symbolism throughout life. It is thought that grandparents eventually establish a comfortable relationship with grandchildren. Problems within these relationships may arise when divorce takes place within a family. The effects of divorce on grandparent-grandchild relationships, especially when the grandparents are the parents of the noncustodial parent, are becoming an important legal and research topic.

Children's Attitudes

Attitudes are learned very early in life. Those attitudes continually influence behavior throughout a person's lifetime. A search of the literature has indicated that negative attitudes toward old people are common throughout the general population. If attitudes children hold of old people are negative, they could have consequences for behavior toward older persons, especially grandparents, and affect the development of an understanding of their own aging.

It is important for children to develop realistic attitudes toward older persons if they are to develop positive interpersonal relations with people of all ages. Children need to learn to recognize the aging process and be given opportunities to understand people who are older. One place this could be fostered is in the schools, but the topics of aging and "growing older" are often neglected in the early childhood curriculum.

A study by Link and Trusty (1980) revealed that children of five, six, and seven held negative attitudes toward older persons. Three groups of children attending the same elementary school were asked to describe what could be done with a baby and what could be done with an older person. A panel of educators involved in a study of aging ranked each response as positive, neutral, or negative. Responses of the students indicated that the children held more negative attitudes toward older persons than infants.

Hickey, Hickey and Kalish (1968) asked 200 third graders to write about "an old person." The most common response was that older persons are "kind." The second most common response was that older persons are "mean." Seefeldt, Jantz, Galper and Serock (1977) found that children between the ages of 3 and 11 described older persons as "sick," "tired," and "unattractive." The children reacted negatively to their perceptions of the physical limitations and physical appearance of older persons. Yet, it is interesting to note that the same children described older people as "wonderful," "kind" or "rich."

A study by Weinberger (1979) of children from ages five through eight indicated that older persons were seen as having fewer friends, being less healthy and less attractive, and being asked for help less often than parents or other adults. These same children indicated that the most desirable people to seek help from, if they were hurt, and as people to whom they would want to give help, would be elderly people.

Schiamberg (1985) reported that children's responses to grandparents vary in terms of the child's age. Younger children seem to react positively to gifts, small favors, and open expressions of affection. Older children seem to respond more favorably to shared activities or having fun with grandparents. A study by Dellmann-Jenkins, Lambert, Fruit, and Dinero (1986) reported that children can develop realistic and positive attitudes about the aging process and the elderly. Children were exposed to both classroom interactions with older people assuming a variety of roles and media presenting accurate information concerning aging. As a result of these experiences positive changes were observed in the perceptions of three and four-year-old children in the way elderly persons look and behave.

Intervention Programs

Although the proportion of elderly persons has increased significantly, and both aging and family relationships are important issues, many programs planned for young children have not considered aging as a curriculum concern. The topic of aging and growing older has been thought to be somewhat unrelated to classroom curriculum topics. However, many educators have become aware of the need to incorporate the concept of aging into the curriculum. A recommendation made as a result of the White House Conference on Aging was that knowledge concerning the aging process should be included as part of the educational curriculum from preschool through higher education (Link, 1978).

While schools cannot assume sole responsibility for the tasks of teaching children about aging, they can provide ideas and the basis for developing learning activities to aid in understanding. Children and their teachers can learn to think, talk, read, and write about the process and the effect of aging. The study of aging and the aging process can easily begin in the preschool years before negative stereotypes solidify. Children and their teachers need to communicate about aging. One way to do this is by focusing on grandparents. Not only will this help children develop attitudes, knowledge, and appreciation, but it has the potential for improving the quality of life of the grandparents.

Zigler and Finn-Stevenson (1987) have noted that the special relationship between a grandparent and a grandchild and the positive reciprocal influences that are inherent in the relationship between children and older persons have been utilized by government and private agencies. Those influences include making provisions for foster grandparent programs. These programs bring together older people who are lonely or needing part-time work and children and teens who need assistance. Programs that capitalize on older persons as valuable resources have been important, not only in terms of the benefits for the children and teens who are helped, but also in terms of the realized benefits by the elderly. Many of these elderly might otherwise be lonely and without a sense of purpose or direction in life.

According to Jantz, Seerfeldt, Galper, and Serock (1977), it is difficult for preschoolers and elementary-school-aged students to negatively stereotype the elderly when they have frequent contact with active and healthy older adults. The phenomena of aging can then be faced more realistically through understanding. The relationship between grandparents and grandchildren varies with the child's perception of the grandparent(s), the child's perception of elderly people in general, and how grandparents behave toward the child. Age of the grandparents as well as grandchildren's ages are other considerations. Intervention programs, including incorporation of aging and grandparent materials and lessons into school curricula can have the potential for improving the quality of life of older Americans.

Conclusions

Relationships between grandchildren and grandparents are an important aspect of the lifestyles of the elderly. The role of grandparent is diverse and varies according to the many characteristics of the people involved, including; age, gender, salience of other roles, and geographic distances. Other factors affecting this role include divorce of the grandchild's parents and the child's attitudes toward, and perceptions of, the elderly. Intervention programs, especially school programs, have the potential to have a positive impact on the attitudes and perceptions of children. This can in turn have a positive impact on the grandparent-grandchild role, which might enhance the lifestyles of older people.

Chapter 14

Teenagers' Reported Interaction with Grandparents
Exploring the Extent of Alienation

Mary Dellman-Jenkins
Department of Individual and Family Studies and Gerontology
Kent State University
Kent, Ohio 44241

Diane Papalia
Department of Psychology and Pediatrics
University of Pennsylvania
Philadelphia, Pennsylvania 19104

Martha Lopez
Struthers High School
Struthers, Ohio 44471

There is some evidence that as grandchildren enter adolescence the grandparent-grandchild relationship weakens (Hoffman, 1979-1980; Kahana & Kahana, 1970). Therefore, the speculation has been made that this stage is a low point in the grandparenting life cycle (Cherlin & Furstenberg, 1985). Perhaps so, but there is an emerging body of grandparenting research that challenges this conjecture and suggests that grandparents view interaction with teenage grandchildren as an important source of satisfaction.

It has been asserted, for example, that during the adolescent grandchild stage, many grandparents derive substantial satisfaction from being bearers of family history (Baranowski, 1982; Spanier & Lerner, 1980). It has also been argued that grandparents who have regular contact with teenage grandchildren derive satisfaction from knowing that their presence helps to dispell stereotyped notions about the aging process and the elderly (Baranowski, 1982; Spanier & Lerner, 1980). Further, research indicates that for some grandparents being around to watch their teenage grandchildren grow up is a source of enjoyment (Cherlin & Furstenberg, 1985).

149

   The above research suggests that many grandparents do maintain close and meaningful relationships with adolescent-aged grandchildren. However, before this conclusion can be drawn, research is needed on the perspective of the other member in this relationship, the teenage grandchild. Obviously, the quality of the grandparent-grandchild relationship is dependent on both members' levels of satisfaction. While there are a number of studies on the value of grandparents for children, such research has generally focused on the young child rather than the adolescent (Baranowski, 1982). The purpose of this chapter, therefore, is to provide some insight on the value of interaction with grandparents *from* the perspective of the teenage grandchild.

Prior Research

Children's Relations with Grandparents

   There is some evidence that the age of the child may be influential in determining the nature of his or her relations with grandparents. Kahana and Kahana (1970), for example, found age-related differences in children's concepts of and attitudes toward grandparents. Young children (aged four to five years) were found to view grandparents almost exclusively in egocentric and concrete terms, focusing on what the grandparent gives the child in the areas of love, food, and presents and, therefore, preferred interacting with indulgent grandparents. There was lack of mutuality in the form of shared activities between young grandchildren and their grandparents. In contrast, eight- and nine-year-olds focused on reciprocity in the relationship. They emphasized what types of fun or pleasurable activities the grandparent shares with the grandchild. This age group valued grandparents more as playmates than as gift-givers. The oldest group (11–12-year-olds) placed little emphasis on the mutual or reciprocal aspects of the grandchild-grandparent relationship. Rather, they intentionally distanced themselves from grandparents or removed themselves completely from interaction with grandparents. Kahana and Kahana (1970) concluded that the preteens' negative or ambivalent attitudes toward contact with grandparents complemented earlier research data (Kahana & Coe, 1969). The older children's attitudes seemed to be mirrored by grandparents' increasingly distant attitudes toward their grandchildren as they grew older.

Teenagers' Relations with Grandparents

The role grandparents play in the lives of adolescents is a neglected area of research. After reviewing the literature on intergenerational relations, both Barranti (1985) and Baranowski (1982) concluded that the topic of grandparent-adolescent relations has received little empirical or theoretical attention. This lack of focus appears to be partially explained by the common assumption that these generations play peripheral roles in each other's lives (Baranowski, 1982). Furthermore, this assumption appears to be supported by the small amount of existing information on the nature of adolescents' interaction with grandparents. Troll (1980) concluded that at least half of the related research indicates that teenagers are alienated from their grandparents.

However, recent studies challenge this notion of alienation and suggest that the role grandparents play in teenagers' lives is one of more importance than originally thought (Troll, 1983). Konopka (1976), for example, interviewed females aged 12-18 years (N = 920), and found that comments about grandparents frequently surfaced during the interviews. She concluded that, next to parents, the family member adolescent girls were most likely to confide in was a grandparent, usually a grandmother.

Further, research has shown that teenagers have positive feelings about their relationships with institutionalized grandparents. Streltzer (1979) found that the most frequent request of adolescents with grandparents residing in a home for the aged was, "What can I do for my grandparent?" Although the Streltzer (1979) data cannot be generalized to the nature of teenagers' relationships with independent living grandparents, it is important to recognize that for this group of adolescents there was a desire to influence their grandparents' lives in positive ways.

In addition, research on young adults' teenage memories of interaction with grandparents does not appear to support the assumption that adolescents are alienated from grandparents. Hartshorne and Manaster (1982), for example, found that the majority of their college student sample (M = 21 years of age) felt their relationships with grandparents was important to them during their high school years. Similarily, Robertson (1976) indicated that the majority (70%) of her young adult sample (aged 18 to 26 years) reported that during their teenage years they viewed interaction with grandparents as satisfying. In terms of young adults' current relationships with grandparents, both Hartshorne and

Manaster (1982) and Robertson (1976) found that the majority of their subjects had positive attitudes about spending time with grandparents.

In reviewing the previous research, it is important to note that the stage of adolescence the grandchild is in may be influential in determining the quality of his or her relationships with grandparents. Kahana and Kahana (1970) described 11–12 year-olds (i.e., preadolescents "making" the transition into adolescence) as tending to distance themselves from grandparents. Other research suggests that those who have "made" the transition into adolescence viewed grandparents as playing important roles in their lives (Konopka, 1976; Streltzer, 1979). Similarly, young adults reported positive teenage memories of their interaction with grandparents (Hartshorne & Manaster, 1982; Robertson, 1976). Because adolescents and young adults appear to have positive feelings about their relations with grandparents, it is possible that if there is alienation during the teenage years, it occurs during early adolescence, is temporary, and generally disappears during middle or late adolescence. Hoffman (1979–1980), one of the few researchers who addressed the issue of age-related differences in teenagers' attitudes toward grandparents, appears to support the validity of this conjecture. He proposed that early adolescence is the period of greatest emotional distance from grandparents, with an increase in involvement and interest in late adolescence.

In summary, a meager amount of information exists concerning the nature of the relationship between teenage grandchildren and their grandparents. Yet in the absence of empirical data, numerous generalizations exist. These include that the majority of today's teenagers are alienated from their grandparents, and that these generations play peripheral roles in each others' lives (Baranowski, 1982; Troll, 1980). The present authors question the validity of such generalizations and propose that the nature of adolescents' relationships with grandparents needs to be better understood.

The purpose of this exploratory study, therefore, is primarily to gather descriptive information with respect to the dynamics of adolescents' voluntary interaction with grandparents. A second objective is to explore whether the age of the adolescent is influential in determining the nature of his or her voluntary exchanges with grandparents. In order to determine whether age-related differences exist, the period of adolescence has been divided into three stages: early (13–14 years); middle (15–16 years); and later (17–18 years).

Methodology

Sample

The sample consisted of 9th-, 10th-, and 11th-grade students attending high schools in urban suburbs of a large Mideastern city. Potential participants were sent a letter describing the nature and goals of the research. Eighty-two percent (N = 225) returned a written consent form indicating that they agreed to participate in the study and had contact with at least one living grandparent. The participants ranged in age from 13 to 18 years (M = 15.48 years; SD = 2.54) and were primarily female (67%). Using parental occupation as an index of socioeconomic status, more than half of the adolescents indicated that they came from blue-collar families (i.e., 57% of the males and 56% of the females). Most of the participants (59%) were living with both parents (35% indicated that their parents were divorced or separated; 4% reported a deceased father; and 2% stated they lived with an aunt or uncle). None of the adolescents indicated that a grandparent currently lived in his or her household.

Instrument

Participants independently completed a self-administered questionnaire devised by the authors for this study. This measure consisted of 20 close-ended items developed to obtain both quantitative and qualitative data on the nature of teenagers' voluntary interaction with their grandparents. Respondents were asked to answer the 20 questions in relation to their sharing recreational time with *one* grandparent. Because preference for a particular grandparent was not assessed in this study, adolescents were not asked to state which grandparent they selected in order to complete the questionnaire. The issue of a favorite grandparent was not explored due to earlier research indicating that preadolescents are often reluctant, in a interview setting, to report a preference for any particular grandparent (Kahana & Kahana, 1970).

Frequency of voluntary interaction between teenagers and grandparents was assessed by asking participants to respond to ten questions ranked on a six-point scale (1 = about twice a month; 2 = about once a month; 3 = about every three months or so; 4 = about twice a year; 5 = about once a year, and 6 = never). These questions primarily focused on how often teenagers invited grandparents to share leisure activities. Example questions include:

> How often do you and your grandmother/father talk on the phone together about things like school or your friends? Do you talk on the phone together . . . ?
>
> When the weather is nice, how often do you and your grandmother/father go for walks? Do you go for walks . . . ?
>
> How often do you and your grandmother/father go shopping? Do you go shopping together . . . ?

Quality of voluntary interaction between these generations was assessed by asking participants to respond to ten questions focused on how they felt when sharing recreational time with grandparents. Responses to these questions were ranked on a six-point scale (1 = completely happy; 2 = mostly happy; 3 = fairly happy; 4 = fairly unhappy; 5 = mostly unhappy; and 6 = completely unhappy). Sample questions include:

> How happy are you when you are talking on the phone with your grandmother/father about personal issues, such as school or your friends? Are you . . . ?
>
> How happy are you when you are taking a walk with your grandmother/father? Are you . . . ?
>
> How happy are you when you are shopping with your grandmother/father? Are you . . . ?

This assessment of teenagers' *voluntary* interaction with grandparents was piloted with a group of adolescents ($N = 30$) and an item analysis indicated that the measure was internally valid and reliable (i.e., the Kuder-Richardson 20 estimate of reliability equalled .93 and the standard error equalled 2.93).

Results and Discussion

Nature of Teenagers' Reported Voluntary Interaction with Grandparents

The frequency of voluntary interaction between teenagers and grandparents appeared to be high. Descriptive data indicated that over half of the subjects (at least 56%) reported sharing ten different types of recreational activities with grandparents on a monthly basis. Table 14.1 lists the ten recreational activities and the percentage of subjects in the three age groups ranking items as shared with grandparents on a frequent basis; that is, "about twice a month" or "about once a month." In terms of the quality of voluntary interaction between teenagers and grandparents, subjects appeared to have positive feelings about sharing leisure time with grandparents. Findings indicated that the majority of respondents (at least 71%) reported feeling happy when sharing all ten types of recreational activities with grandparents. See Table 14.2 for the percentage of subjects in the three age groups responding "completely" or "mostly" happy to reaction questions.

Table 14.1
Frequency of Adolescents' Sharing of Recreational Time with Grandparents

Leisure activity shared with grandparent	Monthly participation with grandparents[a]		
	% of 13–14-year-old group (*n* = 71)	% of 15–16-year-old group (*n* = 79)	% of 17–18-year-old group (*n* = 75)
Talking on the phone about personal issues	95	90	86
Talking face to face about personal issues	95	90	86
Going for walks or car rides	90	86	86
Eating out at formal/fast-food restaurants	86	90	95
Sharing domestic or athletic hobbies	81	86	81
Watching television or going to movies	81	86	81
Shopping	81	86	81
Visiting friends or relatives	76	71	66
Playing cards or table games	71	71	66
Attending social, church, school events	71	76	56

[a] Adolescent reported sharing leisure activity: (a) 1 = about twice a month; or (b) 2 = about once a month.

The nature of teenagers' voluntary interaction with grandparents was further explored by examining subjects' responses to individual questions. This analysis revealed that many of the subjects viewed grandparents as playing an important and multidimensional role in their lives. One dimension of this role appeared to focus on grandparents being confidants. As indicated in Table 14.2, the majority of the subjects (at least 80%) in each of the three age groups reported positive feelings about discussing personal issues with a grandparent (i.e., either through phone calls or face-to-face conversations). A second dimension of this role appeared to focus on grandparents being companions. Most of the

Table 14.2
Reaction of Adolescents to Spending Recreational Time with Grandparents

Leisure activity shared with grandparents	Positive reactions to spending time with grandparents[a]		
	% of 13–14-year-old group (n = 71)	% of 15–16-year-old group (n = 79)	% of 17–18-year-old group (n = 75)
Eating out at formal/fast-food restaurants	95	95	95
Shopping	90	86	90
Talking on the phone about personal issues	90	86	81
Sharing domestic or athletic hobbies	86	81	76
Visiting friends or relatives	86	81	76
Talking face to face about personal issues	81	86	90
Playing cards or table games	76	86	81
Attending social, church, school events	71	80	86
Taking walks or car rides	71	76	80

[a] Adolescent reacted to sharing leisure activity with grandparent as feeling: (a) 1 = completely happy; or (b) 2 = mostly happy.

adolescents in each of the three age groups (at least 70%), as shown in Table 14.2, reported positive feelings about sharing the following activities with grandparents on a regular basis: (a) going for walks or car rides, (b) sharing hobbies, (c) watching television or going to the movies, (d) going shopping, and (e) eating out at formal or fast-food restaurants.

Previous research has reported similar findings concerning the close and companionate nature of adolescents' relationships with grandparents. Konopka (1976), for instance, found that teenage girls viewed grandparents, especially grandmothers, as close confidants. Adolescent-grandparent relationships were described by Kahana and Kahana (1970) as transactional in nature and involving mutual interest and involvement. In a similar context, Streltzer (1979) found that adolescents wanted to learn to give and not just receive in their relationships with institutionalized grandparents. The reciprocal nature of these generations' interactions can be partially explained because grandparents are, on the average, healthier and better educated today than in the past, and are more able to maintain mutual relationships with teenage grandchildren (Kahana & Kahana, 1970).

*Influence of Age on Teenagers' Reported Voluntary
Interaction with Grandparents*

One-way analysis of variance tests were performed to determine the relationships between the independent variable, age, and dependent variables, frequency and quality of voluntary interaction with grandparents. These comparisons were based on subjects' mean frequency and mean quality-of-interaction scores and membership in one of the three age groups: early adolescence (13–14 years), middle adolescence (15–16 years), and later adolescence (17–18 years). The ANOVA analyses revealed that subjects' age was not significantly related to: (1) how often they voluntarily spent recreational time with grandparents, or (2) how they felt about sharing recreational time with grandparents. Specifically, subjects in early adolescence were found to report as frequent and positive interaction with grandparents as did subjects in middle and late adolescence.

These data appear to challenge an earlier proposal that early adolescence is the period of great emotional distance from grandparents (Hoffmann, 1979–1980). In this study, subjects in early adolescence appeared to be maintaining close relations with grandparents. For example, the majority of the 13–14 year-olds (95%), as indicated in Table

14.1, reported discussing personal issues with grandparents at least once a month. In addition, most of this age group (at least 80%), as shown in Table 14.2, expressed positive feelings about being able to regularly share and discuss personal concerns with grandparents. The comparison of these data with those of Kahana's and Kahana's (1970) 11 and 12 yearolds suggests that there may be a positive change in the nature of grandparent-grandchild interaction once the transition into adolescence is made. As noted earlier, Kahana and Kahana (1970) found preteens' perspectives about their relations with grandparents reflecting distance or alienation.

However, it is premature to generalize from the present study's cross-sectional data that the onset of the teenage years results in a positive change in the nature of grandchildren's relationships with grandparents. Obviously, longitudinal analyses are needed to determine whether children's developmental changes are associated with changes in their interaction with grandparents.

Conclusion

The information gathered from the present research contributed to a better understanding of an important, but often neglected, intergenerational bond—teenagers' relationships with grandparents. Data challenged the common assumption that the majority of today's teenagers are alienated from their grandparents. Adolescents, aged 13 to 18 years, were found to view grandparents as playing important and multidimensional roles in their lives; those of confidant and companion.

Although the present study focused on teenagers' perceptions of interaction with their grandparents, it is advanced that some insight was provided on the benefits grandparents derive from interacting with adolescent grandchildren. Data appeared to imply that most of the subjects' grandparents were deeply involved in their teenage grandchildren's lives; especially in the area of mutual assistance (i.e., companionship and advice giving). It is also advanced that this study shed additional light on the dynamics of the grandparenting life cycle; that is, data appeared to suggest that the teenage years are not as much of a low point as originally speculated.

A final note of caution in terms of generalizing the findings of this study to middle-class teenagers' interactions with grandparents. Most of the subjects in this study were members of working class families, which may have had an impact on the role grandparents play in their lives.

There is some evidence that the grandparent in poorer families is far more integrated into daily family life, particularly through the role of extended parent, than the middle-class grandparent (Clavan, 1978). Little empirical attention, however, has been directed toward determining whether or not adolescents' level of interaction with grandparents is influenced by social class (Barranti, 1985). Thus, research assessing teenagers' relationships with grandparents from a social class perspective is recommended.

Additional research is also recommended that explores whether geographic location is a factor which influences the nature of teenagers' relationships with grandparents. The present study's sample consisted of adolescents living in urban suburbs of a major metropolitan area. Rural youth may have different types of interaction with grandparents because their values and orientations have not been subjected to the rapid changes associated with urbanization.

Finally, care must be taken in generalizing this study's findings to adolescent males. The majority of the subjects (67%) were female, which may have had an effect on the nature of their interaction with grandparents (especially grandmothers). Troll (1980) pointed out that the female line of grandmother/mother/daughter appears to display stronger patterns of interaction, affection, and mutual aid than the male line of grandfather/father/son. Turner (1975) suggested that because of societal expectations, daughters are encouraged to maintain close contact with families, whereas, sons are encouraged to be autonomous. Thus, it is recommended that future researchers hold the variable of sex constant in order to explore the effect of teenagers' gender on relations with grandparents.

Part III

Importance of Health

Chapter 15

Home Safety and Health
A Quality-of-Life Issue for the Elderly

Jane M. Cardea
School of Nursing
Azusa Pacific University
Azusa, California 91702
Concetta M. Tynan
Handmaker Jewish Geriatric Center
Tuscon, Arizona 85712

Although many older persons are able to cope with the personal changes of advancing years, more than ever before, this population group needs and demands a variety of health care services. The sensory and physical alterations that normally accompany the aging process can increase the risk potential for accidental falls or burns, affect the time and prognosis for recovery from any illness or injury, and influence the desired effect of prescribed or over-the-counter medications. Although accidents and drug reactions as a result of aging cannot be prevented altogether, any reduction in numbers would be a benefit to individuals, family members, and the currently over burdened health care system. Thus, the planning, implementation, and evaluation of elder health care services is a major concern for the health care system, at large, and particularly for the long-term health care industry.

Literature Review

Documentation has revealed that the leading causes of physical decline and need for long-term care services in the elderly include fractures, burns, and drug complications resulting either from nonadherence to a prescribed medical regimen or from the ingestion of incompatible drugs or medications (Galton, 1976). People over 65 years of age represent three-fourths of all fatal falls (Notelewitz & Ware, 1982), and fractures are the 12th leading cause of death in the United States for all age groups (Louis, 1983). Hip fractures are the most common type of fracture in the elderly population, and approximately 15% of those sustaining a hip fracture die shortly after the injury with 30% dying within 1 year of the injury (Louis, 1976). Interestingly, it has been documented that 50% of all falls are caused by environmental factors such as floor obstacles (electrical cords, scatter rugs, low or broken furniture), poor lighting, improperly fitting shoes or clothes, and congested traffic patterns (Galton, 1976). Relative to the issue of drug complications and the elderly, reports indicated that people over 65 represent approximately 12% of the total American population, yet they account for 38% of all purchased medication (*News Update*, 1984). The noninstitutionalized elderly consume an average of 5.6 drugs per day, with two drugs of this total being prescription medication; 1.8 drugs classified as "over-the-counter" medication; and 1.8 drugs categorized as social drugs such as nicotine, caffeine, and alcohol (Galton, 1976). In addition, 90% of the elderly experience some adverse reactions to drugs with approximately 20% of these reactions requiring hospitalization (Krupkal & Verner, 1979).

Unfortunately, few resources are available to accommodate both the rapidly changing long-term health care needs of the elderly and the current fiscal constraints imposed on health care institutions by federal, state, and private agencies. For example, recent changes in the reimbursement methods for provided long-term care services not only have changed care incentives for hospitals and long-term facilities but have also altered reimbursement protocols (Sandrick, 1983), created a marked influx of more acutely ill patients admitted to long-term care facilities following earlier hospital discharge (*Today's Nursing Home*, 1984), and established payment ceilings (Tobin, 1986). In Arizona, where this project was conducted, the cost of long-term health care poses additional problems for several reasons: (a) At least 25% of the state's $200 million budget for long-term care is allocated to the indigent; (b) Arizona is the only state that does not participate in the Medicaid program for fiscal support to long-term care; and (c) population projections for the next 20 years place Arizona among those states with the highest percentage growth in individuals 65 years of age and older (Pritzlaff, 1984).

In response to the varied health care needs of the elderly and the concomitant demand by funding sources to provide cost-effective health care services, a project was designed to potentially reduce the incidence of falls, fractures, and adverse drug reactions involving the noninstitutionalized elderly. A home-safety assessment service was proposed as one way to provide an institution-sponsored health-promotion service that was not duplicated within the community and to address elder health care needs within a familiar environment. Rationale for this decision was based on the knowledge that approximately 75% of older Americans own their own homes and less than 20% of the elder population live in a nursing home or long-term care institution (Werne, 1987).

Items for the home-safety assessment profile were initially provided by an interdisciplinary group of health care providers from the sponsoring long-term care agency. Next, community experts in gerontology were asked to review the proposed profile for completeness and accuracy. Collected items from both sources were reviewed by several members of the interdisciplinary group and categorized into meaningful divisions. Duplicate items were eliminated, and the profile was revised several times to condense information, replace or clarify awkward wording, simplify recording, improve format, and taken into account information obtained from ten pilot interviews. The final profile consisted of a questionnaire and interview format that assessed areas such as demographic information, current health status, functional abilities, lifestyle habits, use of prescribed and over-the-counter medications, and descriptions of the home environment.

Methodology

Three interviews were proposed: an initial assessment conducted in each elder person's residence, a shortened, second home interview conducted approximately three months after the initial assessment; and a follow-up home interview conducted five months after the second. To reach as many members in the community of 500,000 persons as possible, letters were sent to all known agencies that provided services to the elderly. A flyer was produced to distribute at informal social meetings such as church or school gatherings and throughout community areas known to have a high proportion of elderly residents (mobile home parks and low-income housing). In addition, local newspapers were contacted, and several agencies distributed the provided information through their own communication channels such as newsletters, TV programming, and meeting notices. Information about the project purpose, which included a brief statement about the free home health assessment service and a request for participants accompanied all communications. Referrals for project participation came from persons themselves, family members, neighbors, concerned individuals such as apartment managers or social workers, health care professionals, and organizations such as the local Council on Aging and the American Association of Retired Persons.

Study results reported in this paper represent findings from the first two interviews. The initial interview lasted one-half to two hours. During the first home visit, 15 to 20 minutes was usually allocated for social or introductory purposes. Following this "warm-up" period, findings and recommendations from the room-by-room assessment were recorded. In addition, field notes were added to the questionnaire form whenever clarification of proposed recommendations was deemed necessary. The time for most of the second interviews was considerably shorter, lasting approximately 30 minutes. This brevity can be attributed, in part, to participants' familiarity and increased comfort with the interviewer, and the primary interview focus being one of "follow-up" assessment for compliance with offered suggestions rather than a case-finding focus. All but one of the 126 completed interviews provided useable data.

Sample

The convenience sample consisted of 23 males and 102 females who ranged in age from 60 to 97 years with a mean age of 75.5 years. Over three-fourths (83%) of the participants reported they had achieved a minimum of some high school education. The ethnic or racial distribution of the sample closely matched the dispersion patterns characteristic of the large, southwestern city where data were collected. Sixty-five percent (81) of the sample was identified as Anglo-Saxon; 28% (35) Hispanic; 6% (8) black; and 1% (1) American Indian. Seventy-six percent of the participants stated they lived in their own home or apartment, and 64% reported they personally owned their place of residence. Approximately one half (49%) of the sample lived alone. The majority of participants (80%) noted they were satisfied with the health care they received, but 4% of the respondents reported their health care was inadequate. Almost 40% of the participants reported an income of less than $500 per month with only 10% of the sample reporting greater than $1,100 per month. Ninety-four percent of the participants received Medicare reimbursement for health care; however, 86% of the sample reported additional personal expenses were needed for health care.

An attrition rate of less than 15% was realized following completion of the second interview. Four participants were no longer in the geographic area because they had relocated to be nearer to relatives; two participants had moved to nursing homes due to altered physical or mental capabilities; and four participants had died. Several people were unable to complete the second interview because of feeling overwhelmed by recent family emergencies such as death of spouse or child, hospitalization of spouse for a serious illness, divorce, or recovering from own hospitalization. Only six individuals overtly refused to participate in the second interview.

Results

An overall review of the first assessment data indicated that most of the recommendations could be summarized into five major categories. As expected, two category labels directly aligned with areas of project emphasis: activities or environmental changes to avert falls; and issues of physical health, included medication or drug use. Three additional categories, labeled as Agency Referrals, Emergency Precautions or Referral for Emergency Repairs, and Social-Emotional Support, were not anticipated but do reflect the breadth of exchanged information accomplished during the home visits. These five recommendation categories not only seemed to adequately describe all information collected during the first and second home interview, but also provided a baseline for information comparison across the two assessment periods.

During the first home interview, the vast majority of recommendations made to avert falls centered around the installation of grab bars in the bathroom and the removal or anchoring of scatter rugs (see Table 15.1). Slightly more than one-half (54%) of the participants received recommendations regarding grab bars, and approximately one-third (34%) of the respondents were advised about scatter rugs. Suggestions to purchase a bath seat, shower stool, rubber bath mat, toilet elevator, or hand-held shower also were made to approximately one-third (35) of the participants. Approximately one-third of the participants (35) were also advised to remove obstacles from busy traffic patterns, seek alternatives to lengthy extension cords, use night lights, and install rails along ramps, hallways, or stairs.

Results from the second interview indicated that grab bars had been installed by many participants. Participants reported feeling safer and

Table 15.1
Recommendations to Avert Falls[a]

Recommendations	% of total recommendations	% of participants receiving recommendations
Grab bars	32.8	54.4
Rugs	20.2	34.4
Bath seat or shower stool	11.5	20.0
Rubber bath mat	11.5	19.2
Obstacle removal from traffic pattern	5.7	9.6
Other	18.3	7.0

[a] The percent of participants receiving recommendations exceeds 100% because some individuals received recommendations in more than one category.

more secure while bathing, and several people reported that they were now able to take a bath or shower by themselves. In addition, others reported that the grab bars made it much easier to raise up from the toilet. In contrast to the high compliance rate with recommendations regarding grab bar installation, considerable reluctance was discovered in relation to suggestions for the removal or anchoring of scatter rugs. Although the data did not indicate reasons for this reluctance, it can be implied that scatter rugs were in some way intrinsically valued beyond their material worth or threat of physical harm.

A licensed pharmacist reviewed all information pertinent to medication or drug usage following the first home interview. Recommendations were made to less than 15% of the sample for actions such as blood pressure monitoring, cautioning of potential interactive effects of consumed drugs, or referral for dietary consultation (see Table 15.2). More specific recommendations by the pharmacist warning of a serious interaction potential and the need to seek immediate medical supervision for review of the participant's current medication regimen was made to approximately 3% of those interviewed. Thirteen percent of the participants received additional suggestions from the interviewer, a registered nurse, regarding medication or drug use. Topics such as weight reduction, common side effects of medications, limitation or cessation of harmful drugs (alcohol and caffeine), and clarification of actual schedule information such as time or frequency of dispensed medications were discussed. In addition, the nurse advised 36 (28%) of

Table 15.2
Recommendations Regarding Medications and Physical Health[a]

Recommendations	% of total recommendations	% of participants receiving recommendations
Medications	18.6	12.8
Professional consult		
Physician	17.4	12.0
Dental	12.5	3.6
Podiatry	12.5	3.6
Dietary	10.5	7.2
Monitor lab results	7.7	2.9
Other	20.8	7.3

[a] The percent of participants receiving recommendations exceeds 100% because some individuals received recommendations in more than one category.

the participants to seek assistance from health care professionals such as dietitians, dentists, physicians, and podiatrists. Interestingly, participants often reported a lack of instruction from their physicians regarding prescription medications and a sense that many physicians were uninterested in them.

The pharmacist did not need to review any of the assessment profiles following the second interview. Much of the information recorded within the category of physical needs and medication use during this interview focused on participants' needs for health care teaching. Topics such as nutrition, exercise, and diabetic foot care were discussed.

Recommendations labeled as Agency Referrals were separated into two subcategories: advisements, which focused on an individuals eligibility for community services such as food stamps or Title 20 support; and statements, which encouraged the accessing of direct services provided by agencies such as Adult Protective Services, the Urban League, home health and insurance companies, or the local Handi-Car transportation company (automotive transportation for the physically or emotionally challenged individual). More than three-fourths (80%) of the eligibility recommendations were equally distributed across referrals for Title 20 support (40%) or support from MILC (Metropolitan Independent Living Center) (40%). These referral suggestions were offered to approximately one-fifth (22%) of the participants. Referrals for services from home health agencies were the next most frequent recommendations offered to 10% of the participants.

Within the category labeled Emergency Repairs and Precautions, findings from the first assessment period indicated that 17 participants (14%) were encouraged to purchase smoke alarms and 13 participants (10%) were encouraged to contact emergency city numbers for home repairs. In addition, the gas company was contacted immediately when a smell of gas was detected in one home, and the sewer company was notified quickly when a broken sewer line was observed. Eight percent or 11 participants, were given the number for Life Line, and three (2%) of the participants were given a 911 sticker for their telephone. Two participants did not have an emergency exit from their residence (one had nailed all windows shut to discourage burglars), and three participants did not have access to a telephone. Perhaps the most striking finding in this category was acknowledgment on one participant's profile that her life had been saved. The nurse interviewer had responded to observations of current health status and statements of sharp chest pain lasting over the past several days by transporting the elder woman to her private physician. This emergency appointment resulted in the participant's immediate hospitalization into a coronary care unit.

Few participants had purchased smoke alarms by the time of the second interview. Participants who were found to live in substandard housing also were advised that relocation to low-income housing was delayed beyond a year. In addition to these discouraging observations, waiting periods in excess of six months were reported to participants by sewer and gas emergency numbers operators, necessitating alternative plans for home repairs. A Mennonite group kindly offered their services free of charge and needed repairs were made. Finally, one participant reported that she had followed the nurse's advice to seek medical consultation for a breast lump which had resulted in the diagnosis of cancer and subsequent mastectomy. To the best of her knowledge, her life expectancy had not been greatly compromised due to early detection and treatment of cancer.

The most frequent first interview recommendation (53%) within the category of Social-Emotional Support involved the encouragemet to increase social activity. Ten participants (8%) were advised to contact neighbors or other individuals in their community for social and recreational purposes. Use of the Talking Library, respite care for the spouse, professional counseling services, meditation or yoga, and therapeutic touch or massage were additional recommendations included within this category. Most participants were excited and very willing to have the nurse come into their homes, and anecdotal or field notes indicated that the brief social interaction often was the day's highlighted activity. Findings documented during the second interview indicated a marked increase in the number of times spiritual counseling, thera-peutic touch, meditation, and bereavement counseling were suggested. The number of comments about the helpfulness or concern of neighbors also increased, and it was evident that several participants were maintained in their homes because of the informal caregiving supplied by neighbors.

Conclusion

In summary, specific findings from both interviews have produced expected and unexpected results. From the perspective of the elder consumer, recommendations generally seemed to be well received, except for suggestions relating to scatter rugs and the purchase of smoke alarms. Finances were limited for many participants; however, needed emergency home repairs and the subsidizing of the installation of grab bars by volunteer organizations highlighted for them the generosity and talents of the local community. In addition, many participants enjoyed the interview time as a pleasant sojourn from the usual routine. From the health professionals' perspective, the project has saved two lives, instituted several emergency repair services, and provided a free educational and preventive-health service to the community. None of the interviewed participants had been hospitalized by the time of the second interview because of adverse reactions to drugs or complica-tions from falls, despite the fact that approximately 23% of the participants (27) reported they had fallen between interview periods. When questioned about their falls, most reported their falls had occurred outside the home and were primarily the result of faulty depth perception when trying to maneuver street-to-sidewalk heights. One participant suggested that the city paint all corner curbs white to improve the visual distinction between curb and street height, and this recommendation was forwarded to the city council. Lastly, from an organizational perspective, sponsorship of the project by a long-term care facility not only eased the referral process but also provided an assessment service by health care professionals most familiar with the unique needs of the elder population group. The accessing of known and, (until recently) unknown community resources to promote a safer home environment for the elderly has been challenging.

The project was implemented in an urban-metropolitan area; however, the same project could easily have been adopted in a rural setting. It is hoped that the project can continue to be offered through the fiscal underwriting of activities and personnel time by several insurance companies. In addtion, the assessment profile will be made available to other long-term or health care agencies so that similar projects can be implemented in other communities. Personnel time and financial expenditures were costly to the sponsoring health care facility, but the rewards of an improved quality of life through the continued maintenance of the elder person in the community far outweighed these investments.

Chapter 16

Postponement of Health Care by Widowed, Divorced, and Never-Married Older Men

Pat M. Keith
Department of Sociology
Iowa State University
Ames, Iowa 50011

Research suggests that the health of unmarried men in old age may be more precarious than that of their married counterparts (Hyman, 1983; Verbrugge, 1985). In general, among unmarried men, the separated/ divorced seem most at risk of poor health followed by the widowed and the never-married. This research investigates one aspect of health behavior of unmarried men—postponement of needed treatment. To the degree that seeking care without delay may promote health at any age, why people postpone needed care warrants study.

It was observed that ". . . willingness to care for health problems has had surprisingly little empirical attention" (Verbrugge, 1985, p. 171). Determining why persons postpone or delay care is important because preventive measures can reduce the probability of developing chronic disease and disability (Atchley, 1985). Treatment can sometimes reverse the potentially negative effects of chronic disease, and rehabilitation can aid in restoration of lost functions and provide compensation for unrestorable functions. Early detection and prevention of disability should improve the quality of life by both maximizing independence and reducing health care costs (Besdine, 1981). Because the aged and the unmarried use a disproportionate amount of health services and experience more severe chronic illnesses, investigation of why the aged fail to seek needed care should be informative for those providing health services.

There is little available information on the extent of postponement of needed treatment by the aged. In most research, not seeking care when it is warranted is likely to be included in the general category of non-reported illness or lack of use. Besdine (1981) described the failure of the elderly to report or to conceal illness as a "pervasive behavioral phenomenon." Citing research from Scotland, he suggested that unreported illness may be in part responsible for advanced disease states that foster major disability in the frail elderly (Besdine, 1981). Pioneering Geriatricians in Scotland found a surprisingly large amount of concealed illness despite free care and accessible physicians. "Nonreporting of symptoms reflecting underlying disease in elderly persons is an especially dangerous phenomenon when coupled with the American organizational structure of health care delivery. Our health care system is passive, especially for elderly people, and lacks prevention-oriented or early detection efforts" (Besdine, 1981, p. 19). Postponement of care by the elderly increases the probability that disease will be advanced before the person enters the health care system.

Given the importance of seeking care, how prevalent is postponement of treatment? Harris and associates found that 13% of a sample of 1,836 persons age 65 or over had not seen a doctor about their health when they thought they should have (1981). The most common reason for symptom tolerance and not seeking treatment was expensiveness of care (39%), followed by not being sick enough (21%), not wanting to bother the doctor (21%), and difficulty in getting to the doctor's office or hospital (11%). In the Scottish sample, the most frequent explanation for not seeking care was the belief that illness, functional decline, and feeling sick accompany old age. Depression, intellectual loss, and fear that therapeutic intervention would generate functional loss and impede independent living were additional explanations for not getting treatment (Besdine, 1981). Demographic characteristics that also may be factors in foregoing care were not reported although much research has examined them as correlates of use-nonuse of health services (Coulton & Frost, 1982).

Correlates of Postponement of Health Care

Previous research on factors associated with use of health services is instructive for the study of postponement of care, although delay in seeking or foregoing needed care may often be categorized with other types of nonuse. Therefore, predictors of postponement of care may have been obscured in research on more general issues of nonuse.

A conceptual approach suggesting the use of health services is a consequence of predisposing, enabling, and need variables was selected to guide the multivariate analysis of postponement of care in the present research (Andersen & Newman, 1973). Predisposing variables include personal characteristics that may influence perceptions of need or use of services (e.g., demographic characteristics, age, sex), social structural variables (occupation, education, ethnicity), and beliefs about illness and health care. Enabling factors such as income, transportation, and insurance may facilitate or restrain the use of services after need is recognized. Perceived need (individual perceptions of symptoms and self-assessed health) and needs as determined by physicians comprise the need variables.

Predisposing, enabling, and need variables are differentially associated with use of services (Coulton & Frost, 1982; Mechanic, 1979). In general, although there are limited studies of the aged, assessments of need or illness explain more of the variance in the use of medical services than social, structural, or psychological factors. It is unclear whether models that explain differential use of services in general operate in the same way for unmarried men.

In this research, measures representing predisposing, enabling, and need variables were examined in relation to postponement of needed treatment among unmarried men. Need and enabling variables were represented by self-assessed health and income, respectively. Consistent with the research of Coulton and Frost (1982), social isolation and psychological distress were included as predisposing variables.

Research on the influence of isolation on use of services is somewhat contradictory. Shuval (1970) found that isolates were more likely to secure services, perhaps as a substitution for new contacts while Coulton and Frost (1982) observed that the most isolated used the fewest services. Still other research has indicated that large networks of friends prompt seeking health care while large family networks support delaying behavior (McKinlay, 1981).

In general, various measures of psychological distress have been linked with increased use of health services (Tessler, Mechanic, & Dimond, 1976). Several reasons for this relationship have been given. Distress may be a casual factor in illness; distressed persons may be less skeptical of medical care and believe they have less control over illness; or they may deal with other kinds of problems in their lives by obtaining medical care. Because finances are precarious for many of the unmarried, especially the divorced, perceived financial hardship and comparative financial distress were included as assessments of psychological distress. Financial worries and hardships may figure differently than other types of psychologial distress in decisions about health care. Harris and Associates (1981) found that finances were viewed as a barrier to obtaining care. For this reason, financial distress may diminish use of services and have as a consequence postponement of needed care.

A number of factors suggest that divorced/separated men may be more vulnerable to adverse life conditions that may affect health care decisions. For example, their more negative feelings and outlooks on life and society distinguished them from married and widowed men and women (never-married persons were not studied, Hyman, 1983). They were less integrated into the wider world through the use of media or formal organizations, substantially less satisfied with their finances and health (Hyman, 1983), and more vulnerable to alcoholism (Whittington, 1984). They also may lead more risk-prone lives than widowed or never-married older men, suggesting that they might postpone health care more than their unmarried counterparts. Furthermore, less-certain finances and greater perceived financial hardships may figure more importantly in decisions to delay care by the divorced. A riskier lifestyle may prompt a lack of response to health problems in middle age that continues into old age when effects of earlier overlooked conditions may be exacerbated.

The longitudinal research reported here examined postponement of needed health care by unmarried older men. Relationships between being unmarried (widowed, divorced/separated, never-married) and postponement of treatment, reasons for postponment of care, and changes in health care behavior were considered.

Methods

Sample

Data were analyzed from the 1969 and 1979 waves of the Longitudinal Retirement History Study conducted by the U.S. Bureau of the Census for the Social Security Administration. From an initial sample of 11,153 persons aged 58 to 63 in 1969, a subsample of unmarried men (375) interviewed both in 1969 and 1979 was studied. The subsample included 104 widowed men, 114 divorced/separated men, and 157 never-married men. (See Irelan, 1972, for an extensive description of the sampling plan and the background of the larger study.)

Information was not available to determine the number of years respondents had been widowed or divorced/separated prior to 1969. The men had the same marital status at both interviews. For convenience, the waves of study will be referred to as time 1 and time 2.

Health Care Behavior

To assess whether respondents had postponed health care, they were asked, "Is there some kind of care or treatment that you have put off even though you may still need it? (yes/no). Why have you put it off?" Reasons for postponement were categorized as: financial, convenience, emotional, and "other." Respondents were asked these questions at both time 1 and time 2.

Those who indicated they had not postponed health care may include both persons who needed care and obtained treatment and those who did not need care. Data were not available to determine whether a "no" response meant care had not been sought or care was not needed although in the multivariate analysis, health status was controlled.

Health

Although it is most desirable to have both physician ratings and individual assessments, only self-ratings of health were available. The measure of health assessed functional capacity, responses to two questions were summed: "Do you have any health condition, physical handicap, or disability that limits how well you get around?" and "Does your health limit the kind or amount of work or housework you can do?" (yes, 0; no, 1). Health was measured at both time 1 and time 2.

Income

A measure of income in 1970, obtained in the 1971 wave of the study, was used. Income in 1970 was coded into 14 categories ranging from under $1,000 to $25,000 or over. Income at time 2 was coded into 23 categories ranging from under $1,000 to $30,000 and over. The median income for men at time 1 was in the range of $3,500 to $3,999 and $4,000 to $4,999 at time 2.

Distress

Two measures of distress representing predisposing factors were employed in both interviews. Distress over level of living was assessed by asking: "Generally, how satisfied are you with the way you are living now—that is, as far as money and what you are able to have are concerned? Would you say the way you are living is—More than satisfactory (4) to Very unsatisfactory (1)?"

Financial hardship was measured by responses to: "Which of the following four statements describes your ability to get along on your income? I can't make ends meet (1); I have just enough, no more (2); I have enough, with a little extra sometimes (3); I always have money left over (4)."

Isolation

Isolation from both friends and relatives was considered in relation to postponing care. Respondents indicated the number of friends and relatives whom they contacted in person or by phone daily, weekly, monthly, less than monthly, or not at all. These were recoded so that scores ranged from 4 (daily contact) to 0 (no contact). At the second interview, persons were asked separate questions about how often they phoned or saw friends or relatives (daily–not at all). To correspond more closely to the measure used in the earlier interview, responses were summed for phoning and contact in person, and scores ranging from 0 to 4 were obtained for both friends and relatives.

Analyses

Discriminant analyses were used to determine which combination of factors best differentiated those who had postponed treatment from those who had not. Discriminant function technique identifies the linear combination of variables that best discriminates between discrete groups. Coefficients weighting the variables indicate the relative importance of a factor in the discrimination process and can be interpreted similarly to beta values obtained in multiple regression. In the discriminant analysis, the effect of health status was controlled prior to consideration of the remaining variables.

Results

At time 1, about one quarter of the men (26%) had not received medical care when they felt they needed it, with only a slight increase in those who delayed care by the end of the decade (29%). The proportion of unmarried men who had not sought treatment was more than double that reported by Harris et al. (1981) for a sample of persons 65 years of age or older, although no data were presented by marital status or gender. Marital status did not figure prominently in decisions by men to forego seeking medical care (Table 16.1) although the widowed were somewhat more likely to delay treatment than the never married at time 1. Clearly, the expectation that divorced men would postpone care more than others was not supported.

Reasons for Postponement of Health Care

Respondents indicated why they had put off seeking treatment (see Table 16.2). Reasons included finances, convenience, and emotional factors. Financial reasons were dominant at both the beginning and end of the decade for the majority of men whereas convenience and emotional factors were less likely to intervene in obtaining treatment. For the most part, reasons for postponing care tended to be comparable at both interviews.

The reason men delayed care differed somewhat by marital status both earlier and later in their lives. The relationship between marital status and financial reasons for delaying treatment was similar across time. The widowed and divorced, for example, identified finances much more often (46%-62%) as reasons for not seeking care than the never-married (15%-17%) at both interviews. At the earlier time, widowed men more than any others regarded finances as a barrier to obtaining health care although ten years later they differed little from the divorced in viewing finances as critical to their treatment.

Table 16.1
Postponement of Health Care by Marital Status (Percentages)

Marital status	Time 1	Time 2
Widowed	31	30
Divorced/separated	25	25
Never married	22	27
Total sample	26	29
X^2	2.55, 2 df	.76, 2 df
	ns	ns

Table 16.2
Reasons for Postponement of Health Care by
Marital Status (Percentages)

	Financial		Convenience		Emtional	
Marital status	Time 1	Time 2	Time 1	Time 2	Time 1	Time 2
Widowed	62	52	12	23	15	13
Divorced/separated	46	54	27	21	18	4
Never married	15	17	21	17	27	24

For the never-married, convenience and emotional reasons were at least as important if not more important than finances in their decisions. The extent to which convenience figured in obtaining health care was fairly stable for the divorced and never married but became substantially more important to the widowed over time. Emotional reasons for delaying care were associated with marital status with the never-married more likely to mention them at both times. Marital status had the least effect on decisions based on convenience.

Change in Postponement of Health Care

The data provided an opportunity to observe change in health care behavior. The majority of men who postponed treatment at time 1 continued to delay obtaining treatment (Table 16.3). At both interviews, most of the men, regardless of marital status, reported much the same behavior varying from 69% of the divorced to 74% of the never-married with stable health care behavior. Except for the divorced/separated, men who changed over the decade were more likely to postpone care. Of the men who changed, only 40% of the divorced/separated delayed treatment when they were older compared with about 60% for the never married and widowed.

Need, Enabling, Predisposing Factors, and Postponement of Care

T tests were used to assess the bivariate relationship between need, enabling, and predisposing factors and postponement of care for the three marital statuses. Among the widowed, poorer health ($t = 3.53, p < .001$); lower income ($t = 2.63, p < .01$); greater distress over level of living ($t = 2.59, p < .05$); and financial hardships ($t = 3.67, p < .001$) were

Table 16.3
Change in Postponement of Health Care: Time 1, Time 2

			Those who changed (%)	
Marital status	Stable (%)	Change (%)	Obtained treatment (%)	Postponed treatment (%)
Widowed	70	30	42	58
Divorced/separated	69	31	60	40
Never married	74	26	40	60

associated with postponement of care at the first interview. By the end of the decade, only distress over level of living was related to delaying care among widowed men (t = 3.16, $p < .001$). Poorer health, lower income, and greater financial distress were associated with delaying care by divorced men at time 1 (t = 5.00, $p < .001$; t = 2.10, $p < .05$; t = 3.45, $p < .01$). By time 2, the relationship between health and seeking care had declined somewhat (t = 2.00, ns), whereas distress over their standard of living became more important to decisions about care (t = 3.08, $p < .01$). Among the never-married, low income was associated with foregoing care at both the beginning and end of the decade (t = 2.27, $p < 05$; t = 2.54, $p < .01$), whereas poorer health was related to delayed care at the earlier time (t = 2.27, $p < .05$).

Multivariate Analyses of Postponement Care

Discriminant analyses were used to assess whether need, enabling, or predisposing variables best differentiated men who delayed care from those who did not postpone treatment (Table 16.4). The factors discriminated between health care behavior of the divorced/separated men best and were least salient for the never-married. There was one significant discriminant function for the widowed (X^2 = 16.67, $p < .01$) and divorced (X^2 = 35.19, $p < .001$) at time 1 and one for the divorced at time 2 (X^2 = 12.72, $p < .05$) The variables were better discriminators of postponement of health care earlier in men's lives.

Although low income was associated with delaying care in the bivariate analysis at time 1 for the widowed and at both interviews for the divorced, its influence on postponing treatment diminished when other variables were considered. Rather, income probably contributed to perceptions of financial hardship and distress over level of living, which in turn affected decisions about obtaining care except among the never-married for whom income tended to be associated with obtaining care–especially at the first interview. Financial concerns, either financial hardship or distress over level of living, were more important discriminators for the formerly married than for the never-married, both earlier and later in their lives. Men who were troubled about their finances more often delayed seeking care.

Need, as reflected in health status, was most consistently salient in differentiating health care decisions of the divorced although it was of some importance for other men as well at the first interview. By the end of the decade, however, financial hardship was more important than health in postponing care among the divorced. Contacts with friends and relatives failed to provide a strong consistent influence on decisions about care.

Summary and Discussion

This research investigated the relationship of marital status to postponement of health care, reasons for postponement of treatment, multivariate factors associated with delaying care, and changes in health care behavior over a decade among unmarried men.

Almost 30% of these men did not seek care when their health warranted it, and the tendency to postpone care was quite stable over time. These unmarried men were about twice as likely to delay or forgo health care than Harris et al. (1981) observed in a sample including both married and unmarried older men and women.

Contrary to the expectation that the lifestyle of divorced men might be more conducive to decisions to delay care, marital status was not associated with whether or not treatment was postponed although it was linked to the reasons given for why treatment was delayed. The most striking finding was the marked difference between formerly married and never-married men in attributing finances as reasons for delaying care. More than three times as many formerly married men as never-married claimed finances as reasons for their health care decisions. The lesser importance assigned to finances by the never-married probably reflected their somewhat better economic situation as indicated in unpublished analyses.

The multivariate models revealed that these unmarried men, particularly the formerly married, were vulnerable to life strains that influenced their decisions to seek care. Financial strains must be

Table 16.4
Factors Related to Postponement of Treatment by Marital Status: Standardized Discriminant Function Coefficients

Factors	Widowed		Divorced/ separated		Never married	
	Time 1	Time 2	Time 1	Time 2	Time 1	Time 2
Health	.38	.23	.89	.41	.44	.36
Income	.04	-.32	-.14	-.11	.74	.63
Financial hardship	.63	.23	-.11	.88	-.52	.08
Distress-level of living	.15	.88	.41	-.16	.50	.25
Isolation						
Friends	-.12	.11	.09	.09	.07	.36
Relatives	.34	.05	.10	.28	-.11	-.17
Canonical correlation	.42	.32	.57	.33	.28	.25
$X^2 =$ (df = 6)	16.67*	10.91	35.19**	12.72*	10.99	9.87

*$p < .01$.
**$p < .001$.

regarded as chronic, affecting both earlier and later decisions, and as dominant reasons for not obtaining care especially for the formerly married. Financial concerns of the formerly married tended to be more important than need variables reflected in self-assessed health in either one or both models. This contrasts with other research (Coulton & Frost, 1982), which has generally found need (health condition) as more salient than predisposing variables including psychological distress in determining use of services. The discrepancy between these findings, in part, may be because in some research postponement of needed treatment is not considered separately from other forms of nonuse, even though the origins of postponement of care may be somewhat different. To the degree that distress over finances may be amenable to intervention and change, then these findings may be of use to professionals as they attempt to increase preventive and follow-up care.

The models were not very effective in discriminating health care decisions of the never-married at either time 1 or 2. Models for the never-married might have been improved by including a measure of mental health. In giving reasons for delay, never-married men claimed emotional reasons more than other reasons and mentioned them substantially more often than did the formerly married. It was not possible to determine whether their references to emotional reasons might have been associated with poorer mental health. Measures of mental health might have discriminated between delay and postponement better than physical health or assessments of financial distress for the never-married.

The data indicated the need for preventive education among older unmarried men because the widowed and never-married who changed their health care behavior over time more often changed negatively and postponed treatment than the divorced. Perhaps the most important findings of this research were that proportions of men who failed to obtain care, and their reasons for doing so were fairly stable over time. This indicates there were persistent strains in the lives of older unmarried men that may be attended to by professionals who are able to intervene and address barriers to securing treatment. Reasons given for not seeking care and the discriminant analyses disclosed somewhat divergent needs of the formerly married and never-married that are informative for application. The salience of financial distress of the formerly married and emotional reasons cited by the never-married are factors associated with delay in seeking treatment that would seem to warrant differential attention by practitioners. Early intervention might have diminished or eliminated what over the decade became somewhat stable barriers to seeking care by these men.

Chapter 17

The Social and Psychological Benefits of Involvement in Corporate Fitness Programs through Retirement

William Rudman
Department of Sport Management
Ohio State University
Columbus, Ohio 43210

Over the past 80 years the number of retired workers has increased dramatically. In 1900, only 37% of those over the age of 65 were retired. By 1980, over 80% of those 65 or older were retired from the work force (U.S. Senate Special Committee on Aging, 1981). Whether the individual views retirement as forced unemployment and has difficulty in the transition process (Baum & Baum, 1980; Comfort, 1976), or accepts retirement as an earned privilege and the beginning of new personal responsibilities (Atchley, 1976, 1980), depends on the degree of continuity between preretirement and postretirement activities (Palmore, 1980; Palmore & Kivett, 1976).

In order to meet some of the health, social, and psychological needs of retired employees, several major U.S. corporations have initiated recreation and health/fitness programs. These programs are designed to meet the health needs of retired employees by providing a familiar and safe place for exercise and educational classes on nutrition and stress management. Social and psychological needs are indirectly met through continued contact with the workplace and former work associates.

Although prior research has shown that a positive relationship seems to exist between involvement in exercise and fitness programs for the elderly and good health (Piscopo, 1985; Shepard, 1986), the relationship between belonging to these programs and social psychological benefits

Thanks are accorded to the Campbell Soup Company for funding and support for this study.

for retired employees is not so clear. Indeed, what research that has been conducted in this area has been inconclusive (Kleiber, 1982; Palmore, 1982). Consequently, exercise and health programs designed to attract retired employees have fallen short of program expectations. Only a small percentage of those over the age of 65 participate in organized exercise programs (Rudman, 1985). Recent findings have shown that only 2%-3% of those over the age of 65 participate in exercise programs (Miller Lite Report, 1983). Moreover, among those older adults who begin a regular exercise program, adherence and retention rates are low (Rudman, 1985). Exercise programs designed to attract retirees have often lacked valuable insights into the problems and needs of retired workers (e.g., transportation, support groups).

This study focuses on the social and psychological variables that affect participation in a company sponsored exercise and fitness program from a selected group of retired employees of Campbell Soup Company. Attention is given to: (1) reasons why workers who have recently retired from the Campbell Soup Company have become actively involved in the company's health and fitness program; (2) the desired needs of this specific population of retired employees; (3) various ways in which the Campbell Soup Company can attract a larger number of retired workers into their health and fitness programs.

The key factor that differentiates this study from others is that research was conducted on an exercise and fitness program located at the workplace. This is important in that "work" and work-related factors are important determinants of personal identity and self-worth (Difazio, 1985). By locating a health and fitness center at the workplace, a greater degree of continuity in the preretirement to postretirement transition may be achieved for those individuals involved in the postretirement programs (Kleiber, 1982; Palmore, 1980). As will be noted later, retired workers involved in the health and fitness programs did not limit their contact with the workplace to the health and fitness center. Trips were made to the cafeteria, company store, and old work offices. The involvement in the health and fitness programs legitimized the retired workers' continued contact with the company. In other words, the retiree had an acceptable reason to continue direct contact with the workplace through company-sponsored programs.

The Retirement Transition

Most people believe retirement is the cause of many health, social, and psychological pathologies among the elderly (e.g., anomia, depression, illness, loss of self-esteem and self-worth) (Palmore, 1980). Current research, however, suggests that in general significant differences do not exist between the elderly who have retired and those who have remained in the work force (Atchley, 1985; Kleiber, 1982; Rosenberg, 1984). Moreover, studies using both longitudinal and cross-sectional data seem to indicate that a certain degree of continuity exists in preretirement and postretirement attitudes. For example, current research has shown that significant differences do not exist between those in the work force and those who have retired on measures of depression (Cottrell & Atchley, 1969); physical illness (Ekerdt, Bossé, & LoCastro, 1983; Streib & Schneider, 1971); mental illness (Lowenthal & Berkman, 1967); or life satisfaction (Glamser, 1981; Palmore, 1980). The "negative" effects of retiring (loss of occupational role) are balanced off by the positive reactions to retirement (Atchley, 1976; Ward, 1979).

Involvement in the Preretirement and Postretirement Programs

Although research suggests that for most retirement per se is not the cause of health, social, or psychological disorders, there are several questions that all retirees must deal with during this stage in their life. Practical and personal questions such as: How will I live on my current income? What will I do with my free time now that I do not have to go to work? What are my new goals and ambitions? How will society, my friends, and family react to me now that I am retired? Preretirement and postretirement programs sponsored by corporations are intended to ease the transition into retirement by providing a certain degree of continuity in lifestyle routines. Research has shown that those involved in preretirement programs seem to adjust better in the areas of health, life satisfaction, social integration, and productive leisure (Palmore, 1982). Moreover, it has been shown that those who are involved in active leisure behaviors at older ages adapt better to retirement and score higher on life satisfaction measures (Darnley, 1975; DeCarlo, 1974; Draper, 1967). Surprisingly, however, prior studies have not dealt with how on-site corporate exercise and health retirement programs are related to the successful adaptation to retirement. In addition to meeting the practical needs of retirees by offering classes concerning the benefits of proper nutrition, exercise, and stress management, as well as a place to exercise under supervised conditions, on-site programs offer the additional benefit of providing a meeting place with other retired employees and former work associates. This helps to maintain a level of continuity in lifestyle activities through the retirement process.

Data

Data for this study were collected from observations and personal interviews of retired employees of the Campbell Soup Company located in Camden, New Jersey. The analysis is restricted to only those retired employees currently active in programs offered by the onsite health and fitness center. Thirteen[1] out of 900 retired workers living in the Camden area were active at the fitness center's programs at the time this study was conducted. Issues related to the small number of retirees involved in the program will be discussed later in this chapter. Ten out of the 13 actively involved retired employees were interviewed. Respondents ranged in age from 65 to 76; in tenure at Campbell Soup from 12 to 40 years; and held prior occupational statuses ranging from warehouse workers, secretaries, middle management, to upper level management. There were nine male and one female retired employees interviewed.

Prior Exercise and Leisure Involvement

Most of the theories developed to explain adult involvement in structured leisure or exercise programs are based on disengagement theory (Cummings & Henry, 1961). Briefly, this position suggests that as an individual ages there is a tendency to withdraw from social activity. The diversification of family roles and the need to concentrate on acruing the economic necessities of life are often cited as reasons for this disengagement. Because leisure and, in this case, involvement in structured exercise programs are not viewed as being necessary for existence, participation in these activities is expected to decrease as other family, social, or work obligations increase.

The group of retirees from the Campbell Soup Company generally followed this pattern of disengagement from structured exercise and social leisure behavior. Only two out of ten individuals interviewed had been involved in either a regular exercise or sport activity as an adult. In both cases, however, involvement was limited to coaching youth teams, and involvement had ceased at least 20 years prior to their retirement.

From these interviews, three general patterns of responses seemed to emerge. First, all those interviewed felt that the education they had received had not adequately explained the benefits of either maintaining a regular exercise program or proper dietary habits. There was a general belief among the retirees that young and middle-aged adults did not need to have a regular exercise routine to maintain good health. This lack of understanding led to unhealthy eating and personal habits (e.g., overeating, frying instead of baking, smoking). After joining the on-site health and fitness center, however, all 13 retirees noticed positive changes in their personal health habits. Either they had stopped smoking, become aware of cholesterol intake, or begun to reduce their weight by modifying their diet.

Second, there was a belief among those interviewed that daily work habits and nonregulated exercise behavior would provide the necessary exercise for adults. Working in the yard (e.g., mowing the lawn, chopping wood, working in the garden), or involvement in work-related tasks (e.g., carrying bags of potatoes, lifting boxes onto trucks) were initially believed to provide the individual with sufficient exercise to remain healthy. For example, a 65-year-old former assembly-line worker had believed that trimming hedges and chopping wood throughout his middle years was enough to provide sufficient exercise. Similarly, a 75-year-old former warehouse worker believed his daily work routine, which consisted of loading 400-pound bags of potatoes onto trucks, provided the necessary exercise to remain healthy while he was a "younger man." Involvement in the on-site health and fitness center's programs had increased the awareness levels of the retirees for the need to exercise properly, stretch, and to develop aerobic capacity.

Third, the white-collar retirees felt that work and family obligations had restricted their involvement in leisure and exercise programs. As these individuals became more involved in their work, social obligations, or in rasing a family, personal time for involvement in a structured exercise program decreased. As a 66-year-old former upper-level white-collar worker explained, as he and his wife began raising a family, and as he was promoted through the ranks at Campbell Soup Company, there was a definite need to "prioritize time commitments." Time previously spent on exercising was spent attending school or social functions for their children, or at work earning money to support his family. It was not until he had retired from work did he begin involvement in the ongoing exercise and fitness programs offered by Campbell Soup Company.

Of those interviewed in this study, eight out of ten retirees stated that physical problems were the primary reason for their initial involvement in the health and fitness center's programs. Chronic conditions ranged from weight problems, high blood pressure, arthritis, lower-back pains, to the rehabilitation of a cardiovascular condition. One retired employee who had recently suffered a heart attack was told by a consulting physician that unless a regular and supervised exercise and fitness program was started, the probability of another heart attack would greatly increase. Regardless of whether the retired employees began for health or social reasons, all ten strongly believed that their current involvement in the fitness center programs would add both years to their life and quality to their years.

Participation in Fitness: A Positive Experience

Although initial involvement centered around physiological concerns, adherence to the fitness program was based primarily on social and psychological parameters. Each retiree believed that the positive atmosphere encountered at the fitness center was the main reason for continued involvement in the program. The retirees felt welcome, and they also believed they had a friend at the fitness center. The point was emphatically made that the fitness center was open to anyone regardless of race, sex, or socio-economic status. Not only did the retirees feel welcome, but they strongly believed that the Campbell Soup Company cared about their personal health needs even though they had retired. A 71-year-old former designer/draftsman who had 30 years of work experience at Campbell Soup Company spent a great deal of time explaining the "turnaround philosophy," and how that philosophy had visibly revolved around opening the health and fitness center. As noted by this retiree, the "turnaround philosophy" suggests that, in order to make long-term changes in behavior, the individual must take responsibility for personal actions. The fitness center programs provided employees with information concerning the benefits of regular exercise, proper dietary habits, and ways to accomplish these goals. By providing these services, this was a "sign" to employees that Campbell Soup Company cared about their personal health needs.

In addition to the direct positive impact of staff employees of the fitness center encouraging the retiree to come into the center involvement in this program provided the retiree with a feeling of security through continued contact with the company. A predominant theme among those retired employees interviewed concerned the positive strokings that appeared to perpetuate feelings of self-worth. As noted by two retirees, involvement in the fitness center's programs made "you feel a part of the company" and helped you feel that you were "still worth something."

As might be expected, most of the retirees had spent the majority of their working lives at Campbell Soup Company. As noted earlier, the employment span at the Camden plant ranged from 12 to 43 years, and the average length of tenure was 32 years. To end such a relationship abruptly could be psychologically as well as socially harmful. Involvement in the fitness center's programs still provided the retired employee with a link to the company, and more importantly allowed for retirees to believe they have a direct means of continued input into the company. For example, a 66-year-old retiree who had been a director of strategic planning (38 years of tenure at Campbell Soup Company), had recently been hired to teach financial planning courses for new employees at Campbell Soup Company. A 66-year-old former maintenance worker who had 43 years of experience at Campbell Soup Company proudly noted that younger employees were continually asking him ways to improve their work efficiency when he would come into the health and fitness center to "work out." In other words, participation in the fitness programs provided a justifiable excuse to come into the Camden office.

Visitations were not limited to the fitness center, but extended to the company store, cafeteria, and old work offices. Contact with old friends who are currently employed at the Campbell Soup Company allowed retirees the opportunity to discuss work matters and offer suggestions based on their personal work experiences. Several retirees noted with great pride recent involvement and consultation with current employees. By offering suggestions that were listened to by employees, the retirees were made to feel that they still made a difference in the company. Given these circumstances (i.e., an on-site program) social needs to interact as well as feelings of self-worth were both directly and indirectly met through participation in the fitness program.

These findings were consistent with those of Difazio (1985) who studied the effects of long-term "unemployment" among longshoremen. Difazio found that although the longshoremen did not work, they reported on a daily basis to the union hiring halls in order to maintain contact with work associates and with the workplace. Difazio concluded that by simply continuing to come to the union hall, an important degree of continuity was achieved in the workers' lifestyles. Continued contact with the workplace helped the workers to organize time, it provided meaning to their existence, combated the boredom of unemployment, and provided a measure of dignity of belonging to the community (Difazio, 1985).

Responses from the interview suggest that continuation in the exercise and fitness program offered by Campbell Soup Company provides retirees with similar social and psychological benefits to those experienced by the longshoremen. For some it "provided a reason to get up in the morning" when they did not feel like getting out of bed. For others, it allowed for continued contact with "friends and associates they had known for the last 25 to 30 years." For others, it provided an opportunity to remain "mentally" active by providing consultation (on a formal and informal basis) to working company employees. Finally, for all of the retired employees, it provided the much-needed impetus to remain active in organized social activities. If, for example, a retired employee did not come in for his/her regular workout, a member of the fitness staff would contact that individual to find out the reason for not coming. Consequently, the retiree remained socially active and felt a part of a work community organization.

Increased Participation: An Issue

Although the ten retirees who were interviewed were enthusiastic and provided positive feedback concerning their involvement in the fitness center, it must be noted that the entire number of retired employees in the Camden area is approximately 900. In other words, only 1% of the Campbell Soup Company retirees living in the area were currently active in the health and fitness center programs. The real issue needing to be addressed is ways to increase the participation rate of retired employees who are not active in the fitness center programs.[2] Moreover, as noted earlier, those employees currently involved in the fitness program began as a result of physical problems and not because they simply wanted the opportunity to exercise.

What seems to be needed are programs and incentives that will attract others before medical problems occur. From discussions directed toward issues related to exposure and access, the retirees seemed to agree that the primary reasons why more employees are not involved in the current program are: (a) the lack of knowledge concerning the benefits of eating right and exercising, and (b) transportation and parking limitations. For example, all six of the blue-collar retirees had heard about the fitness program through friends. Not one of these individuals remembered any formal contact from Campbell Soup Company concerning the existence or availability of the health and fitness center programs. The suggestion was made that the health and fitness center publish a newsletter for retired Campbell Soup Company employees informing them about the existence of the program and the benefits of a more healthy lifestyle.

The second reason behind beliefs concerning the low number of retired employees in the health and fitness center programs were related to transportation and parking. Either expanding the area available for parking or providing transportation to and from the fitness facilities were suggested as means of increasing retiree participation. Finally, those interviewed felt that having a whirlpool or sauna would benefit and attract retired employees to the fitness center. There was a belief among retirees that the programs offered and the equipment available were designed to attract younger members of the company. Offering facilities or programs directed to the retirees would make the fitness center more attractive in the eyes of the retired population in the Camden area.

Although there were concerns about the types of programs offered (e.g., programs directed toward the younger employees) there was unanimous agreement among the retirees that the fitness center should not implement programs directed only for the older (retired) population. All ten noted the importance of interaction on the exercise floor with current employees. The retirees believed that offering separate programs for the retirees would segregate and reduce interactions with current employees. There was also concern that separate program for the retirees would enhance a negative stereotype of "what it is like to be old."

Discussion and Issues

Corporate health and fitness programs that are open to retirees often meet many of the social and psychological needs of older adults. These programs provide meeting places where retirees can interact with each other and with former colleagues. Finally, these programs provide an atmosphere where retirees can feel useful and needed. Lack of attendance in fitness programs can be a direct result of the lack of knowledge about the program itself or about the benefits of proper dietary and exercise behavior, or the lack of transportation to facilities. Providing information about the fitness center and increasing access by providing transportation are ways in which involvement in health and fitness center programs can be increased.

Although these findings suggest that continued association with the work place helps to meet certain types of social (e.g., belonging) and psychological needs (e.g., feelings of self-worth), much more work in this area is needed. The first step would be to collect information from retired employees who are not actively involved in corporately sponsored retirement programs. These data would help in providing information:

(1) concerning ways in which corporations might attract a larger number of retirees to company sponsored programs, and (2) this would provide the necessary information contrasting actual differences between retirees involved and those not involved in company programs and whether this involvement makes a difference in the retirement transition. The second step concerns redefining how we think about the retirement process per se. Retirement is not the end of the individual's productive years, but rather a beginning of a new stage in the life cycle. For most of the retirees interviewed in this study, retirement is not wasted by simply watching television or laying around. Rather, it is a time where activity with the family (primarily the spouse) takes on a new meaning. The shift from work roles to social/domestic roles is often a source of great pleasure. This was noted by all of the retirees interviewed, in statements such as: "I am busier now than when I worked," "I am busy all day long now," or "I have less time now (because of yard work) to socialize with my friends than I did when I was working." If corporations view retirement programs in this manner, the implementation of on-site health and fitness programs may be seen as a way of helping the retiree remain physically healthy, socially active, and meet psychological needs of belonging by providing continuity between lost work roles and new social roles associated with the home.

Notes

1. Twelve out of the 13 retirees active in the program are males.
2. Since the initial findings were reported to employees of the Campbell Soup Company, efforts have been made to attract a larger number of retired employees. From late March, the time when this study was conducted, to December, the number of retired employees who were active in the health and fitness center programs increased from 13 to 44.

Part IV

Caregiving Issues

Chapter 18

Parents of Adults with Developmental Disabilities
Age and Reasons for Reluctance to Use Another Caregiver

Jean L. Engelhardt
Southwest Ohio Development Center
Batavia, Ohio 45103

Victoria D. Lutzer
188 Lewis Roberts Way
Williamsburg, Virginia 23186

Timothy H. Brubaker
Family and Child Studies Center
Miami University
Oxford, Ohio 45056

The lifestyles of older people vary considerably. Differences can be attributed to various family patterns and situations (Brubaker, 1985a). Some older families are financially secure and some are not. Some experience health difficulties and others do not. Many change their relationships and responsibilities as they age. As these situations and relationships change, the needs of older families change. One group of older persons who have unique lifestyles and needs are parents of adults with developmental disabilities. These older persons need to deal with their own aging as well as the needs of their dependent adult child.

The process of meeting the needs of aging persons had been identified as stressful (Springer & Brubaker, 1984), and the level of stress may be magnified when a child with developmental disabilities is a member of the family. Within recent years, attention has been directed toward the

We express our gratitude to the Family Resource Services Program of the Butler County (Ohio) Board of Mental Retardation and Developmental Disabilties for their help, and to the Jacob G. Schmidlapp Trust of Cincinnati for financial support during the writing of this article.

needs of the growing population of aging adults with developmental disabilities (Janicki & MacEachron, 1984; Seltzer, 1985; Seltzer & Seltzer, 1985; Seltzer, Seltzer & Sherwood, 1982). However, little research has focused on the needs of older persons who help care for their adult children with developmental disabilities. Recently, Lutzer and Brubaker (1988) examined the respite needs of older parents of adults with developmental disabilities and this article further examines the caregiving relationship.

As older parents of these adults with handicaps age, their needs for both themselves and their child increase. A number of these parents have been the primary caregivers of their handicapped child, and their decreasing ability to provide care for their dependent child and themselves creates a difficult situation. One way to reduce this difficulty for the elderly caregiver is to have someone else help care for the dependent adult. However, in spite of the apparent solution this presents, practitioners who work with these families notice a reluctance to relinquish the caregiving task to others. This article examines the relationship between parental age and reasons parents give for not leaving an adult child with developmental disabilities with someone else. The primary question addressed in this study is: Are the reasons for not leaving an adult child with developmental disabilities with someone else correlated with parental age?

This article examines data from a county wide survey of parents of mentally retarded adults. The primary focus of the survey is the respite needs of families with mentally retarded members. Lutzer and Brubaker (1988) in one analysis of this survey data, focused on the age of the parents and their expressed needs for respite care. This first analysis showed that as age increased, parents reported differential needs for respite services. Older parents, more than younger parents, reported a need for out-of-home respite care and care that would limit their involvement with intra- and extrafamilial support systems. Because it seems that the lifestyles of older parents of adults with developmental disabilities could be enhanced if the parents enlisted someone else as a caregiver, it is unclear why some parents are reluctant to use another caregiver.

The current analysis, rather than examining the need for services, examines the reasons for underutilization of services that are currently available. Do older parents or younger parents find it more difficult to use services because of financial reasons? Is parental age related to parental unwillingness to leave their child in anyone else's care? Answers to these questions will provide critical information about how current services may more efficiently meet the needs of this special population and, possibly, improve their lifestyles.

Method

The survey was developed by the Family Resource Service Program, a state-funded, locally administered program, whose mission is twofold: to prevent institutionalization and improve the quality of family life for families including an individual with mental retardation. The goal of the survey was to ascertain respite needs of families currently receiving services from the county Board of Mental Retardation and Developmental Disabilities in a semirural county in southwestern Ohio.

Surveys were mailed to the 636 families with a member receiving services of the Board. One hundred fifty-five families (155) or 24% of the sample replied. Not all respondents completed all items. The 1980 Ohio Census indicates that this county had a population of 258,787, and the Ohio Prevalence and Needs Survey of 1984 of the Ohio State Plan indicates a statewide prevalence of mental retardation of .008 to .01. These figures suggest that there were between 2070 and 2,588 individuals with mental retardation in the southwestern Ohio county sampled. Therefore, the survey sample included approximately 24% to 30% of the total estimated number of families with a mentally retarded member. The survey instrument consisted of 32 questions covering specific respite needs, including time, place and personnel; and population demographics of parental age, number of family members and developmentally disabled member's age and sex. Response choices describing parental difficulty in leaving handicapped child with others were:

1. "My son/daughter does not relate well to strangers and/or new environments."
2. "I have not found anyone willing to stay with him or her."
3. "I have not found anyone qualified."
4. "My son/daughter has too many problems."
5. "My husband/wife does not allow it."
6. "I cannot afford it."
7. "I do not wish to impose on others."
8. "I am not willing to leave him/her with anyone."

Six age groupings were developed to account for 10-year parental age ranges between 15 and 65 and 65 and over. Approximately 25% of the respondents reported a parental age range of over 56 years (see Table 18.1). Identity of respondents was not requested, only the age range of both parents. For all respondents the handicapped child/adult was currently living in the home. No follow-up attempt was made.

Results

Spearman rank-order correlation coefficients were determined for the variables of parental age and reasons for difficulty in leaving the dependent adult (see Table 18.2). Significant positive correlations occurred between age of parent and difficulty of leaving the child because the parent couldn't find anyone qualified (p = .0314) and difficulty leaving the dependent adult because the parent couldn't afford it (p = .0019). Older parents, more than younger parents, reported that they have difficulty leaving their handicapped child because they feel they cannot find anyone qualified to care for their child. Also, older parents, more than younger parents, reported that they have difficulty leaving their handicapped child with anyone because they cannot afford it.

Table 18.1
Age Ranges of Survey Respondents

Age	Frequency	Percent
16–25	13	8.4
26–35	37	23.9
36–45	29	18.7
46–55	29	18.7
56–65	32	20.6
Over 65 years	8	5.2
No age given	7	4.5
Total	155	100.0

A moderate positive correlation occurred between the age of parent and difficulty leaving child because the child has too many problems ($p =$ .0556). That is, older parents, more than younger parents, reported difficulty leaving their handicapped child with anyone because of their feelings that their child has too many problems.

No significant correlations occurred for age of parent and difficulty in leaving a handicapped child because:

1. "My son/daughter does not relate well to strangers and/or new environments."
2. "I have not found anyone willing to stay with him/her."
3. "My husband/wife does not allow it."
4. "I do not wish to impose on others."
5. "I am not willing to leave them with anyone."

Age of parent does not correlate with these perceptions of the handicapped child's dependence.

Table 18.2
Spearman Correlation Coefficients: Age of Respondent with Perceived Difficulty of Leaving Child with Anyone

Reason	r	p
"My son/daughter does not relate well to strangers and/or new environments."	.0089	.9207
"I have not found anyone willing to stay with him/her."	.1035	.2449
"I have not found anyone qualified."	.1903	.0314
"My son/daughter has too many problems."	.1696	.0056
"My husband/wife does not allow it."	-.0128	.8860
"I cannot afford it."	.2718	.0019
"I do not wish to impose on others."	-.1520	.0867
"I am not willing to leave them with anyone."	.0095	.9149

Discussion

The discussion of results must be introduced with the caution that the returned sample may be biased and may not be representative of: (1) those families who do not receive services from the Board of Mental Retardation and Developmental Disabilities and (2) those families who received but did not return the survey.

The findings indicate that older parents of handicapped children differ from younger parents of handicapped children in that they reflect different reasons for not leaving their handicapped child with someone else. That is, older parents were more likely to report that (1) they could not afford someone else; (2) they could not find a qualified person with whom to leave their handicapped child, and (3) their children had too many problems. However, older parents did not differ from younger parents in their report of their willingness to leave their child. This suggests that older persons' reluctance to use other caregivers is related to a perceived feeling of too much cost and the lack of the available, qualified caregivers.

Parental perceptions that there are not qualified personnel available may reflect feelings related to experiences with nonfamilial caregivers during their handicapped child's life. Also, these feelings may stem from negative experiences with professionals as well. Turnbull and Turnbull (1985) present writings by parents of children with developmental disabilities that describe their numerous negative and painful interactions with professionals. Thus, negative experiences by older parents may result in a lack of confidence in professionals and a general tendency to avoid painful interactions by not seeking professional help. On the other hand, younger parents may not have experienced as many negative professional interactions and, therefore, are less likely to report a lack of qualified personnel as a reason for not seeking respite care.

Parent feelings that their children have too many problems and there is a lack of qualified, nonfamilial caregivers are probably related. It is likely that over time nonfamilial caregivers repeatedly convey to parents the idea that their children have many problems. Turnbull and Turnbull's (1985) collection of parental reports suggests that this is the case.

Parental reports of a lack of qualified personnel may also reflect that: (1) parents are actually experiencing more problems with their adult children because of the complications associated with the advancing age of the retarded child (Seltzer et al., 1982), (2) as the parent ages a generalized feeling of increased difficulty associated with all tasks occurs (Brubaker, 1985), or (3) these feelings reflect a lack of parental knowledge and information regarding the qualified programs and persons available to meet the needs of their dependent adult.

The results suggest that practitioners in this field need to be aware of the parents' perceptions related to their reluctance to utilize other caregivers for their handicapped adults. Information needs to be provided to these parents regarding the quality of programs and professionals that are currently available to meet their needs.

Summary

Older parents of individuals with mental retardation receiving Board of Mental Retardation and Developmental Disabilities services, who responded to a questionnaire, reported difficulty in leaving their child with someone else because (1) they could not find anyone qualified, (2) their child had too many problems, and (3) they couldn't afford it. Although further research on aging parents of mentally retarded adults is necessary to more clearly interpret these preliminary findings, the results of the current study suggest aging parents are willing to leave their child with someone but they require financial assistance and education regarding program quality and availability.

This study deals with both the aging process in a caregiving parent and in an adult child with developmental disabilities. The findings suggest that this interaction may result in differential utilization of service patterns. This differential utilization may reflect both the needs of the caregiving parent and the dependent adult. This complex issue requires both systematic research and individual diagnostic efforts in order to better understand parental decisions to utilize respite care systems.

Future Research

More specific reasons for the underutilization of services by parents of handicapped children needs to be examined. Parental reports of utilization of and satisfaction with services would provide a richer data base from which to propose theoretical structures. In the current investigation, there is a confounding of parental age with the aging of the dependent adult. Research that separates these two factors in order to study their separate effects is necessary in order to more fully understand the interaction between parental age and reluctance to utilize respite care. The effect of the prolongation of parenting into the years of aging and retirement needs additional work. This work probably cannot occur in isolation from the study of the effect of specific handicapping conditon on the family as parents and children age. The current work suggests the fruitfulness of this area of study and delineates the variables of parental perception of the child and parental needs as important.

Chapter 19

The Sibling Relationship as a Housing Alternative to Institutionalization in Later Life

Dolores Cabic Borland
Department of Family and Child Ecology
Michigan State University
East Lansing, Michigan 48824–1030

Research suggests that the kinship network provides the individual with many resources, including social relationships, psychological support, mutual aid, residential migration, and a comparative reference group. Because spouse-spouse and parent-child relationships are believed to be the most imporant and intimate of all family relationships, they have received the greatest attention in research, whereas, the nature, quality, and function of the sibling relationship, especially in adulthood, has been relatively overlooked (Irish, 1964; Scott, 1983). Most studies about the aging family that have included questions on siblings have done so in passing or have included siblings within the category of other relatives. However, during the early 1980s the first two major books were written that focused on the sibling relationship over the life span (Bank & Kahn, 1982; Lamb & Sutton-Smith, 1982).

Sibling relationships are believed to be unique among family relationships in at least four ways (Cicirelli, 1982). Siblings share a common heritage, environment and childhood, which may lead to perspectives on life not shared by others. The sibling relationship tends to be highly egalitarian in that one sibling does not have any prescribed power over the other as is found in the parent-child relationship. The sibling role is an ascribed role into which a person is born. Finally, the sibling relationship may be the family relationship of longest duration.

This research was supported in part by a grant from the Michigan State University Foundation, Grant # (ORD 26081) and parts were presented at the 1986 National Council on Family Relations Annual Conference.

The sibling relationship may become more important as a person grows older. Bank and Kahn (1975) suggested that because the sibling relationship often lasts through a lifetime of 50 to 80 years as compared with the parent-child relationship, which lasts 30 to 50 years, it may become the primary family subsystem in later years. The increased importance of the sibling relationship in later years was also suggested by Cummings and Schneider (1961) when they found that solidarity or subjective closeness increased with age and that the sibling bond appeared to partially replace a person's ties with adult children after the children left the family home.

Availability of living siblings and frequency of contact between siblings over the life cycle has been investigated by several researchers. In studies reviewed by Brubaker (1985a) and Troll, Miller, and Atchley (1979), research results indicated that approximately 75% to 90% of the elderly had at least one living sibling. Shanas (1979b) found that over one-half of her elderly respondents reported seeing a sibling in the previous week. Cicirelli (1980) found that 17% of his sample of siblings saw each other weekly, 33% visited at least monthly and 56% had face-to-face contact several times a year. Several other researchers have found that the frequency of interaction varied with other life circumstances, including physical proximity (Scott, 1983), presence of living parents (Adams, 1968; Rosenberg & Anspach, 1973; Young & Willmott, 1957), marital status of siblings (Manney, 1975; Rosenberg & Anspach, 1973), geographical and social mobility, life cycle stage, age differences, childhood experiences, perceived compatibility, feelings toward sibling's spouse and degree of sibling affection, socioeconomic class (Allan, 1977), and involvement in other social roles after retirement (Troll et al., 1979). Brubaker (1985a) and Cicirelli (1982) concluded that although sibling contact is likely to decline during adulthood as they advance in age and focus more on their family of procreation, siblings continue to maintain some form of contact and seldom sever their relationship.

Several studies have investigated the type of contact that takes place between siblings. Adams (1968) found that social interaction between siblings consisted mainly of brief visits and that even though there was not a feeling of obligation to give help or assistance to a sibling, there did appear to be a feeling of obligation to keep in touch to some degree, if only through asking parents about the other siblings. Scott (1983) reported that contact was most frequent with siblings who lived within an hour's travel distance, was most frequently maintained by face-to-face contact or by telephone and was done infrequently by written communication. Social interaction was greater than the amount of assistance exchanged and consisted most frequently of sharing happy occasions, visiting briefly, and engaging in commercial and home recreational activities together.

Although most studies confirm that children are the primary source of support for older persons, siblings have been found to be an important source of support in time of need, even though there does not appear to be a feeling of obligation to provide assistance (Adams, 1968). When Shanas (1961) asked respondents 65 years of age and older whom they would contact, other than their spouse if they became ill or needed long-term care and wanted to discuss the situation with someone, 9.5% named a sibling and 8.5% named another relative. Approximately 70% of those persons without living children said they would ask help from relatives including siblings. In a study of 199 randomly selected white, middle-class, elderly persons 65 years and older, Scott (1983) found that respondents exchanged significantly more help with their children than they did with grandchildren and siblings. The most frequently exchanged types of assistance between siblings was assistance when ill, help in making important decisions, and transportation. The exchange of assistance between siblings was greater when children and spouse were not available as in the case of single, widowed and childless persons. Troll, Miller, and Atchley (1979) also suggested that the narrower the social support network of older persons, the more likely they would be to see a sibling as a source of aid in time of need.

Several researchers (Adams, 1968; Allan, 1977; Cicirelli, 1980, 1982; Ross & Milgram, 1982) found that the degree of perceived closeness of the sibling relationship was related to several critical family factors, including age differential, amount and type of family interaction, and affectional bonds in childhood. Large age differences, physical separation in childhood, family interaction patterns that discouraged a sense of closeness, parenting values and practices that did not emphasize the family unit or equality among members, and the lack of opportunities to share common experiences appeared to prevent a close sibling bond from developing in childhood. Ross and Milgram (1982) suggested that rarely was solidarity developed and maintained in adulthood if it had not developed in childhood. The preexisting bond between siblings in childhood was also found to be directly related to their reactions to critical events in adulthood such as sickness or loss of parents, divorce, and sickness or death of siblings.

Research results on gender differences in sibling relationships are inconclusive. Affectional ties were found to be stronger between sisters as compared to brothers and between same-sex siblings as compared with cross-sex siblings (Adams, 1968). Sisters were found to be more influential and emotionally supportive with each other than were brothers who appeared to be more competitive and jealous (Cicirelli, 1977). Scott (1983), however, did not find any gender differences in the amount of contact or in affectional ties between siblings.

Despite the availability of a sibling throughout most persons' lives, and Troll, Miller, and Atchley's (1979) suggestion that siblings are the best prospect next to adult children for providing permanent homes for older people, few siblings live together. Riley and Foner (1968) and Glick (1979) reported that approximately 5% of their subjects 65 and older lived with a sibling. No research was found that focused on trying to explain why this has not been a more viable living arrangement. The sibling relationship may provide an alternative for a significant number of the elderly whom Shanas (1979b) has called the "frail elderly" and who disproportionately are forced to enter institutionalized settings in later life. Thus, the purpose of this research was to explore the nature of the sibling relationship in later life and to assess its potential as a housing alternative. As the normal life span extends and the population shifts to an increasing number and proportion of older individuals who are single by choice, deaths, or changes in marital patterns, and who may not have children, knowledge of this potential sibling social support system as it exists in different cultural groups will become increasingly critical.

Sample Characteristics

Semi structured interviews were conducted for approximately 1½ hours in several small and medium-sized cities in a midwestern state. The cities were stratified by population size and a random selection of cities from each stratum was drawn. Retired individuals were randomly selected from the city directories and were contacted in person for possible inclusion in the study. Only persons with at least one living sibling were eligible for inclusion in the study. Seventy-eight persons were identified as eligible participants through screening interviews. Forty-one agreed to be interviewed, resulting in a 53% response rate.

Of the 41 persons involved in the study, 32% were males and 68% were females, ranging in age from 56 to 84 years with a median age of 73 years. Eighty-five percent were white and 12% were black. Eighty-eight percent identified themselves ad Protestant, 10% as Roman Catholic, and 2% as not belonging to any established religion. Most were married (56%) or widowed (37%). An additional 5% were divorced and 2% never married.

Of the number who were married, 79% were in their first marriage and 96% had been married 30 or more years. In terms of educational attainment, 39% had less than a high school education, 39% had completed high school, 7% had finished some college or professional degree, and 15% had obtained a college degree. Although all respondents considered themselves retired (81%) or full-time housewives (19%), one person worked part-time. Occupationally, 8% had been farmers, 33% had been in blue-collar occupations, 54% had been in white-collar occupations, and 5% had always been full-time housewives. The median family income was $10,000, with 56% earning less than $10,000, 31% earning between $10,000 and $19,999 and 13% earning $20,000 – $30,000 annually. The majority (88%) lived in and owned a single family dwelling and had lived in their present community for over 20 years (75%). A little over one-third (39%) of the respondents lived alone, or with one other person (39%) and the rest (22%) lived with two or more persons.

The Nature of the Sibling Relationship

The sibling relationship in middle and later life was assessed by asking about the structure, availability, geographical proximity, and emotional affinity. The frequency and type of contact between siblings was also investigated. To be included in the study, respondents had to have at least one living sibling. In this sample, the size of the living and deceased sibling systems ranged from none to ten with 46% having four or more siblings in their family. The birth orders of the respondents were evenly distributed with approximately one-fifth falling within each category of the oldest, next to oldest, a middle child, next to the youngest, and the youngest of all siblings. Twenty-nine percent had only one living sibling, 46% had two or three living siblings, and 24% had four to seven siblings still living.

Respondents were asked how far away each sibling lived. Thrity-eight percent lived less than one hour away, 16% lived one to two hours away, 14% lived between three and ten hours away, and 32% lived over ten hours from the respondent. Thus, the majority of the respondents lived in moderate-sized sibling structures and at this late stage in life still had at least two or three living siblings available to them.

Respondents were asked to rate their degree of emotional affinity to each living sibling on a five-point scale. The respondents rated 11% of their siblings as not at all or not particularly close, 22% as moderately close and 67% as quite or extremely close.

Frequency of contact with all siblings varied by type of contact. Letters were exchanged at least once a month with 17% of the siblings and several times a year with an additional 30% of the siblings. Fifty percent of the siblings were contacted by telephone at least once a month and an additional 31% were telephoned several times a year. Personal visits took place with one-third of the siblings at least monthly, one-third were visited several times a year, and one-third were visited less than once a year or never.

Frequency of contact was believed to be affected by degree of emotional affinity and by geographical proximity. Frequency of contact was correlated with degree of emotional affinity for each type of contact studied. For telephone contact the correlation was moderate (gamma = .38), for frequency of letter writing the correlation was low (gamma = -.24), and for personal visits there was almost no correlation (gamma = .10). Thus, although contact with siblings took place even if the degree of emotional affinity was low, the more personalized forms of contact were most likely to be utilized with siblings with whom the respondents felt closest.

Frequency of contacts was somewhat more highly correlated with geographical proximity than with emotional affinity. As expected, respondents were more likely to write letters to siblings living at a distance than those living close (gamma = .28), were somewhat more likely to telephone siblings living close more often those siblings at a distance (gamma = -.15) and were likely to visit siblings who lived at a distance less frequently than those siblings living nearby (gamma = -.57).

The respondents were asked additional indepth questions about the one sibling they would be willing to live with or, if unwilling to live with a sibling, the sibling to whom they felt closest. When asked about their contact with each other, two-thirds of the contacts whether by letter, telephone, or actual visiting were described as usually initiated equally by both siblings. Nearly two-thirds of the respondents indicated their visits were not due just to special occasions or emergencies. Only 18% said visits were usually due to emergencies or special occasions and of this group nearly three-fourths (73%) said they would visit as often anyway. None of the respondents reported they would like to see that sibling less than they did, 28% said they saw them just enough, and nearly two-thirds (62%) said they would like to see that sibling a little more or much more than they did at present.

Respondents were asked to choose the reasons they kept in touch with this identified sibling. Ninety-five percent indicated enjoyment was very important, 57% indicated emotional support was very important, and obligation was rated as very important by 50%. Twelve respondents volunteered other reasons for keeping in touch including family ties, caregiving, and family business. Thus, contact with siblings was described as being reciprocal, voluntary, and not as much as desired. Contact was maintained because of enjoyment, emotional support, obligation, caregiving, or family ties.

Assessing Cohabitation Potential

One of the major objectives of this study was to assess the acceptability of the idea of living with a sibling in later life when independent living was no longer possible. This was assessed in several ways. First, respondents were asked if they had ever considered alternative living arrangements if they could not live alone in later life. Those who had considered alternatives were asked about the nature of those alternatives, at what approximate age that consideration had occurred and what had prompted them to consider alternatives. The majority of the respondents (68%) indicated they had already thought about where they would like to live later in life if they could not live in their present home by themselves. Although two persons first considered alternative living arrangements prior to the age of 50, most individuals (72%) considered other living arrangements in late middle age or after retirement age. As one respondent stated, "The older you get, the more you think about it." Although a variety of critical events were given as prompting such considerations, the most frequently mentioned critical events were a change in the health of either the respondent or the spouse (32%), observing other people's situations (14%), the spouse asking what the respondent would do in such a situation (11%), and growing older (11%). Other critical events mentioned by one person each included retirement, financial reasons, a desire to be near family, loss of a close friend, weather problems, an abusive child, having children, and transportation problems. The most frequently mentioned alternatives were smaller living quarters such as an apartment or mobile home (36%), a retirement or senior citizens home (29%), living with a child (18%), and having someone come into the home to live and provide help (7%). Only one person had considered living with a sibling. Thus, living with a sibling was an alternative living arrangement that was not initially considered by 97% of the respondents.

A second way of assessing the acceptability of living with a sibling in later life was to pose a hypothetical situation. The respondents were asked:

I would like you to consider a make-believe situation. Mr. (Mrs.) Jones, who is 67, is recovering from an accident. The doctor has advised him (her) that he (she) should not try to live alone for the next year. When you visit him (her) in the hospital, he (she) asks your advice about some possible living arrangements available to him (her). There are possible living arrangements your friend could try. (Respondent has handed a card with six possible arrangements to consider.) In what order would you advise them? Begin with what you feel is most advisable and end with what you would least advise.

One person felt he could not rank the choices. Of the remaining 40 persons, almost one-fifth ranked living with a sibling as their first choice, one-fourth ranked it as their second choice, and one-third as their third choice (see Table 19.1). As a first choice, living with a sibling was less acceptable than living in a nursing home, but was comparable in ranking with living with one child or several children on a rotating basis.

The third way of assessing the acceptability of living with a sibling in later life was to ask a more direct question. All of the respondents were asked:

If you were living alone in later life and something happened that you could no longer live by yourself, would you consider living with any of your brothers or sisters for a period of time?

Table 19.1
Rank Order of Selected Living Arrangements Respondents Said They Would Suggest to a Friend (%)

Choice rank	Nursing home (n = 40)	Several children in rotation (n = 40)	Sibling (n = 39)	One child (n = 39)	Friend (n = 40)	Older parent (n = 40)
1st	32	20	18	18	13	03
2nd	18	18	23	21	15	05
3rd	05	15	33	21	08	18
4th	05	18	10	21	30	15
5th	08	20	13	15	25	20
6th	32	10	03	05	10	40
Total[a]	100	101	100	101	101	101

[a]Totals do not always add to 100 due to rounding to nearest whole percentages.

Slightly more than one-half said they would (37%) or might (17%) consider living with a sibling in later life. These proportions were essentially the same when analyzed by gender.

Several social characteristics and life experiences have been sugested by researchers as being related to sibling closeness in later life (see Table 19.2). These were factors investigated as possible predictors of willingess to live with a sibling in later life. The aforementioned question concerning willingness to live with a sibling in later life was correlated with each of these factors related to sibling closeness.

Among the social characteristics studied, willingness to live with a sibling in later life was found to be moderately correlated with age (gamma = -.30), number of children (gamma = -.40), and educational level (gamma = .41).

Several life experiences were hypothesized as possibly affecting a person's willingness to consider living with a sibling in later life (see Table 19.2). Respondents were asked if they had ever lived with a sibling previously during their adult life, who had lived with whom, the situation prompting that living arrangement, why it ended, and whether they would consider living with that sibling again. Of the total group, 49% had lived with a sibling in adulthood at least once. Living with a sibling in adulthood was more common among the male respondents (62%) than among the female respondents (43%). Of the 20 respondents who had lived with a sibling in adulthood, 75% had lived with a sister and 25% had lived with a brother. In 50% of the cases, it was a sister-sister living arrangement, 45% were brother-sister arrangements, and one case was a brother-brother arrangement. In 90% of the living arrangements, a female was the host sibling. Thus, men were somewhat more likely to live with a sibling than were women, but when a sibling, male or female, went to live with another sibling, it was usually to a female sibling's home. In only one case each did a brother move in with a brother and a sister move in with a brother.

Nearly three-fourths of the cohabiting siblings lived together for more than one year, and 48% cohabited for over three years. Siblings reported living together for both functional and emotionally supportive reasons. The most frequent reason given was financially related (53%), with the most frequent financial need being that one sibling was unemployed and the other sibling provided both a job and housing. Other financial reasons included providing housing following a return of one sibling from the military service and providing housing while one sibling completed college. The second most frequent reason siblings lived together was

Table 19.2
Willingness to Live with a Sibling in Later Life by Selected Social Characteristics and Life Experiences[a]

Social characteristics and life experiences	(n)	Willingness to live with a sibling			Correlation with willingness to live with a sibling
		Yes (%)	Maybe (%)	No (%)	
Age of respondent					-.30[b]
56–64	(07)	43	00	57	
65–74	(18)	61	17	22	
75–84	(16)	06	25	69	
Gender of respondent					0[c]
Male	(13)	31	23	46	
Female	(28)	39	14	47	
Marital status					.14[c]
Married	(23)	39	22	39	
Divorced	(02)	100	00	00	
Widowed	(15)	20	13	57	
Never married	(01)	100	00	00	
Number of children					-.40[b]
None	(07)	57	14	28	
1–3	(19)	42	16	42	
4–7	(15)	20	20	60	
Household membership					.24[b]
Lives alone	(16)	31	13	56	
Lives with another	(25)	40	20	40	
Ethnicity					.05[c]
White	(35)	40	20	40	
Black	(05)	00	00	100	
Other	(01)	100	00	00	
Educational level					.41[b]
< High school degree	(16)	19	19	62	
High school, non-college degree	(19)	37	16	47	
College degree	(06)	83	17	00	
Occupational head of household					.10[c]
Farmer	(03)	00	67	33	
Blue collar	(13)	39	15	46	
White collar	(21)	48	09	43	
Housewife	(02)	00	00	100	

Table 19.2 *(Continued)*

Social characteristics and life experiences	(n)	Willingness to live with a sibling			Correlation with willingness to live with a sibling
		Yes (%)	Maybe (%)	No (%)	
Family income					.27[b]
< $10,000	(22)	33	23	54	
$10,000–19,999	(12)	59	08	33	
$20,000–29,999	(05)	60	00	40	
Religious affiliation					.14[c]
Protestant	(36)	33	17	50	
Catholic	(04)	75	25	00	
None	(01)	00	00	100	
Church attendance					.05[b]
Never, once/month	(17)	47	18	35	
1–3/Month	(09)	11	11	78	
Weekly or more	(15)	40	20	40	
Importance of religion					-.16[b]
Not at all, not very	(02)	50	00	50	
Somewhat	(05)	40	20	40	
Important, very important	(34)	32	18	50	
Living with a sibling in adulthood					0[c]
Yes	(20)	35	20	45	
No	(21)	38	14	48	
Know siblings living together					0[c]
Yes	(12)	42	08	50	
No	(29)	34	21	45	
Closeness in childhood, teenage years					.25[b]
Not at all close	(07)	13	00	26	
Somewhat	(01)	00	00	05	
Fairly	(07)	07	29	21	
Quite	(14)	53	29	21	
Extremely	(12)	27	43	26	
Closeness in early adult years					.41[b]
Not at all close	(00)	00	00	00	
Somewhat	(05)	13	00	16	
Fairly	(15)	13	57	47	
Quite	(10)	27	29	21	
Extremely	(11)	47	14	16	

(continued)

Table 19.2 *(Continued)*

Social characteristics and life experiences	(n)	Willingness to live with a sibling			Correlation with willingness to live with a sibling
		Yes (%)	Maybe (%)	No (%)	
Closeness in middle age (45-retirement)					.65[b]
Not at all close	(00)	00	00	00	
Somewhat	(03)	07	00	11	
Fairly	(11)	00	29	47	
Quite	(15)	40	43	32	
Extremely	(12)	53	29	11	
Closeness across life span					.18[b]
Less close over years	(04)	20	00	05	
Unchanged over years	(15)	40	71	21	
Up and down	(03)	07	00	11	
Increasingly close	(19)	33	29	63	

[a]N =42.   [c]Lambda
[b]Gamma $*p < .05$, two-tailed.

because of the absence of a family environment (35%) for one or both siblings. This was usually due to the death of a parent or spouse.

Respondents were asked about the advantages and disadvantages of that shared living arrangement and the reasons for its termination. The advantages perceived included sharing of financial resources, companionship, emotional support, exchange of services, and a sense of having been able to help a sibling in a time of need. When asked about the problematic aspects of this living arrangement and why the shared living was terminated, most could not recall any major problems. The few problems reported included two persons for whom differences in personality or living habits were issues. One respondent indicated that the spouse of the sibling was alcoholic and abusive. Two respondents related problems due to overcrowding and lack of space. The shared living arrangement ended most frequently because (1) the critical event prompting the shared living arrangement ended (i.e., jobs were found or jobs or schooling ended), (2) a change occurred in the family structure (i.e., one sibling married) or (3) the specified time for living together ended (i.e., it was only intended to be seasonal or for a specified period).

It was hypothesized that having had a previous experience with a sibling-sibling living arrangement in adulthood that was positive might make a person more willing to consider living with a sibling again in later life. This hypothesis was not supported by the data. The respondents were almost equally divided in their willingness to live with that sibling again, 55% indicated they would or might, and 45% indicated they would not. This was true for those who reported problematic or negative shared-living experiences as well as for those who reported no major problems. Thus, nearly one-half of the respondents had lived with a sibling at least once during adulthood, and of these, 55% would or might consider living with that sibling again in later life.

It was hypothesized that knowing siblings who lived together might affect people's willingness to consider the living arrangement for themselves. This was not found to be the case as respondents were nearly equally divided in their willingness to consider living with a sibling when controlled for acquaintance with siblings living together (see Table 19.2).

Although closeness in childhood was suggested by Ross and Milgram (1982) to be the best predictor of closeness in adulthood, in this study closeness in childhood was not strongly correlated with willingness to live with a sibling in later life (gamma = .25) (see Table 19.2). Closeness in early adulthood (leaving home to age 45) and closeness in middle age (45 to retirement) were found to be moderately and strongly correlated with willingness to live with a sibling in later life (gamma = .41 and .65, respectively). Consistency of closeness across the life span was not found to be highly correlated with willingness to live with a sibling (gamma = .18). Of all the relationships analyzed and reported in Table 19.2, only closeness in middle age was found to be significant at the .05 level, and therefore generalizable beyond this sample. Thus, among respondents in this study, willingness to live with a sibling in later life was found to be most related to increasing age, a higher level of education, fewer children, and emotional affinity with a sibling, particularly in their current stage of life.

In an effort to understand why persons would or would not consider living with a sibling in later life, several questions were asked. Respondents who said they would consider living with a sibling in later life and who named a particular sibling were asked, "Why would you consider living with that particular sibling?" Most frequently mentioned reasons were social and nonobligatory in nature: that they felt they would get along well, that they enjoyed each other's company, or that their personalities and views on life were similar. Less frequently mentioned reasons were more functional and obligatory in nature: that the health of one sibling was good and the other needed assistance because of poor health, they disliked living alone, they would have a place to live, it would provide mutual help, and this sibling was the only living sibling.

Persons who would not consider living with a sibling or who were uncertain about wanting to live with a sibling in later life were asked, "Why is it you would not consider living with one of your brothers or sisters?" The most frequent reasons given were that they were concerned they would not get along or that their lifestyles or dispositions were too different. Other reasons included: They preferred to live with one of their children; they preferred to be alone or independent; they didn't want to be a burden or to interfere with their sibling's life; they felt either their own or their sibling's health would be a problem; their siblings were too old; they lived too far apart; and they felt their siblings would not agree to the idea. Thus, a desire to help one's siblings, how well they felt they would get along, and perceived similarity of interests and viewpoints were the major factors on which willingness to consider living with a sibling was based.

Summary

The 41 respondents in this study indicated that nearly three-fourths had two or more siblings still living, 38% of the living siblings lived one hour or less travel time from the respondents, and an additional 16% lived between one and three hours away. Two-thirds of the living siblings were rated as being quite or extremely close emotionally to the respondents. One-third to one-half of all living siblings were contacted at least monthly by letter, telephone or personal visits. Of the three types of contact studied, telephone contact was most strongly associated with emotional affinity, and personal visits were most strongly associated with geographical proximity to the respondents. Contact with the sibling they felt closest to or the sibling they would live with was described as reciprocal, voluntary, less frequent than desired, and maintained because of enjoyment, emotional support, obligation, caregiving, and/or family ties.

Respondents were asked about their willingness to live with a sibling in later life. While only one respondent had previously considered living with a sibling in later life, slightly over one-half said they would or might consider it in the future. When asked to rank six alternative living arrangements in a hypothetical case, living with a sibling was less acceptable than living in a nursing home as a first choice, but comparable in rank order to living with one or more children on a rotating basis.

Although nearly one-half of the respondents had lived with a sibling in adulthood for emotional and functional reasons and most recalled it as a positive experience, this experience was not found to be related to their willingness to live with that sibling again in later life. In 90% of the living arrangements a female was the host sibling. Willingness to live with a sibling in later life was found to be most acceptable to those persons with a higher level of education, few children, and a feeling of closeness to the chosen sibling. For most respondents, their willingness to live with a sibling was because they wanted to help a sibling, they felt they would get along, they enjoyed each other's company, or they felt their personalities and views on life were similar.

This study goes beyond previous research in that some of the data were collected on the whole sibling constellation of each respondent rather than on only one identified sibling. Second, it gathered data on an assistance or help pattern not considered in previous research, namely the host function. Previous research indicates that the sibling role does not carry with it an obligation to interact with or to exchange services with other siblings. This research found that many siblings expressed a desire for contact and interaction with their siblings and a desire to help a sibling in the time of need even if the assistance was not an obligatory function of the sibling role. Because most of the questions focused on whether persons would consider living with a sibling in later life, data are not available as to if they would actually do this in the future. Research is needed to assess the situation of siblings who actually decide to live together. What are the characteristics of siblings who choose to live together? How is that decision made? What is the quality of that living arrangement? What makes such a living arrangement successful? Living with a sibling was not initially considered as an alternative living arrangement, but it appeared to become a more acceptable alternative after some consideraton. If the dynamics and strengths of this living arrangement were understood, educators, therapists, and other helping professionals might encourage families and older persons to consider this alternative. With a sibling structure available to many who do not have children or other family members to care for them in later life, it may be that this would be a viable alternative, particularly for those whom Shanas has referred to as the "frail elderly," those most likely to enter institutional living in later life.

Chapter 20

Adult Day Care Participation among Impaired Elderly

Charles M. Barresi
Department of Sociology
and
Institute for Life Span Development and Gerontology
The University of Akron
Akron, Ohio 44325
Donna J. McConnell
Mahoning County Transitional Homes
Youngstown, Ohio 44504

According to the gerontological literature, there is a movement away from institutional care toward community-based services. Some residents in nursing homes do not need 24-hour skilled nursing care although they do need some assistance in order to live in the community. In addition, families reluctantly place their elderly relatives in nursing homes and do so only after various solutions have been attempted (Dunlop, 1980; Shanas, 1979a; Ward, 1985). In response to these concerns, adult day care and other community-based care have been given growing attention as an alternative to nursing home care (Capitman, 1986; Goldstein, 1983).

It has been found that the majority of the elderly population are able to live independently without help; however, a small percentage have severe limitations that place them at risk of being institutionalized. Jette and Branch (1981) investigated the noninstitutional elderly of Framingham, Massachusetts and found that the vast majority were self-sufficient. However, 7% of the respondents reported needing assistance

Revision of a paper presented at the 37th Annual Scientific Meeting of the Gerontological Society of America, San Antonio, Texas, November 16-20, 1984. The authors would like to thank John Allen, Ronald Huiatt, and the Summit Senior's Team Corporation, for making the PISCES Project data available. Dennis Byrne and Geoffrey Greer provided helpful suggestions with the analysis.

to perform one or more of the basic activities of daily living. In another investigation (Branch & Jette, 1981) 6% of the respondents had unmet social needs. Clearly, these studies indicate that within this population there are people who urgently need assistance in order to live independently within the community.

In recent years, adult day care has increasingly been offered as a noninstitutional long-term program. Weissert (1976, 1977) has defined two discrete models of adult day care. Model I, a medical model, provides skilled care for clients who frequently are discharged hospital patients. Model II provides less skilled care with more emphasis on social orientation.

Adult day care in this study is defined as Model II, in which the older adult is provided with social activities, and nutritional and health care services under a protective environment during the day. Although the types of day care services have been defined, and several studies (Wan, Weissert, & Livieratos, 1980; Wan & Weissert, 1981; Weissert, Wan, Liverieratos, & Katz, 1980) have done a comparative analysis of day care with homemaker services or nursing home admissions (Arling, Harkins, & Romaniuk, 1984; Weissert, 1978), individual characteristics of adult day care clients in comparison with community impaired elderly remains untapped. Ullmer, Abrahams, & Brown (1982) have provided additional information in defining the target group of elderly who are in need of adult day care services. However, their study is limited to various activities of daily living. The present study includes a broader range of variables, thus providing a more practical identification of those elderly persons who are prospective day care clients.

The purpose of this study is (a) to provide a more comprehensive analysis of characteristics that distinguish adult day care participants and (b) to determine if they are a group of people distinguishable from other impaired elderly residing in the community. Figure 20.1 illustrates a model of those variables which are identified in the above literature as being related to day care participation among impaired elderly.

Methods

Sample

The data for the community elderly in this study were obtained from a 1981 study of older adults residing in Summit County, Ohio by the Program for an Integrated System of Community Elderly Services. This

Impaired elderly   Domains   Discriminating variables

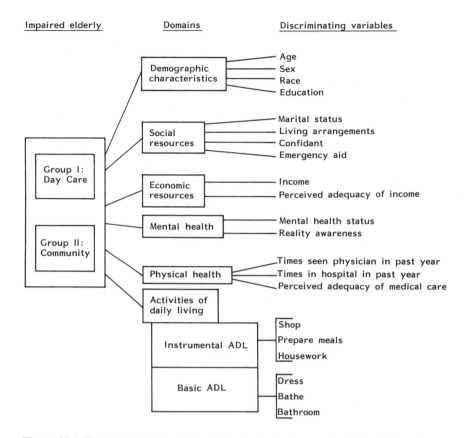

Figure 20.1. Relationship between impaired elderly adults and discriminating variables.

program, known locally as the PISCES Project, is one of eight national demonstration projects funded by the Robert Wood Johnson Foundation to survey, evaluate, and integrate the diverse array of services needed by elderly citizens with health problems (Barresi & McConnell, 1984).

The survey employed a two-stage random sampling procedure. In the initial stage, a list of addresses were randomly selected from the list of 50,000 elderly residents of Summit County who are Golden Buckeye cardholders, a state-wide discount system for persons over 65 years of age. This list contains approximately 70% of all Summit County elders.

A second stage supplemental area probability sampling procedure was also utilized to increase the representativeness of the total sample and to be more certain that some homogeneous categories such as the extremely impaired, highly independent, low or high income elderly were included. The list and supplemental samples resulted in approximately 700 potential respondents each. A total of 1,139 completed interviews were obtained for an 81% response rate. The demographic characteristics of the resulting sample do not vary significantly from those of the total county elderly population.

The data for the adult day care were collected in 1982 by face-to-face interviews of 50 elderly adults, 60 years of age and older, who attended a day care center in Summit County, Ohio. This day care is based on the Model II concept and provides social and recreational services to both private-pay and Title XX participants. The latter make up approximately 90% of the daily census. Of the total number of 56 participants available for interviews, two refused and four were not available during the interview period. This provided an 89% response rate.

Measurement Instrument

The Duke University Older Americans Resources and Services (OARS) multidimensional functional assessment questionnaire was used in this study (Duke University, 1978). The OARS instrument has been found to be a valid and reliable measure of the conditions and needs of the elderly (Fillenbaum & Smyer, 1981). It assesses the functioning level of the older adult on each of the five domains:

1. Social resources
2. Economic resources
3. Mental health
4. Physical health
5. Activities of daily living (ADL)

Each respondent is rated on each of the five domains in a six-point scale. They are identified as having excellent or good capacity in the domain or as being mildly, moderately, severely or completely impaired according to their present level of performance in the domain. Professional interviewers were thoroughly trained in the use of the OARS instrument.

The General Accounting Office (Comptroller General, 1977) in a study of Cleveland elderly, devised a composite eight-point scale describing overall impairment levels. This scale considers the scores of the individual on the five domains of the OARS instrument and translates them into a single "well-being" description. The categories of well-being and their descriptions are:

1. Unimpaired—excellent or good in all five domains of functioning.
2. Slightly Impaired—excellent or good in four domains.
3. Mildly Impaired—mildly or moderately impaired in two areas, or mildly or moderately impaired in one domain and severely or completely impaired in another.
4. Moderately Impaired—mildly or moderately impaired in three domains, or mildly or moderately impaired in two and severely impaired in one.
5. Generally Impaired—mildly or moderately impaired in four domains.
6. Greatly Impaired—mildly or moderately impaired in three domains and severely or completely impaired in another.
7. Very Greatly Impaired—mildly or moderately impaired in all five domains.
8. Extremely Impaired—mildly or moderately impaired in four areas and severely or completely impaired in two or more domains.

From each of the samples, those individuals classified either as generally impaired, greatly impaired, very greatly impaired, or extremely impaired were selected for analysis. This eliminated all those elderly in both the day care and community samples who are unimpaired or are evaluated as only slightly, mildly, or moderately impaired. A total of 35 impaired day care clients and 116 impaired community elderly were used in the study.

While this decision eliminates any generalization regarding day care clients who are less impaired, it also eliminates any invidious comparisons. For example, there are no unimpaired among the day care sample, while 48% of the community elderly were so rated. Furthermore, comparison of the percentage distribution of persons in the four well-being categories of generally through extremely impaired reveals a close approximation between the two samples. This gives further strength to the decision to limit the analysis to those respondents who are classified as generally impaired or worse.

Indeed, when the two samples are compared on the usual social correlates using a t-test of means, we find that they are generally similar with no significant differences in age, sex, education, living arrangement or income range. The only differences noted regard race (the day care sample has proportionately more blacks) and marital status (the community elderly sample is proportionately more married). In addition, comparing the use of homemaker services in the past six months indicates no statistically significant differences between the two samples.

Measures

The independent variables include: social resources, economic resources, mental health, physical health, activities of daily living, and demographic characteristics. Based on previous studies (Kohen, 1983; Wan & Weissert, 1981) social resources are measured by the following four indicators that address the availability of social networks: marital status, measured as (1) married or (0) widowed, divorced, separated or never married; living arrangement measured as (1) for those living with others and (0) for those who live alone; presence of a confidant as measured by having someone outside of the home to trust and confide in, (1) yes and (0) no; and finally the availability of someone who can provide emergency help, (1) yes and (0) no.

Economic resources are measured by an income ladder ranging from (1) 0–$499 up to (13) $40,000 or more. Respondents were also asked their perception of the adequacy of their income with responses scored as (1) poorly, (2) fairly well, or (3) very well.

Mental health is measured by two indicators of mental status. Reality awareness is determined by a series of preliminary questions with the number of errors coded from 0 to 10. A brief MMPI Test indicates the degree of emotional impairment in each respondent with scores ranging from 0 to 15.

The physical health of respondents is measured by three items. The first two identify the number of times a medical doctor was seen and/or the number of hospital stays experienced in the last 12 months. The last question in this domain asked for the respondent's perception regarding the need for more medical treatment. A yes is coded as (1) and no (0).

An index of Activities of Daily Living (ADL) was constructed for both instrumental and basic ADL. This follows suggestions from previous studies (Branch & Jette, 1983; Stoller & Earl, 1983) to differentiate between the two types for more accurate measure of functional abilities. Instrumental ADL include functioning levels in grocery shopping, meal preparation, and housework. Basic ADL consist of dressing, bathing, and toileting. A score of (1) is assigned for those who can function without assistance in each of the functioning levels, otherwise a score of (0) is assigned. The IADL and BADL indexes are computed from the sum of the total scores in each type of daily activity.

The final set of independent variables selected for this analysis consists of four demographic characteristics: age, race, sex, and education. Those who reported their age as between 60 through 74 are scored (0), and those indicating their age as 75 and over are scored (1). These two age cohorts distinguish between the "young-old" and the "old-old" (Neugarten, 1974). Sex is measured as (1) male and (0) female. Race is measured as (1) white and (0) non white, whereas education is measured in intervals of completed education ranging from (1) indicating 0 to 4 years of schooling up to (8) designating postgraduate college.

Results

The data were analyzed using a multiple stepwise discriminant analysis (MDA). Discriminant analysis is a technique which weights and linearly combines the discriminating variables into two or more classes or categories that are made as statistically distinct as possible. This method determines the optimum coefficient for each predictor variable so that it will produce the maximum separation between the discriminant scores for the classes. These variables are seen as comprising a discriminant function that distinguishes between them. Disciminant analysis can also be used to classify persons, on the basis of these variables, into one of several mutually exclusive and exhaustive groups. MDA can thus serve both the purpose of analysis and classification of data, and is particularly useful in determining the multivariate effects on predicting class or group membership (Klecka, 1980, Legge & Ziegler, 1979).

The 17 discriminating variables which are identified in Figure 20.1 were entered into the MDA to determine their relative power in distinguishing between those elderly persons who are more likely to use day care facilities and those who are not. The Rao method of MDA was selected because it identifies those variables which produce the largest increase in *Rao's V*. *Rao's V* is a generalized measure of the overall separation between the groups.

Discriminators of Day Care Participation

Table 20.1 shows that 10 of the 17 variables contribute enough discriminating power to be included in the analysis. In order of the changes in *Rao's V* marital status, mental health, reality orientation, income, living arrangement, age, perceived adequacy of income, physical health, and sex are the most important variables. The significance level for the

Table 20.1
Summary Table for Discriminators of Day Care Participation According to Step Entered, Multivariate *F* Ratio, and Change in *Rao's V*

Step variable	*F* ratio (Multivariate)	*Rao's V*	Change in *Rao's V*	Significance of change
1. Mental health	5.84*	14.83	14.83	.000
2. Reality orientation	6.72*	25.61	10.77	.001
3. Living arrangement	14.96*	33.25	7.65	.006
4. Marital status	22.16*	50.31	17.06	.000
5. Income	5.36*	60.62	10.31	.001
6. Age	5.25*	67.12	6.50	.011
7. Physical health	3.57*	71.65	4.54	.033
8. Sex	1.57ns	75.45	3.80	.051
9. Confidant	4.35*	78.03	2.58	.108
10. Adequacy of income	2.95*	83.44	5.41	.020

F insufficient to enter analysis beyond this step ($F < 1.0$)

11. Race
12. Education
13. Emergency aid available
14. Times in hospital in past year
15. Perceived adequacy of medical care
16. Instrumental activities of daily living
17. Basic activities of daily living

Overall $F = 7.68*$ (10,104)

*$p < .01$ (significance of *F* ratio).

change in *Rao's V* is less than .05 for each of these variables. The presence of a confidant contributes to the separation of the elderly into the two groups, but is less important.

Variables which did not contribute to the separation, when all the other variables are taken into account are: race, education, availability of emergency aid, number of times in the hospital in the past year, perceived adequacy of medical care, and both instrumental and basic activities of daily living.

The analysis created one discriminant function as shown in Table 20.2. The linear combination of variables produce the ability to separate the elderly in the sample into two groups according the likelihood of using or participating in a day care setting. The amount of variance in the discriminant function explained by the classifying variables is 42.3%.

The analysis identified the group centroids, or means of the discriminant function, as positive for the community group and negative for the day care group (Table 20.3). A positive coefficient indicates that a high score on the variable is associated with being in the community and a negative coefficient indicates that persons with high scores on the variable are more likely to be day care participants.

The profile that emerges is that those persons in the sample who are more likely to use day care are younger, more often widowed, divorced,

Table 20.2
Standardized Discriminant Function Coefficients

Variable	Coefficients
Age (60-74 = 0, 75 = 1)	.36*
Sex (female = 0, male = 1)	-.22
Marital status (non-married = 0, married = 1)	.91
Living arrangement (live alone = 0, live with others = 1)	-.68*
Confidant (no = 0, yes =1)	.66*
Income (low = 0, high = 13)	-.37*
Adequacy of income (poor = 1, fair = 2, very well = 3)	-.56*
Mental health (excellent = 0, very poor = 15)	.51*
Reality orientation (excellent = 0, very poor = 10)	-.41*
Physical health (excellent = 0, very poor = 10)	.29*
Canonical correlation	Rc = .65**
Variance explained by classifying variables	Rc^2 = .423

*$p < .01$.
**$p < .001$.

Table 20.3
Canonical Discriminant Functions Evaluated at Group Means
(Group Centroids)

Group	Mean
Day care	-1.43
Community	0.50

or never married; they more often live with others than alone; are less likely to have a confidant; have more income and perceive that income as adequate; have fewer emotional disturbances, are more likely to be disoriented, but are in overall better physical health. The larger the magnitude of the coefficient, the greater the contribution of that variable as a discriminator between the two groups.

Classification of Cases

The last part of the analysis is the evaluation of the degree to which the discriminant function allows for the correct classification of cases into groups using the discriminating variables. As shown in the Table 20.4, the percentage of "grouped" cases correctly classified is 82.8%. This is a 32.8% increase over chance assignment. This is also a 66% improvement over the assignment of cases on the basis of prior probabilities.

Table 20.4
Classification Results—Percent of Cases Correctly Classified
According to Group Membership[a]

Actual Group	n	Predicted group membership	
		Group 1	Group 2
1. Day care	35	71.4[b]	28.6
2. Community	93[c]	12.9	87.1[b]

[a]Percentage of "grouped" cases correctly classified for total sample: 82.8.
[b]Percentage correctly classified in each group.
[c]Only 93 cases were used in the analysis.

The variables in this analysis are somewhat better at identifying community impaired individuals because only 12.9% are incorrectly identified as compared with 28.6% of the day care participants who are identified as community persons.

Interpretation and Discussion

The results of this study, similar to those of Ullmer et al. (1982), indicate that those persons who participate in adult day care make up a distinct group. The profile of characteristics provided by the function gives us an overall description of typical day care participants.

When the standardized function coefficients are ranked in order of magnitude, a pattern begins to emerge by which the discriminant function can be identified (Table 20.5). The variables with the three largest coefficients are all in the social resources domain. More importantly, when these coefficients are more closely examined we see an underlying dimension of dependence–independence emerging.

Table 20.5
Discriminators of Adult Day Care Participation by Rank Order of Standardized Function Coefficient and Variable Domain[a]

Variable	Coefficients	Domain
Marital status	.91	
Living arrangement	-.68	Social resources
Confidant	.66	
Adequacy of income	-.56	Economic
Mental health	.51	Mental health
Reality orientation	-.41	
Income	-.37	Economic
Age	.36	Demographic
Physical health	.29	Physical health

[a] A positive coefficient denotes a high score on the variable is associated with being in the community. A negative coefficient denotes a high score on the variable is associated with day care participation.

Those persons who are not married and are living with others are more usually in a dependent condition than those elderly who are married and living with spouse. Another facet of this dependence is also indicated by the lack of a confidant as reported by the typical day care participant.

The second domain that the function highlights is the economic. Day care users report higher income and perceive their income as adequate for their needs. This domain clearly illustrates that despite their use of Title XX assistance, day care participants are economically better off than their community counterparts. While the absolute measure of income would seem to place them in a higher category than community elderly, the relative judgment of adequacy of income might be a further indicator of the dependent condition of the day care population. Because of this dependent condition, they may perceive their income as adequate in relative terms.

Mental health is the third domain that is seen in the discriminant function. The day care elderly display better mental health by virtue of the assessment of fewer emotional disturbances. They are also more disoriented when given a series of questions to determine their acuity regarding everyday matters. Apparently the condition of dependency can contribute to an overall better outlook on life and reduce worries while at the same time creating a condition in which the elderly person is so sheltered as to be "out of touch" with day-to-day events.

The remaining coefficients that make up the discriminant function indicate that day care participants are younger and in better health. Ordinarily, it would seem that these characteristics would indicate an ability to remain in the community group, but given the dependent condition as indicated by the social resources indicators, it is apparent that they do not prevent the elderly person from being placed in the day care setting. Indeed, if these persons, given their dependent condition, were older and in poorer health, they would no doubt be placed in a permanent long-term care setting.

In summary, there is a distinct group of elderly that day care facilities serve. Given the underlying dimension of dependence, those unmarried elderly living with family members are more often labeled as dependent. It may be that those elderly who are in the community are in many ways dependent also, but because there is no one there to observe their failings they do not become labeled as dependent and are thus allowed to continue in a community setting until they are absolutely incapable of managing for themselves. The situation might be likened to the adolescent who is capable of more mature behavior than his/her doting parents will allow. The relationship between social labeling and decreasing competence among the elderly has been clearly stated by Kuypers and Bengtson (1973). The argument they make regarding increasing dependence and the lack of self-confidence that comes about through social labeling following role loss, role changes, and lack of supportive reference group seems to apply to day care participants.

This should not be interpreted as meaning that day care centers create or contribute to dependence among elderly clients. Indeed, the staff of the day care center used in this study reported that clients usually display increased levels of social skills and independence after a number of months of attendance. This analysis does, however, call into question the role of social supports of the elderly and day care participation.

References

Adams, B. (1968). *Kinship in an urban setting.* Chicago: Markham.

Adams, D. (1969). Analysis of a life satisfaction index. *Journal of Gerontology, 24,* 470-474.

Ade-Ridder, L., & Brubaker, T. (1983a). The quality of long-term marriages. In T. Brubaker (Ed.), *Family relationships in later life* (pp. 21-30). Beverly Hills, CA: Sage.

Ade-Ridder, L., & Brubaker, T. (1983b). Sexuality and marital quality of community and residential older couples. *The Gerontologist, 23,* 236. (Abstract)

Aldous, J. (1978). *Family careers: Developmental changes in families.* New York: Wiley.

Allan, G. (1977). Sibling solidarity. *Journal of Marriage and the Family, 39,* 177-184.

Andersen, R., & Newman, J. (1973). Societal and individual determinants of medical care utilization in the United States. *Milbank Memorial Fund Quarterly, 51,* 95-124.

Anderson, S., Russell, C., & Schumm, W. (1983). Perceived marital quality and family life-cycle categories: A further analysis. *Journal of Marriage and the Family, 45,* 127-139.

Arling, G., Harkins, E., & Romaniuk, M. (1984). Adult day care and the nursing home. *Research on Aging, 6,* 225-241.

Arth, M. (1980). American culture and the phenomenon of friendship in the aged. In C. Tibbitts & W. Donahue (Eds.), *Social and psychological aspects of aging* (pp. 529-546). New York: Arno.

Atchley, R. (1976). Selected social and psychological differences between men and women in later life. *Journal of Gerontology, 31,* 204-211.

Atchley, R. (1976). *The sociology of retirement.* Cambridge, MA: Schenkman.

Atchley, R. (1980). *The social forces in later life* (3rd ed.). Belmont, CA: Wadsworth.

Atchley, R. (1982). The process of retirement: Comparing women and men. In M. Szinovacz (Ed.), *Women's retirement* (pp. 153-168). Beverly Hills, CA: Sage.

Atchley, R. (1985). *Social forces and aging* (4th ed.). Belmont, CA: Wadsworth.

Atchley, R., & Miller, S. (1983). Types of elderly couples. In T. Brubaker (Ed.), *Family relationships in later life* (pp. 77-90). Beverly Hills, CA: Sage.

Bain, C. (1974). *Marital adjustment of golden wedding anniversary couples.* Master's thesis, Virginia Polytechnic Institute and State University, Blacksburg.

Ballweg, J. (1967). Resolution of conjugal role adjustment after retirement. *Journal of Marriage and the Family, 29,* 277-281.

Bank, S., & Kahn, M. (1975). Sisterhood-brotherhood is powerful: Sibling sub-systems and family therapy. *Family Process, 14,* 311-337.

Bank, S., & Kahn, M. (1982). *The sibling bond.* New York: Basic Books.

Bankoff, E. (1983). Aged parents and their widowed daughters: A support relationship. *Journal of Gerontology, 38,* 226-230.

Baranowski, M. (1982). Grandparent-adolescent relations: Beyond the nuclear family.

Adolescence, 17, 575-584.

Barranti, C. (1985). The grandparent/grandchild relationship: Family resource in an era of voluntary bonds. *Family Relations, 34,* 343-352.

Barresi, C., & McConnell, D. (1984). *Service utilization and service needs: Final Report of the PISCES project. A survey of Summit County's older adults.* Akron, OH: Summit Senior's Team Corporation.

Barrett-Lennard, G. (1962). Dimensions of therapist response as causal factors in therapeutic change. *Psychological Monographs, 76,* 43.

Baum, M., & Baum, R. (1980). *Growing old: A societal perspective.* Englewood Cliffs, NJ: Prentice-Hall.

Beam, W. (1979). College students' perceptions of family strengths. In N. Stinnett, B. Chesser, & J. DeFrain (Eds.), *Building family strengths* (pp. 31-37). Lincoln, NE: University of Nebraska Press.

Bengtson, V. (1985). Diversity and symbolism in grandparental roles. In V. Bengston & J. Robertson (Eds.), *Grandparenthood* (pp. 11-25). Beverly Hills: Sage.

Berger, P., & Kellner, H. (1964). Marriage and the construction of reality: An exercise in the microsociology of knowledge. *Diogenes, 46,* 1-23.

Bernard, J. (1972). *The future of marriage.* New York: World Publishing.

Bernard, J. (1982). *The future of marriage.* New Haven, CT: Yale University Press.

Besdine, R. (1981). Health and illness behavior in the elderly. In D. Parron, & J. Rodin (Eds.), *Health, behavior, and aging* (pp. 15-24). Washington, DC: National Academy Press.

Bianchi, S., & Spain, D. (1983). *American women: Three decades of change* (No. CDS 80-8). Washington, DC: Bureau of the Census, U.S. Government Printing Office.

Birren, J., Butler, R., Greenhouse, S., Sokoloff, L., & Yarrow, M. (1963). *Human aging* (U.S. Public Health Service Publication No. 986). Washington, DC: U.S. Government Printing Office.

Blood, R., & Wolfe, D. (1960). *Husbands and wives.* New York: Free Press.

Branch, L., & Jette, A. (1981). The Framingham disability study: Social disability among the aging. *American Journal of Public Health, 71,* 1202-1210.

Branch, L. & Jette, A. (1983). Elders' use of informal long-term care assistance. *The Gerontologist, 23,* 51-56.

Brim, O., Jr. (1976). Theories of the male midlife crisis. *Counseling Psychologist, 6,* 2-9.

Brown, A. (1974). Satisfying relationships for the elderly and their patterns of disengagement. *The Gerontologist, 14,* 258-262.

Brubaker, T. (1983). Introduction. In T. Brubaker (Ed.), *Family relationships in later life* (pp. 9-18). Beverly Hills, CA: Sage.

Brubaker, T. (1985a). *Later life families.* Beverly Hills, CA: Sage.

Brubaker, T. (1985b). Responsibility for household tasks: A look at golden wedding anniversary couples aged 75 years and older. In W. Peterson & J. Quadagono (Eds.), *Social bonds in later life* (pp. 27-36). Beverly Hills, CA: Sage.

Brubaker, T., & Ade-Ridder, L. (1986). Husbands' responsibility for household tasks in older marriages: Does living situation make a difference? In R. Lewis & R. Salt (Eds), *Men in families* (pp. 85-96). Beverly Hills, CA: Sage.

Brubaker, T., & Brubaker, E. (1984). Family support of older persons in long-term care: Recommendations for practice. In W. Quinn & G. Hughston (Eds.), *Independent aging: Family and social systems perspectives* (pp. 106-114). Rockville, MD: Aspen Systems.

Brubaker, T., & Hennon, C. (1982). Responsibility for household tasks: Comparing dual-earner and dual-retired marriages. In M. Szinovacz (Ed.), *Women's retirement: Policy implications of recent research* (pp. 205-219) Beverly Hills, CA: Sage.

Bull, C., & Aucoin, J. (1975). Voluntary association participation and life satisfaction: A replication note. *Journal of Gerontology, 30,* 73-76.

Bultena, D., Powers, E., Falkman, P., & Frederick, D. (1971). Life after 70 in Iowa. *Sociology Report, 95.* Ames, IA: Iowa State University Press.

Burgess, E., & Wallin, P. (1953). *Engagement and marriage.* Philadelphia: Lippincott.

Cameron, P. (1968). Masculinity/femininity of the aged. *Journal of Gerontology, 23,* 63-65.

Cameron, P. (1976). Masculinity/femininity of the generations: As self-reported as stereotypically appraised. *International Journal of Aging and Human Development, 7,* 143-151.

Cameron P., & Biber, H. (1973). Sexual thought throughout the life-span. *The Gerontologist, 13,* 144-147.

Campbell, A., Converse, P., & Rodgers, W. (1976). Marriage and family life. In *The quality of American life: Evaluations and satisfactions* (pp. 321-346). New York: Russell Sage.

Campbell, D., & Stanley, J. (1963). *Experimental and quasi-experimental designs for research.* Chicago: Rand-McNally.

Capitman, J. (1986). Community-based long-term care models, target groups, and impacts on service use. *The Gerontologist, 26,* 389-397.

Cavan, R., Burgess, E., Havighurst, R., & Goldhamer, J. (1949). *Personal adjustment in old age.* Chicago: Science Research Associates.

Cherlin, A., & Furstenberg, F. (1985). Styles and strategies of grandparenting. In V. Bengston & J. Robertson (Eds.), *Grandparenthood* (pp. 97-116). Beverly Hills, CA: Sage.

Chiriboga, D. (1982). Adaptation to marital separation in later and earlier life. *Journal of Gerontology, 37,* 109-114.

Cicirelli, V. (1977). Relationships of siblings to the elderly person's feelings and concerns. *Journal of Gerontology, 32,* 317-322.

Cicirelli, V. (1980). Sibling relationships in adulthood: A life span perspective. In L. Poon (Ed.), *Aging in the 1980's: Psychological issues.* Washington, DC: American Psychological Association.

Cicirelli, V. (1982). Sibling influence throughout the life span. In M. Lamb, & B. Sutton-Smith (Eds.), *Sibling relationships: Their nature and significance across the lifespan* (pp. 267-284). Hillsdale, NJ: Erlbaum.

Clark, A., & Wallin, P. (1965). Women's sexual responsiveness and the duration and quality of their marriages. *American Journal of Sociology, 71,* 187-196.

Clavan, S. (1978). The impact of social class and social trends on the role of grandparents. *The Family Coordinator, 27,* 351-357.

Cole, C. (1984). Marital quality in later life. In W. Quinn & G. Hughston (Eds.), *Independent aging: Family and social systems perspectives* (pp. 72-90). Rockville, MD: Aspen Systems.

Cole, C., & Cole, A. (1985). Toward a marriage of equals. In H. Feldman & M. Feldman (Eds.), *Current controversies in family studies* (pp. 131-141). Beverly Hills, CA: Sage.

Comfort, A. (1976). *A good age.* New York: Crown.

Comfort, A. (1980). Sexuality in later life. In J. Birren & R. Sloane (Eds.), *Handbook of mental health and aging* (pp. 885-892). Englewood Cliffs, NJ: Prentice-Hall.

Comptroller General of the United States. (1977). *The well-being of older people in Cleveland, Ohio.* Washington, DC: United States General Accounting Office.

Cottrell, F., & Atchley, R. (1969). *Women in retirement: A preliminary report.* Oxford, OH: Scripps Foundation.

Coulton, C., & Frost, A. (1982). Use of social and health sources by the elderly. *Journal of Health and Social Behavior, 23,* 330-339.

Cronbach, L. (1951). Coefficient alpha and the internal structure of tests. *Psychometrika*, *16*, 297-334.

Cuber, J., & Harroff, P. (1965). *The significant Americans*. New York: Appleton-Century-Crofts.

Cummings, E., & Henry, E. (1961). *Growing old: The process of disengagement*. New York: Basic Books.

Cummings, E., & Schneider, D. (1961). Sibling solidarity: A property of American kinship. *American Anthropologist*, *63*, 498-507.

Darnley, F. (1975). Adjustment to retirement: Integrity or despair? *Family Coordinator*, *24*, 217-226.

DeCarlo, T. (1974). Recreation patterns and successful aging. *Journal of Gerontology*, *29*, 416-422.

Dellmann-Jenkins, M., Lambert, D., Fruit, D., & Dinero, T. (1986). Old and young together: Effect of an educational program on preschoolers' attitudes toward older people. *Childhood Education*, *62*, 206-212.

Difazio, W. (1985). *Longshorcmen: Community and resistance on the Brooklyn waterfront*. South Hardley, MA: Bengin & Garvey.

Donnenworth, D., Guy, R., & Norvell, M. (1978). Life satisfaction among older persons: Rural-urban and racial comparison. *Social Science Quarterly*, *57*, 578-583.

Dowd, J. (1975). Aging as exchange: A preface to theory. *Journal of Gerontology*, *30*, 584-594.

Dowd, J. (1980). Stratification among the aged. Monterey, CA: Brooks/Cole.

Dowd, J., & LaRossa, R. (1982). Primary group contact and elderly morale: An exchange/power analysis. *Sociology and Social Research*, *66*, 184-197.

Draper, J. (1967). *Work attitudes and retirement adjustment*. Madison, WI: University of Wisconsin Bureau of Business Research.

Dressler, D. (1973). Life adjustment of retired couples. *International Journal of Aging and Human Development*, *4*, 335-349.

Duke University Center for the Study of Aging and Human Development. (1978). *Multidimensional functional assessment: The OARS methodology*. Durham, NC: Duke University Press.

Dunlop, B. (1980). Expanded home-based care for the impaired elderly: Solution or pipe dream? *American Journal of Public Health*, *70*, 514-518.

Duvall, E. (1957). *Family development*. Philadelphia: Lippincott.

Dworetzky, J. (1984). *Introduction to child development* (2nd ed.). St. Paul, MN: West.

Edmonds, V. (1967). Marriage conventionalization: Definition, and measurement. *Journal of Marriage and the Family*, *29*, 681-688.

Edwards, J., & Klemmack, D. (1973). Correlates of life satisfaction: A re-examination. *Journal of Gerontology*, *28*, 497-502.

Ekerdt, D., Bosse, R., & LoCastro, J. (1983). Claims that retirement improves health. *Journal of Gerontology*, *38*, 231-36.

Ericksen, J., Yancy, W., & Ericksen, E. (1979). The division of labor. *Journal of Marriage and the Family*, *41*, 301-313.

Eskew, R. (1978). *Investigation of cohort differences in the marriage relationships of older couples*. Doctoral dissertation, Purdue University, West Lafayette, IN.

Farkas, G. (1976). Wage rates and the division of labor between husband and wife. *Journal of Marriage and Family*, *38*, 473-483.

Fengler, A. (1975). Attitudinal orientation of wives toward their husbands' retirement. *International Journal of Aging and Human Development*, *6*, 139-152.

Fengler, A., & Jensen, L. (1981). Perceived and objective conditions as predictors of the life satisfaction of urban and non-urban elderly. *Journal of Gerontology, 36,* 750-752.

Fields, N. (1983). Satisfaction in long-term marriages. *Social Work, 18,* 37-41.

Fillenbaum, G., & Smyer, M. (1981). The development, validity, and reliability of the OARS multidimensional functional assessment questionnaire. *Journal of Gerontology, 36,* 428-434.

Fiore, A., & Swensen, C. (1977). Analysis of love relationships in functional and dysfunctional marriages. *Psychological Reports, 40,* 708-714.

Friedman, A., & Todd, J. (1983). *Power, intimacy, and happiness in long-term marriages.* Manuscript submitted for publication.

Galton, L. (1976). Drugs and the elderly. *Nursing, 76,* 39-43.

Garza, J., & Dressel, P. (1983). Sexuality and later-life marriages. In T. Brubaker (Ed.), *Family relationships in later life* (pp. 91-108). Beverly Hills, CA: Sage.

Gilford, R., & Bengtson, V. (1979). Measuring marital satisfaction in three generations: Positive and negative dimensions. *Journal of Marriage and the Family, 41,* 387-398.

Gilford, R., & Black, D. (1972). *The grandchild-grandparent dyad: Ritual or relationship.* Paper presented at the annual meeting of the Gerontological Society, San Juan, PR.

Glamser, F. (1976). Determinants of a positive attitude toward retirement. *Journal of Gerontology, 31,* 104-07.

Glamser, F. (1981). The impact of preretirement programs on the retirement experience. *Journal of Gerontology, 30,* 529-600.

Glass, S., & Wright, T. (1977). The relationship of extra-marital sex, length of marriage and sex differences on marital satisfaction and romanticism. Athanasiou's data reanalyzed. *Journal of Marriage and the Family, 39,* 691-703.

Glenn, N., & McLanahan, S. (1981). The effects of offspring on the psychological well-being of older adults. *Journal of Marriage and the Family, 43,* 409-421.

Glick, P. (1979). Future marital status and living arrangements of the elderly. *The Gerontologist, 19,* 301-310.

Glick, P., & Norton, A. (1977). Marrying, divorcing, and living together in the U.S. today. *Population Bulletin, 32,* 5.

Goldhaber, D. (1986). *Life-span human development.* New York: Harcourt Brace Jovanovich.

Goldstein, R. (1983). Adult day care: Expanding options for service. In G. Getzel & M. Mellor (Eds.), *Gerontological social work practice in long-term care* (pp. 157-168). New York: Haworth.

Grad, S., & Foster, K. (1979). *Income of the population 55 and older.* Washington, DC: Social Security Administration.

Grover, K., Paff-Bergen, L., Russell, C., & Schumm, W. (1984). The Kansas marital satisfaction scale: A further brief report. *Psychological Reports, 54,* 629-630.

Gubrium, J. (1974). Marital desolation and the evalution of everyday life in old age. *Journal of Marriage and the Family, 36,* 107-113.

Gutmann, D. (1975). Parenthood: Key to the comparative psychology of the life cycle. In N. Datan & L. Ginsburg (Eds.), *Developmental psychology: Normative life crisis* (pp. 167-184). New York: Academic Press.

Gutmann, D. (1977). The cross-cultural perspective: Notes towards a comparative psychology of aging. In J. Birren & K. Schaie (Eds.), *Handbook of the psychology of aging* (pp. 167-184). New York: Van Nostrand.

Hampe, C., & Blevins, A. (1972). *Survey of the aged for the State of Wyoming.* Laramie, WY: University of Wyoming Press.

Harris, L., & Associates. (1975). *The myth and reality of aging in America.* Washington, DC: National Council on Aging.

Harris, L., & Associates. (1981). *Aging in the eighties: America in transition.* Washington, DC: National Council on Aging.

Harry, J. (1976). Evolving sources of happiness for men over the life cycle: A structural analysis. *Journal of Marriage and the Family, 38,* 289-296.

Hartshorne, T., & Manaster, G. (1982). The relationships with grandparents: Contact, importance, and role conception. *International Journal of Aging and Human Development, 15,* 233-245.

Hess, B. (1979). Sex roles, friendship, and the life course. *Research on Aging, 1,* 494-515.

Heyman, D., & Jeffers, F. (1968). Wives and retirement: A pilot study. *Journal of Gerontology, 23,* 488-496.

Hickey, T., Hickey, L., & Kalish, R. (1968). Children's perceptions of the elderly. *Journal of Geriatric Psychology, 12,* 227-235.

Hicks, M., & Platt, M. (1970). Marital happiness and stability: A review of research in the sixties. *Journal of Marriage and the Family, 32,* 553-573.

Hill, E., & Dorfman, L. (1982). Reaction of housewives to the retirement of their husbands. *Family Relations, 31,* 195-200.

Hill, R., Foote, N., Aldous, J., Carlson, R., & McDonald, R. (1970). *Family development in three generations.* Cambridge, MA: Schenkman.

Hiller, D., & Philliber, W. (1982). Predicting marital and career success among dual-worker couples. *Journal of Marriage and Family, 44,* 53-62.

Hof, L., & Miller, W. (1981). *Marriage enrichment: Philosophy, process and program.* Bowie, MD: Brady.

Hoffman, E. (1979-1980). Young adults' relationships with their grandparents: An exploratory study. *International Journal of Aging and Human Development, 10,* 299-310.

Houseknecht, S. (1981). Combining marriage and career: The marital adjustment of professional women. *Journal of Marriage and Family, 43,* 651-661.

Hughes, F., & Noppe, L. (1985). Family Relationships. In F.P. Hughes & L.D. Noppe (Eds.), *Human development: Across the life span* (pp. 413-416). St. Paul: West Publishing Co.

Hutchinson, I. (1975). The significance of marital status for morale and life satisfaction among lower-income elderly. *Journal of Marriage and the Family, 37,* 287-293.

Huyck, M. (1977). Sex and the older woman. In L. Troll, J. Israel, & K. Israel (Eds.), *Looking ahead: A woman's guide to the problems and joys of growing older.* Englewood Cliffs, NJ: Prentice-Hall.

Hyman, H. (1983). *Of time and widowhood.* Durham, NC: Duke University Press.

Irelan, L. (1972). Retirement history study: Introduction. *Social Security Bulletin, 35,* 3-9.

Irish, D. (1964). Sibling interaction: A neglected aspect in family life research. *Social Forces, 42,* 269-288.

Janicki, M., & MacEachron, A. (1984). Residential, health and social service needs of elderly developmentally disabled persons. *The Gerontologist, 24,* 128-137.

Jantz, R., Seefeldt, C., Galper, A., & Serock, K. (1977). Children's attitudes toward the elderly. *Social Education, 41,* 518-523.

Jaslow, R. (1976). Employment, retirement and morale among older women. *Journal of Gerontology, 31,* 212-218.

Jette, A., & Branch, L. (1981). The Framingham disability study: Physical disability among the aging. *American Journal of Public Health, 71,* 1121-1216.

Kahana, E., & Coe, R. (1969). Perceptions of grandparenthood by community and institutionalized aged. *Proceedings of the Seventy-Seventh Annual Convention of the American Psychological Association, 4,* 735-736.

Kahana, E., & Kahana, B. (1970). Grandparenthood from the perspective of the developing grandchild. *Developmental Psychology, 3*, 98-105.

Kalish, R. (1982). *Late adulthood: Perspectives on human development* (2nd ed.). Monterey, CA: Brooks/Cole.

Karp, D., & Yoels, W. (1982). *Experiencing the life cycle: A social psychology of aging.* Springfield, IL: Charles C. Thomas.

Keating, N., & Cole, P. (1980). What can I do with him 24 hours a day?: Changes in the housewife role after retirement. *The Gerontologist, 20*, 84-89.

Keith, P. (1982). Working women versus homemakers: Retirement resources and correlates of well-being. In M. Szinovacz (Ed.), *Women's retirement* (pp. 77-91). Beverly Hills, CA: Sage.

Keith P., & Brubaker, T. (1977). Sex-role expectations associated with specific household tasks: Perceived age and employment differences. *Psychological Reports, 41*, 15-18.

Keith, P., & Brubaker, T. (1979). Male household roles in later life: A look at masculinity and marital relationships. *Family Coordinator, 28*, 497-502.

Keith, P., & Brubaker, T. (1980). Adolescent perception of household work: Expectations by sex, age, and employment situation. *Adolescence, 15*, 171-182.

Kerckhoff, A. (1966). Family patterns and morale in retirement. In I. Simpson & J. McKinney (Eds.), *Social aspects of aging* (pp. 173-192). Durham, NC: Duke University Press.

Kinsey, A., Pomeroy, W., Martin, C., & Gebhard, P. (1953). *Sexual behavior in the human female.* Philadelphia: Saunders.

Kivinick, H.Q. (1982). *The meaning of grandparenthood.* Ann Arbor, MI: University of Michigan Institute of Gerontology.

Klecka, W. (1980). *Discriminant analysis.* Beverly Hills, CA: Sage.

Kleiber, D. (1982). Optimizing retirement through lifelong learning education and leisure education. In N. Osgood (Ed.), *Life after work:* (pp. 319-330). New York: Praeger.

Kline, C. (1975). The socialization process of women. *The Gerontologist,* 489-492.

Kohen, J. (1983). Old but not alone: Informal social supports among the elderly by marital status and sex. *The Gerontologist, 23*, 57-63.

Konopka, G. (1976). *Young girls: A portrait of adolescence.* Englewood Cliffs, NJ: Prentice-Hall.

Koopman-Boyden, P., & Wells, L. (1979). The problems arising from supporting the elderly at home. *New Zealand Medical Journal, 89*, 265-268.

Krupkal, L., & Verner, A. (1979). Hazards of drug use among the elderly. *The Gerontologist, 19*, 90-94.

Kuypers, J., & Bengtson, V. (1973). Social breakdown and competence: A model of normal aging. *Human Development, 16*, 181-201.

Lamb, M., & Sutton-Smith, B. (Eds.). (1982). *Sibling relationships: Their nature and significance across the lifespan.* Hillsdale, NJ: Erlbaum.

Lawton, M. (1970). Ecology and aging. In L. Paslalan & D. Carson (Eds.), *The spatial behavior of older people.* Ann Arbor, MI: University of Michigan Institute of Gerontology.

Lawton, M., & Cohen, J. (1974). The Generality of housing impact on the well-being of older people. *Journal of Gerontology, 29*, 194-204.

Lee, G. (1978). Marriage and morale in later life. *Journal of Marriage and the Family, 40*, 131-139.

Lee, G. (1979). Children and the elderly: Interaction and morale. *Research on Aging, 1*, 335-360.

Lee, G., & Ellithorpe, E. (1982). Intergenerational exchange and subjective well-being among the elderly. *Journal of Marriage and the Family, 441*, 217-224.

Lee, G., & Tallman, M. (1980). Sibling interaction and morale: The effects of family relations on older people. *Research on Aging, 2,* 367-391.

Legge, J., Jr., & Ziegler, H. (1979). Utilizing discriminant analysis in social research: An explanation and illustration, *7,* 27-35.

Lemert, E. (1963). Paranoia and the dynamics of exclusion. *Sociometry, 25,* 2-20.

Levinger, G. (1966). Systemic distortion of preferred and actual sexual behavior. *Sociometry, 26,* 291-299.

Lewin, K. (1951). *Field theory in social science.* New York: Harper.

Lewis, J. (1979). *How's your family?* New York: Brunner/Mazel.

Lewis, J., Beavers, W., Gossett, J., & Phillips, V. (1976). *No single thread.* New York: Brunner/Mazel.

Lewis, R., & Spanier, G. (1979). Theorizing about quality and stability of marriage. In W. Burr, R. Hill, F.I. Nye, & I. Reiss (Eds.), *Contemporary theories about the family: Vol. 1. Research-based theories* (pp. 268-294). New York: Free Press.

Liang, J., Dvorkin, L., Kahana, E., & Mazian, F. (1980). Social integration and morale: A re-examination. *Journal of Gerontology, 35,* 746-757.

Link, M. (1978). Reading activities on aging for children. *Indiana Reading Quarterly, 11,* 25-27.

Link, M., & Trusty, K. (1980). Bridging the generation gap: A study of aging. *Mid-Western Educational Researcher, 1,* 10-11.

Lipman, A. (1961). Role conceptions and morale of couples in retirement. *Journal of Gerontology, 16,* 267-271.

Livson, F. (1983). Gender identity: A life span view of sex role development. In R. Weg (Ed.), *Sexuality in the later years* (pp. 105-127). New York: Academic Press.

Locke, H., & Wallace, K. (1959). Short marital-adjustment and prediction tests: Their reliability and validity. *Marriage and Family Living, 21,* 251-255.

Loevinger, J. (1976). *Ego development.* San Francisco: Jossey-Bass.

Loevinger, J., & Wessler, R. (1970). *Measuring ego development.* San Francisco: Jossey-Bass.

Lohmann, N. (1977). Correlations of life satisfaction, morale and adjustment measures. *Journal of Gerontology, 32,* 73-75.

Louis, M. (1983). Falls and their causes. *Journal of Gerontological Nursing, 9,* 143-149.

Lovell-Troy, L. (1983). Anomia among employed wives and housewives: An exploratory analysis. *Journal of Marriage and the Family, 45,* 301-310.

Lowenthal, M. Thurner, M., Chiriboga, D., & Associates. (1975). *Four stages of life: A comparative study of women and men facing transitions.* San Francisco: Jossey-Bass.

Lowenthal, M., & Berkman, P. (1967). *Aging and mental disorder in San Francisco.* San Francisco, CA: Jossey-Bass.

Lutzer, V., & Brubaker, T. (1988). Differential respite needs of aging parents of individuals with mental retardation. *Mental Retardation, 26,* 13-15.

Maas, H., & Kuypers, J. (1974). *From thirty to seventy.* San Francisco: Jossey-Bass.

Mace, D. (1972). Contemporary issues in marriage. In R. Albrecht & E. Bock (Eds.), *Encounter: Love, marriage, and family* (pp. 5-14). Boston: Holbrook.

Mace, D. (1982). *Close companions.* New York: Continuum.

Mace, D. & Mace, V. (1974). *We can have better marriages if we really want them.* Nashville, TN: Abingdon.

Maddox, G. (1968). Retirement as a social event in the United States. In B. Neugarten (Ed.), *Middle age and aging.* Chicago: University of Chicago Press.

Mancini, J. (1979). Family relationships and morale among people 65 years of age and older. *American Journal of Orthopsychiatry, 49,* 195-203.

Manney, J. (1975). *Aging in American society.* Ann Arbor, MI: Institute of Gerontology.

Markides, K. & Martin, H. (1979). A causal model of life satisfaction among the elderly. *Journal of Gerontology, 34,* 86-93.

Martin, W. (1973). Activity and disengagement: Life satisfaction of inmovers into a retirement community. *The Gerontologist, 13,* 224-227.

Masters, W., & Johnson, V. (1964). *Human sexual inadequacy.* Boston: Little, Brown.

Matthews, S. (1986). *Friendships through the life course: Oral biographies in old age.* Beverly Hills, CA: Sage.

McCubbin, H., Larsen, A., & Olson, D. (1982). F-COPES. Family coping strategies. In D. Olson, H. McCubbin, H. Barnes, A. Larsen, M. Muxen, & M. Wilson (Eds.), *Family inventories: Inventories used in a national survey of families across the family life cycle* (pp. 101-120). Minneapolis: University of Minnesota Press.

McKain, W. (1969). *Retirement marriages.* Agriculture Experiment Station Monograph No. 3. Storrs, CT: University of Connecticut Press.

McKinlay, J. (1981). Social network influences on morbid episodes and the career of help seeking. In L. Eisenberg & A. Kleinman (Eds.), *The relevance of social science for medicine.* Dordrecht, Holland: D. Reidel.

Mechanic, D. (1979). Correlates of physician utilization: Why do major multivariate studies of physician utilization find trivial psychosocial and organizational effects? *Journal of Health and Social Behavior, 20,* 387-396.

Medley, M. (1976). Satisfaction with life among persons 65 years and older. *Journal of Gerontology, 31,* 448-455.

Medley, M. (1977). Marital adjustment in the post-retirement years. *Family Coordinator, 26,* 5-11.

Medling, J., & McCarrey, M. (1981). Marital adjustment over segments of the family life cycle: The issue of spouse's value similarity. *Journal of Marriage and the Family, 43,* 195-203.

Meneghan, E. (1983). Marital stress and family transitions: A panel analysis. *Journal of Marriage and the Family, 45,* 371-386.

Merton, R. (1969). The role-set: Problems in sociological theory. In L. Coser & B. Rosenberg (Eds.), *Sociological theory: A book of readings* (pp. 365-375). New York: Macmillan.

Michaelson, R., Michaelson, C., & Swensen, C. (1982). *Factors related to coping strategies employed by older adults.* Paper presented at the meeting of the American Psychological Association, Washington, DC.

Miller, B. (1976). A multivariate developmental model of marital satisfaction. *Journal of Marriage and the Family, 38,* 643-657.

Miller Lite Report. (1983). *Report on Americans' attitudes towards sports.* Milwaukee, WI: Miller Brewing Company.

Minnigerode, F., & Lee, J. (1978). Young adults' perceptions of social sex roles across the life span. *Sex Roles, 4,* 563-569.

Mitchell, S., Newell, G., & Schumm, W. (1983). Test-retest reliability of the Kansas marital satisfaction scale. *Psychological Reports, 53,* 545-546.

Moore, K., & Sawhill, I. (1978). Implications of women's employment for home and family life. In A. Stromberg & S. Harkess (Eds.), *Women working* (pp. 201-225). Palo Alto, CA: Mayfield.

National Data Program for the Social Sciences. (July, 1976). *Codebook for the spring 1976 general social survey.* Chicago: National Opinion Research Center, University of Chicago.

Neugarten, B. (1974). Age groups in American society and the rise of the young-old.

American Academy of Political and Social Science, 415, 187-198.

Neugarten, B., Havighurst, R., & Tobin, S. (1961). The measurement of life satisfaction. *Journal of Gerontology, 16,* 134-143.

Newman, G., & Nichols, C.R. (1970). Sexual activities and attitudes in older persons. In E. Palmore (Ed.), *Normal aging: Reports from the Duke longitudinal study* (Vol. 1). Durham, NC: Duke University Press. *News Update.* (1984). *9,* 622.

Nie, N. (1983). *SPSSx User's guide.* New York: McGraw-Hill.

Notelewitz, M., & Ware, M. (1982). *Stand tall.* Gainesville, FL: Triad.

Nye, I.F. (1979). Choice, exchange, and the family. In W. Burr, R. Hill, F.I. Nye, & I. Reiss (Eds.), *Contemporary theories about the family: Vol. 2. General theories/theorival orientations* (pp. 1-41). New York: Free Press.

Nye, F.I., White, L., & Frideres, J. (1973). A preliminary theory of marital stability: Two models. *International Journal of the Sociology of the Family, 3,* 102-122.

Olson, D., & Barnes, H. (1982). Quality of life. In D. Olson, H. McCubbin, H. Barnes, A. Larsen, M. Muxen, & M. Wilson (Eds.), *Family inventories: Inventories used in a national survey of families across the family life cycle* (pp. 137-148). Minneapolis: University of Minnesota Press.

Olson, D., Fournier, D., & Druckman, J.M. (1982). ENRICH: Enriching and nurturing relationship issues, communication, and happiness. In D. Olson, H. McCubbin, H. Barnes, A. Larsen, M. Muxen, & M. Wilson (Eds.), *Family inventories: Inventories used in a national survey of families across the family life cycle* (pp. 46-68). Minneapolis: University of Minnesota Press.

Olson, D., Larsen, A., & McCubbin, H. (1982). Family strengths. In D. Olson, H. McCubbin, H. Barnes, A. Larsen, M. Muxen, & M. Wilson (Eds.), *Family inventories: Inventories used in a national survey of families across the family life cycle* (pp. 121-136). Minneapolis: University of Minnesota Press.

Olson, D., & Wilson, M. (1982). Family satisfaction. In D. Olson, H. McCubbin, H. Barnes, A. Larsen, M. Muxen, & M. Wilson (Eds.), *Family inventories: Inventories used in a national survey of families across the family life cycle* (pp. 25-32). Minneapolis: University of Minnesota Press.

Orthner, D. (1975). Leisure activity patterns and marital satisfaction over the marital career. *Journal of Marriage and the Family, 37,* 91-102.

Otto, H. (1962). What is a strong family? *Marriage and Family Living, 24,* 77-81.

Otto, H. (1964). The personal and family strength research projects: Some implications for the therapist. *Mental Hygiene, 48,* 439-450.

Palmore, E. (1980). Preparation for retirement: The impact of preretirement programs on retirement and leisure. In N. Osgood (Ed.), *Life after work* (pp. 330-341). New York: Praeger.

Palmore, E., & Kivett, V. (1976). Change in life satisfaction: A longitudinal study of persons 40-70. *Journal of Gerontology, 32,* 311-316.

Palmore, E., & Luikart, C. (1972). Health and social factors related to life satisfaction. *Journal of Health and Social Behavior, 13,* 68-80.

Papalia, D., & Olds, S. (1986). *Human development* (3rd ed.). New York: McGraw-Hill.

Parron, E., & Troll, L. (1978). Golden wedding couples: Effects of retirement on intimacy in long-standing marriages. *Alternative Lifestyles, 1,* 447-464.

Perlin, L., & Schooler, D. (1978). The structure of coping. *Journal of Health and Social Behavior, 19,* 2-21.

Peterson, J. (1968). *Married love in the middle years.* New York: Association Press.

Peterson, J. (1975). *Love in the Later Years.* New York: Association Press.

Petrowsky, M. (1976). Marital status, sex, and the social network of the elderly. *Journal of Marriage and the Family, 38,* 749-756.

Pfeiffer, E., & Davis, G. (1972). Determinants of sexual behavior in middle and old age. *Journal of the American Geriatric Society, 20,* 151-158.

Pfeiffer, E., Verwoerdt, A., & Davis, G. (1972). Sexual behavior in middle life. *American Journal of Psychiatry, 128,* 1262-1267.

Pineo, P. (1961). Disenchantment in the later years of marriage. *Marriage and Family Living, 3,* 3-11.

Piotrowski, C., & Crits-Christoph, P. (1981). Women's jobs and family adjustment. *Journal of Family Issues, 2,* 126-147.

Piscopo, J. (1985). *Fitness and aging.* New York: Wiley.

Prentis, R. (1980). White collar working women's perception of retirement. *The Gerontologist, 20,* 90-95.

Pritzlaff, J., Jr. (1984). *Pritzlaff Commission on long term care in Arizona: Final report.* Submitted to the Governor of Arizona, and the Arizona House of Representatives and Senate Committees.

Puglisi, J. (1983). Self perceived age changes in sex role concept. *International Journal of Aging and Human Development, 16,* 183-191.

Puglisi, J., & Jackson, D. (1980-1981). Sex role identity and self esteem in adulthood. *International Journal of Aging and Human Development, 12,* 129-138.

Quinn, W. (1983). Personal and family adjustment in later life. *Journal of Marriage and the Family, 45,* 57-73.

Riechard, S., Livson, F., & Peterson, P. (1962). *Aging and personality.* New York: Wiley.

Reiss, I. (1976). *The family system in America.* Hinsdale, IL: Dryden.

Rhyne, D. (1981). Bases of marital satisfaction among men and women. *Journal of Marriage and the Family, 42,* 841-955.

Rice. F. (1983). *Contemporary marriage.* Boston: Allyn & Bacon.

Riley, M., & Foner, A. (1968). *Aging and society: An inventory of research findings* (Vol. 1). New York: Russell Sage.

Roberto, K., & Scott, J. (1986). Friendships of older men and women: Exchange patterns and satisfaction. *Psychology and Aging, 1,* 103-109.

Roberts, W. (1980). Significant elements in the relationship of long-married couples. *International Journal of Aging and Human Development, 10,* 3, 265-272.

Robertson, J. (1975). Interaction in three generational families, parents as mediators: Toward a theoretical perspective. *International Journal of Aging and Human Development, 6,* 103-110.

Robertson, J. (1976). Significance of grandparents: Perceptions of young adult children. *The Gerontologist, 16,* 137-140.

Robinson, B. (1983). Validation of a caregiving strain index. *Journal of Gerontology, 38,* 344-348.

Robinson, B., & Thurnher, M. (1979). Taking care of aged parents: A family cycle transition. *The Gerontologist, 19,* 586-593.

Robinson, P. (1983). The sociological perspective. In R. Weg (Ed.), *Sexuality in later life* (pp. 82-100). New York: Academic Press.

Rollins, B., & Cannon, K. (1974). Marital satisfaction over the life cycle: A reevaluation. *Journal of Marriage and the Family, 36,* 271-292.

Rollins, B., & Feldman, H. (1970). Marital satisfaction over the family life cycle. *Journal of Marriage and the Family, 32,* 20-28.

Rosenberg, E. (1984). Sport voluntary association involvement and happiness among middle-aged and elderly Americans. In B. McPherson (Ed.), *Sport and aging* (pp. 25-36). Champaign, IL: Human Kinetics.

Rosenberg, G., & Anspach, D. (1973). Sibling solidarity in the working class. *Journal of Marriage and Family, 35,* 108-113.

Rosenblatt, P. (1977). Needed research on commitment in marriage. In G. Levinger & H. Raush (Eds.), *Close relationships: Perspectives on the meaning of intimacy* (pp. 73-85). Amherst: University of Massachusetts Press.

Rosow, I. (1967). *Social integration of the aged.* New York: Free Press.

Ross, H., & Milgram, J. (1982). Important variables in adult sibling relationships: A qualitative study. In M. Lamb & B. Sutton-Smith (Eds.), *Sibling relationships: Their nature and significance across the lifespan* (pp. 225-249). Hillsdale, NJ: Erlbaum.

Rowe, G., & Meredith, W. (1982). Quality in marital relationships after twenty-five years. *Family Perspective, 16,* 149-155.

Rowitz, L. (1985). Social support: Issue for the 1980's. *Mental Retardation, 23,* 165-167.

Rudman, W. (1985). Lifecourse socioeconomic transitions and sport involvement: A theory of restricted opportunity. In B. McPherson (Ed.), *Sport and aging* (pp. 25-36). Champaign, IL: Human Kinetics.

Sandrick, K. (1983). *What doctors should know about DRG's.* Chicago: Care Communications.

Schiamberg, L. (1985). *Human development.* (2nd ed.). New York: Macmillan.

Schram, R. (1979). Marital satisfaction over the family life cycle: A critique and proposal. *Journal of Marriage and the Family, 41,* 7-12.

Schultz, J. (1980). *The economics of aging* (2nd ed.). Belmont, CA: Wadsworth.

Schumm, W., Anderson, S., Race, G., Morris, J., Griffin, C., McCutchen, M., & Beniga, J. (1983). Construct validity of the marital communication inventory. *Journal of Sex and Marital Therapy, 53,* 153-162.

Schumm, W., Benigas, J., McCutchen, M., Griffin, C., Anderson, S., Morris, J., & Race, G. (1983). Measuring empathy, regard and congruence in the marital relationship. *Journal of Social Psychology, 119,* 141-142.

Schumm, W., Bollman, S., & Jurich, A. (1981). The dimensionality of an abbreviated version of the relationship inventory: An urban replication with married couples. *Psychological Reports, 48,* 51-56.

Schumm, W., Jurich, A., & Bollman, S. (1981). Dimensionality of an abbreviated relationship inventory for couples. *Journal of Psychology, 105,* 225-230.

Schumm, W., Nichols, C., Shectman, K., & Grigsby, C. (1983). Characteristics of responses to the Kansas marital satisfaction scale by a sample of 84 married mothers. *Psychological Reports, 53,* 567-572.

Schumm, W., Scanlon, E., Crow, C., Green, D., & Buckler, D. (1983). Characteristics of the Kansas marital satisfaction scale in a sample of 79 married couples. *Psychological Reports, 53,* 583-588.

Scott, J. (1983). Siblings and other kin. In T. Brubaker (Ed.), *Family relationships in later life* (pp. 47-62). Beverly Hills, CA: Sage.

Seefeldt, C., Jantz, R., Galper, A., & Serock, K. (1977). Children's attitudes toward the elderly: Educational implications. *Educational Gerontology, 2,* 301-310.

Seleen, D. (1982). The congruence between actual and desired use of time by older adults: A predictor of life satisfaction. *The Gerontologist, 22,* 95-99.

Seltzer, M. (1985). Informal supports for aging mentally retarded persons. *American Journal of Mental Deficiency, 90,* 259-265.

Seltzer, M., & Seltzer, G. (1985). The elderly mentally retarded: A group in need of service. *Journal of Gerontological Social Work, 7,* 99-119.

Seltzer, M., Seltzer, G., & Sherwood, C. (1982). Comparison of community adjustment of older vs. younger mentally retarded adults. *American Journal of Mental Deficiency, 87,* 9-13.

Shanas, E. (1961). Living arrangements of older people in the United States. *The Gerontologist, 1,* 27-29.

Shanas, E. (1973). Family kin networks and aging in cross cultural perspective. *Journal of Marriage and the Family, 35,* 505-511.

Shanas, E. (1979a). Social myth as hypothesis: The case of the family relations of old people. *The Gerontologist, 19,* 3-9.

Shanas, E. (1979b). The family as a social support system in old age. *The Gerontologist, 19,* 169-174.

Shanas, E. (1980). Older people and their families: The new pioneers. *Journal of Marriage and the Family, 42,* 9-15.

Shepard, R. (1986). *Economic benefits of enhanced fitness.* Champaign, IL: Human Kinetics.

Sherman, S. (1975). Patterns of contacts for residents of age-segregated and age-integrated housing. *Journal of Gerontology, 30,* 103-107.

Shuval, J. (1970). *The social functions of medical practice.* San Francisco, CA: Jossey-Bass.

Simos, B. (1973). Adult children and their aging parents. *Social Work, 18,* 3, 78-85.

Simpson, I., Back, K., & McKinney, J. (1966). Work and retirement. In I. Simpson & J. McKinney (Eds.), *Social aspects of aging* (pp. 45-54). Durham, NC: Duke University Press.

Smart, M., & Smart, R. (1975). Recalled, present, and predicted satisfaction in stages of the family life cycle in New Zealand. *Journal of Marriage and the Family, 37,* 408-415.

Spanier, G. (1976). Measuring dyadic adjustment: New scales for assessing the quality of marriage and similar dyads. *Journal of Marriage and Family, 38,* 15-28.

Spanier, G., & Filsinger, E. (1983). The dyadic adjustment scale. In E. Filsinger (Ed.), *Marriage and family assessment: A sourcebook for family therapy* (pp. 155-168). Beverly Hills, CA: Sage.

Spanier G., & Lerner, R. (1980). *Adolescent development: A life span perspective.* New York: McGraw-Hill.

Spanier, G., & Lewis, R. (1980). Marital quality: A review of the seventies. *Journal of Marriage and the Family, 42,* 825-839.

Spanier, G., Lewis, R., & Cole, C. (1975). Marital adjustment over the family life cycle: The issues of curvilinearity, *Journal of Marriage and the Family, 37,* 263-275.

Spanier, G., Sauer, W., & Larzelere, R. (1979). An empirical evaluation of the family life cycle. *Journal of Marriage and the Family, 41,* 27-38.

Spanier, G., & Thompson, L. (1982). A confirmatory analysis of the dyadic adjustment scale. *Journal of Marriage and Family, 44,* 731-738.

Sporakowski, J., & Hughston, G. (1978). Prescriptions for happy marriage: Adjustments and satisfactions of couples married 50 or more years. *The Family Coordinator, 27,* 321-327.

Spreitzer, E., & Snyder, E. (1974). Correlates of life satisfaction among the aged. *Journal of Gerontology, 29,* 454-458.

Springer, D., & Brubaker, T. (1984). *Family caregivers and dependent elderly.* Beverly Hills, CA: Sage.

Stinnett, N. (1979). In search of strong families. In N. Stinnett, B. Chesser, & J. DeFrain

(Eds.), *Building family strengths* (pp. 23-29). Lincoln: University of Nebraska Press.

Stinnett, N., Carter, L., & Montgomery, J. (1970). Marital need satisfaction of older husbands and wives. *Journal of Marriage and the Family, 32,* 428-434.

Stinnett, N., Carter, L., & Montgomery, J. (1972). Older persons' perceptions of their marriages. *Journal of Marriage and the Family, 34,* 665-670.

Stinnett, N., Sanders, G., & DeFrain, J. (1981). Strong families: A national study. In N. Stinnett, J. DeFrain, K. King, P. Knaub, & G. Rowe (Eds.,) *Family Strengths 3: Roots of well being.* Lincoln: University of Nebraska Press.

Stinnett, N., Sanders, G., DeFrain, J., & Parkhurst, A. (1982). A nationwide study of families who perceive themselves as strong. *Family Perspective, 16,* 15-22.

Stinnett, N., & Sauer, K. (1977). Relationship characteristics of strong families. *Family Perspective, 11,* 3-11.

Stoller, E. & Earl, L. (1983). Help with activities of everyday life: Sources of support for the non-institutional elderly. *The Gerontologist, 23,* 64-70.

Strain, L., & Chappell, N. (1982). Confidants: Do they make a difference in quality of life? *Research on Aging, 4,* 479-502.

Streib, G., & Schneider, C. (1971). *Retirement in American society.* Ithaca, NY: Cornell University Press.

Streltzer, A. (1979). A grandchildren's group in a home for the aged. *Health Social Work, 4,* 167-183.

Swensen, C. (1971). Commitment and the personality of the successful psychotherapist. *Psychotherapy: Theory, Research and Practice, 8,* 31-36.

Swensen, C. (1972). The behavior of love. In H. Otto (Ed.), *Love today: A new exploration* (pp. 86-101). New York: Association Press.

Swensen, C. (1973). A scale for measuring the feelings and behaviors of love. In J. Pfeiffer & J. Jones (Eds.), *The 1973 annual handbook for group facilitators* (pp. 71-86). La Jolla, CA: University Associates.

Swensen, C. (1977). Ego development and interpersonal relations. In D. Nevill (Ed.), *Humanistic psychology: New frontiers* (pp. 36-66). New York: Gardner Press.

Swensen, C. (1983). Post-parental marriages. *Medical Aspects of Human Sexuality, 17,* 171-194.

Swenson, C., Eskew, R., & Kohlhepp, K. (1981). Stage of family life cycle, ego development, and the marriage relationship. *Journal of Marriage and the Family, 43,* 841-853.

Swenson, C., & Fiore, A. (1982). The marriage problems scale. In P. Keller (Ed.), *Innovations in clinical practice: A sourcebook:* Sarasota, FL: Professional Resource Exchange.

Swenson, C., & Moore, C. (1979). Marriages that endure. In E. Corfman (Ed.), *Families today* (Vol. 1) (pp. 249-286). Rockville, MD: National Institute of Mental Health, Science Monographs 1.

Swensen, C., & Trahaug, G. (1979). *Mental problems of older married couples.* Bergen, Norway: Psychology Institute, University of Bergen.

Szinovacz, M. (1977). Rule allocation, family structure and female employment. *Journal of Marriage and the Family, 39,* 781-791.

Szinovacz, M. (1980). Female retirement: Effects on spousal roles and marital adjustment. *Journal of Family Issues, 1,* 423-440.

Szinovacz, M. (1982). Introduction: Research on women's retirement. In M. Szinovacz (Ed.), *Women's Retirement* (pp. 13-21). Beverly Hills, CA: Sage.

Tagnoli, J. (1979). The flight from domestic space: Men's roles in the household. *Family Coordinator, 28,* 599-607.

Tessler, R., Mechanic, D., & Dimond, M. (1976). The effect of psychological distress on physician utilization: A prospective study. *Journal of Health and Social Behavior, 17*, 353-364.

Tobin, B. (1986). Prospective payment: A good idea gone awry? *Nursing Life*, 18-20.

Today's Nursing Home, 5 (1984). Nofield, IL: McKnight Medical Communications.

Todd, J., Friedman, A., & Lomranz, J. (1983). *Post-retirement changes in happiness, power and intimacy in long term marriages*. Manuscript submitted for publication.

Towsend, P. (1963). *The family life of old people*. Harmondsworth, England: Penguin.

Traupmann, A., & Hatfield, E. (1981). Love and its effect on mental and physical health. In *Change in the family* (pp. 253-274). New York: Academic Press.

Troll, L. (1971). The family of later life: A decade review. *Journal of Marriage and the Family, 33*, 263-290.

Troll, L. (1980). Grandparenting. In L. Poon (Ed.), *Aging in the 1980s: Psychological issues* Washington, DC: American Psychological Association.

Troll, L. (1983). Grandparents: The family watchdogs. In T. Brubaker (Ed.), *Family relationships in later life*. Beverly Hills, CA: Sage.

Troll, L., Miller, S., & Atchley, R. (1979). Siblings and other kin. In L. Troll, S. Miller, & R. Atchley (Eds.), *Families in later life* (pp. 121-127). Belmont, CA: Wadsworth.

Turnbull, H., & Turnbull, A. (1985). *Parents speak out: Then and now*. Columbus, OH: Merrill.

Turner, R.H. (1975). *Family interaction*. New York: John Wiley.

Ullmer, J., Abrahams, L., & Brown, D. (1982). Adult day care clients: A distinct population. *Journal of Gerontological Social Work, 4*, 53-166.

U.S. Bureau of the Census. (March, 1977). Household and family characteristics. *Current Population Reports* (Series P-20, No. 326). Washington, DC: U.S. Government Printing Office.

U.S.Bureau of the Census. (March, 1982). Household and family characteristics. *Current Population Reports* (Series P-20, No. 381). Washington, DC: U.S. Government Printing Office.

U.S. Senate Special Committee on Aging. (1981). *Developments in aging: 1980*. Washington, DC: U.S. Government Printing Office.

Valliant, G. (1977). *Adaptation to Life*. Boston: Little, Brown.

Verbrugge, L. (1979). Marital status and health. *Journal of Marriage and the Family, 41*, 267-285.

Verbrugge, L. (1985). Gender and health: An update on hypotheses and evidence. *Journal of Health and Social Behavior, 26*, 156-182.

Wampler, K., & Powell, G. (1982). The Barret-Lennard relationship inventory as a measure of marital satisfaction. *Family Relations, 31*, 139-145.

Wan, T., & Weissert, W. (1981). Social support networks, patient status, and institutionalization. *Research on Aging, 3*, 240-256.

Wan, T., Weissert, W., & Livieratos, B. (1980). Geriatric day care and homemaker services: An experimental study. *Journal of Gerontology, 35*, 256-274.

Wand, R. (1979). *The aging experience*. New York: Lippincott.

Ward, R. (1985). Informal networks and well-being in later life: A research agenda. *The Geronotologist, 25*, 55-61.

Watson, J., & Kivett, V. (1976). Influences on the life satisfaction of older fathers. *The Family Coordinator, 25*, 482-488.

Weinberger, A. (1979). Stereotyping of the elderly: Elementary school children's responses. *Research on Aging, 1*, 113-136.

Weissert, W. (1976). Two models of geriatric day care. *The Gerontologist, 16*, 420-427.

Weissert, W. (1977). Adult day care programs in the United States: Current research projects and a survey of ten centers. *Public Health Reports, 92*, 49-56.

Weissert, W. (1978). Costs of adult day care: A comparison to nursing homes. *Inquiry, 15*, 10-19.

Weissert, W., Wan, T., Livierieratos, B., & Katz, S. (1980). Effects and costs of day-care services for the chronically ill: A randomized experiment. *Medical Care, 18*, 567-584.

Weren, J. (1987), January 11). Barrier-free housing is vital. *The Arizona Daily Star*, Tucson, AZ.

Whittington, F. (1984). Addicts and alcoholics. In E. Palmore (Ed.), *Handbook on the aged in the United States* (pp. 279-294). Westport, CT: Greenwood.

Wood, V., & Robertson, J. (1978). Friendship and kinship interaction: Differential effect on the morale of the elderly. *Journal of Marriage and the Family, 40*, 2, 367-375.

Yarrow, M., Blank, P., Quinn, O., Youmans, F., & Stein, J. (1971). *Human aging* (Pub. No. [HSM] 71-9051). Washington, DC: U.S. Government Printing Office.

Youmans, E. (1963). *Aging patterns in a rural and urban area of Kentucky*. Agricultural Experiment Station, Bulletin No. 681. Lexington: University of Kentucky.

Young, M. & Willmott, P. (1957). *Family and kinship in East London*. London: Routledge & Kegan Paul.

Zigler, E., & Finn-Stevenson, M. (1987). *Children: Development and social issues*. Lexington, MA: Heath.

Zube, M. (1982). Changing behavior and outlook of aging men and women: Implications for marriage in the middle and later years. *Family Relations, 31*, 147-156.

About the Contributors

Leland V. Axelson, Ph.D., is Professor at Virginia Polytechnic Institute and State University in Blacksburg, Virginia. His current research interests and publications include topics in intergenerational family relationships and homelessness.

Charles M. Barresi, Ph.D., is Professor of Sociology and a Senior Fellow in the Institute for Life Span Development and Gerontology at the University of Akron in Akron, Ohio and is a Fellow in the Gerontological Society of America. He earned his Ph.D. at the State University of New York at Buffalo. His research interests include ethnicity in aging, gender differences in widowhood, and patterns of family caregiving. He is currently working on a book on ethnicity and long-term care.

Dolores Cabic Borland, Ph.D., earned her degree in Sociology from Texas Women's University. Currently, she serves as Associate Professor in Family and Child Ecology at Michigan State University in East Lansing, Michigan. Her research interests include middle age and sibling relationships in middle age and in later life.

Ellie Brubaker, Ph.D., is Associate Professor of Sociology and Anthropology at Miami University in Oxford, Ohio. Her degree is in Social Work from the Ohio State University. Currently, she is researching in the area of social service delivery to older families.

Timothy H. Brubaker, Ph.D., is Professor and Director of the Family and Child Studies Center, Department of Home Economics and Consumer Sciences, at Miami University in Oxford, Ohio. His Ph.D. in Sociology is from Iowa State University. He is currently conducting research about later-life families and on the older parents of developmentally disabled children.

Margaret A. Bugaighis, Ph.D., is currently serving as the Director of a social service agency in Bethlehem, Pennsylvania. She received her degree from Kansas State University.

Jane M. Cardea, Ph.D., is Associate Professor and Director of Graduate
Nursing at the Azusa Pacific University in Azusa, California. Her
degree is from Texas Tech University, in Human Development and
Family Studies. Her research interests include the chronically mentally ill, social networks, and families of oncology patients.

Charles Lee Cole, Ph.D., is Associate Professor of Family Environment
at Iowa State University in Ames, Iowa. His research interests
include marital quality, family wellness, and therapy.

Janette M. Copeland is currently completing her work for the Ph.D. at
Kansas State University.

Mary Dellman-Jenkins, Ph.D., is Associate Professor of Individual and
Family Studies and Gerontology at Kent State University in Kent,
Ohio. She earned her degree from the University of Wisconsin in
Madison. Her research interests center around the psychological
and social functioning of older adults.

Jean L. Engelhardt, Ph.D., is a Research Consultant with Southwest
Ohio Development Center, Batavia, Ohio. She earned her Ph.D. from
Notre Dame University, in Psychology. Currently, her interests are
with mental retardation.

Ron W. Eskew, Ph.D., is currently the Chief of Psychology at the Buffalo
Psychiatric Center in Buffalo, New York. His current research interests focus upon geriatrics.

Mary L. Franken, Ed.D., is Assistant Professor of Home Economics at
the University of Northern Iowa. She is co-director of a teenage
pregnancy project at the present time.

Pat M. Keith, Ph.D., is Professor of Sociology at Iowa State University in
Ames, Iowa. Her degree was earned from St. Louis University, in
Sociology. Her current research interests are in the areas of gender
roles in later life and in rural-urban differences among the elderly.

Beth I. Kinsel, M.G.S., earned her degree in Gerontology from Miami
University in Oxford, Ohio.

Karen A. Kohlhepp is employed by Kennebec Valley Mental Health
Center.

Mary S. Link, Ed.D., is Associate Professor and Coordinator of the Child
Studies Laboratory, Department of Home Economics and Consumer
Sciences, Miami University in Oxford, Ohio. She earned her degree
from Ball State University in Muncie, Indiana. Current research
interests include child care and parenting and grandparenting
issues.

Martha Lopez is currently a high school Home Economics teacher at
Struthers High School in Struthers, Ohio. She collected the data for

the study reported in Chapter 14 of this volume.

Victoria D. Lutzer, Ph.D., is a school psychologist for the York County Public Schools in Grafton, Virginia. Her recent research interests have focused upon older parents of developmentally disabled children.

Carol E. MacKinnon, Ph.D., is Associate Professor at the University of North Carolina in Greensboro, North Carolina. She received her degree from the University of Georgia, in Child and Family Development. Her current research interests are in the area of family interaction, with particular interest in the developmental outcome for children.

Robert F. MacKinnon, Ph.D., is Director of Best Friends, Youth Services Bureau in Greensboro, North Carolina. His degree is from the University of Georgia, in Child and Family Development. His research interests are in the area of family interaction.

Donna J. McConnell, M.A., is a graduate student at the University of Akron in the Department of Sociology in Akron, Ohio. Her degree is a Specialist in Gerontology. She currently serves as a rehabilitation counselor for the Mahoning County Transitional Homes in Youngstown, Ohio.

Diane Papalia, Ph.D., is Adjunct Professor of Psychology and Pediatrics in the school of Medicine at the University of Pennsylvania. Her degree is from West Virginia University at Morgantown, West Virginia. She is currently involved in research in the area of adult intellectual functioning.

Karen A. Roberto, Ph.D., is Assistant Professor and Coordinator of the Gerontology Program at the University of Northern Colorado. Her degree in Human Development is from Texas Tech University. She is interested in women's health issues in aging and in older people's involvement with informal support networks.

William Rudman, Ph.D., is Assistant Professor of Sports Management, The Ohio State University in Columbus, Ohio. His degree is from the University of Illinois. Currently, he is conducting research on the impact of implementing physical fitness programs on work culture. Specifically, programs on fitness, attitudes of fitness, and how fitness affects lifestyle over the life cycle are being explored.

Gregory F. Sanders, Ph.D., is Assistant Professor in the Department of Child Development and Family Relations at North Dakota State University in Fargo, North Dakota. His research interests center around gerontological issues.

Walter R. Schumm, Ph.D., is Associate Professor in the Department of

Human Development and Family Studies at Kansas State University in Manhattan, Kansas. His current research interests focus upon marital satisfaction and interaction.

Jean Pearson Scott, Ph.D., is Associate Professor in the Department of Human Development and Family Studies at Texas Tech University in Lubbock, Texas. She earned her degree from the University of North Carolina at Greensboro, and is currently researching Alzheimer's disease in the family and among rural elderly.

Michael J. Sporakowski, Ph.D., is Professor of Family and Child Development at Virginia Polytechnic Institute and State University, in Blacksburg, Virginia. His current research interests include long-term marriages and perceptions of spouse abuse.

Clifford H. Swenson, Ph.D., is Professor of Clinical Psychology at Purdue University in Lafayette, Indiana. Currently, he is conducting research on marriage and family relationships and on the quality of life in cancer patients.

Georgeanna M. Tryban, Ph.D., is Assistant Professor of Sociology at Indiana State University. Recently returned from Japan, she gathered data for a National Institute on Aging funded project on self-care behavior of aged Japanese.

Concetta M. Tynan, M.S.N., is the Director of Health Services at the Handmaker Jewish Geriatric Center in Tucson, Arizona. Her degree is from Columbia University. Currently, she is interested in health promotion among institutionalized and independent living elderly.

James Walters, Ph.D., is Professor and Department Head of the Child and Family Development Department at the University of Georgia in Athens, Georgia. His degree is from The Florida State University. His current research interests focus on teenage sexuality.

About the Editors

Linda Ade-Ridder, Ph.D., received her degree in Marriage and Family Therapy in the Interdivisional Program between Sociology and Home and Family Life from the Florida State University in Tallahassee, Florida. She is Associate Professor of Individual and Family Studies, an affiliate of Women's Studies, and is an Associate of the Family and Child Studies Center at Miami University in Oxford, Ohio. Her research interests are focused around women's roles in the family, including women in long-term marriages, parenting, eating disorders, and family violence.

Charles B. Hennon, Ph.D., received his degree in Sociology from Case Western Reserve University in Cleveland, Ohio. He is Professor of the Department of Home Economics and Consumer Sciences, and is Associate Director of the Family and Child Studies Center at Miami University in Oxford, Ohio. He is Editor of *Lifestyles: Family and Economic Issues.* His research interests include family roles, family stress, and rural families.

Index

Activities of Daily Living (ADL), 227, 228, 230, 231, 232
Actual Household Responsibility Index, 105
Adaptability, 54, 56, 66, 70, 72
Adult Protection Services, 171
Affection, 161, 211, 213, 214, 221, 222; *see also* Love
Aging parents, 13, 111, 202, 207, 211; *see also* Treatment of the older person
Aging process, 12, 144, 147, 148, 149, 150, 151, 165
American Association of Retired Persons, 168
Aspiration, 17
Autonomy, 39, 66, 67, 68, 69, 70, 71, 75, 96, 97, 113, 175, 176, 215, 222, 225, 226, 228, 235, 237

Barrett-Lennard Relationship Inventory, 32
Blacks, 13, 168, 212, 218, 230, 231
Blue collar: *see* Socioeconomic status (SES)
Board of Mental Retardation and Developmental Disabilities, 206, 207

Campbell Soup Company, 5, 187n, 188, 190, 191, 192, 193, 194, 196n
Caregiving, 2, 4, 5, 39, 111, 113, 121, 129, 132, 173, 202, 206, 207, 211, 215, 220, 222; *see also* Children; Health; Relationships; Support networks
Children, 3, 39, 68, 96, 126; *see also* Caregiving; Relationships
  aid from 3, 113, 211
  visits with, 3, 127, 129, 130
Church: *see* Religion
Cohesion, 40, 54, 56, 66, 124

Commitment, 3, 27, 51, 55, 64, 66, 68, 70, 71, 74, 75, 76, 78, 80, 82, 97
Communication, 2, 31, 36, 51, 52, 56, 57, 59, 66, 69, 70, 71
Companionship, 4, 31, 42, 50, 83, 84, 131
Conflict, 56, 59, 64, 66, 67, 68, 70, 72, 77, 78, 82
Congruence, 19, 26, 31, 32, 33, 34, 35, 36, 37, 40, 84, 105
Control, 54
Coping, 2, 3, 55, 57, 165; *see also* Family
Council on Aging, 168
Couples, *see also* Relationships
  activities, 73, 127, 128
  dual-earner, 3, 83, 87, 88, 89, 90, 91, 92, 93, 94, 95, 97, 98n, 99, 100
  dual-retired, 99, 100
  married, 2, 11, 12, 13, 32, 73, 74, 76, 77, 82, 85, 91, 106, 107, 125, 129; *see also* Marital/marriage
  normative scores, 29
  older, 41, 42, 73, 74, 76, 77, 78, 101, 124, 125, 129
  retired, 3, 14, 48, 78, 114
  traditional, 3, 27, 61, 83, 84, 87, 88, 89, 90, 91, 92, 93, 94, 95, 97, 98n
Cross-sectional studies, 28, 41, 43, 86, 160, 189

Day care, adult, 5, 225, 226, 227, 228, 229, 231, 232, 233, 234, 235, 236, 237; *see also* Health; Living situtation; Respite care
Death, 11, 12, 64, 74, 125, 155, 166, 169, 173, 211, 212, 220

DATE DUE